From Curse to Blessing? Using Natural Resources to Fuel Sustainable Development

Irakli Khodeli

This edition first published 2009
© 2009 UNESCO

Blackwell Publishing was acquired by John Wiley & Sons in February 2007. Blackwell's publishing program has been merged with Wiley's global Scientific, Technical and Medical business to form Wiley-Blackwell.

Registered Office
John Wiley & Sons Ltd, The Atrium, Southern Gate, Chichester, West Sussex, PO19 8SQ, United Kingdom

Editorial Offices
350 Main Street, Malden, MA 02148-5020, USA
9600 Garsington Road, Oxford, OX4 2DQ, UK
The Atrium, Southern Gate, Chichester, West Sussex, PO19 8SQ, UK

For details of our global editorial offices, for customer services, and for information about how to apply for permission to reuse the copyright material in this book please see our website at www.wiley.com/wiley-blackwell.

The rights of Moufida Goucha and John Crowley to be identified as the editors of this work has been asserted in accordance with the Copyright, Designs and Patents Act 1988.

Library of Congress Cataloging-in-Publication Data applied for

ISBN 978-1-4051-9263-7

A catalogue record for this book is available from the British Library.

Set in 10 on 12 points, Times by Macmillan India
Printed in Singapore by C.O.S. Printers Pte Ltd

International Social Science Journal

From Curse to Blessing? Using Natural Resources to Fuel Sustainable Development

Irakli Khodeli

A view from the industry

Abstracts

Resolving conflicts of interest in state-owned enterprises

Jenik Radon and Julius Thaler

State-owned enterprises (SOEs) face conflicts of interest that stem from a government's dual role as an owner, operator and businessman on the one hand and as the protector of the public interest and therefore a regulator of the SOE on the other hand. Besides pursuing profit maximisation like any private business, SOEs often have a mandate if not an obligation, for broader social goals, such as community education and employment generation. In its function as regulator, a government has to ensure that certain standards, for instance labour and environmental regulations, will be implemented and enforced. These two conflicting goals are difficult to reconcile. The proposed solution to the conflicts of interest is to provide for a clear separation of the ownership and regulatory functions. A SOE should be granted entrepreneurial independence to enable the management to pursue exclusively commercial goals. In order to fulfil its regulatory function the government should also establish separate and independent regulatory bodies. However, a necessary precondition for positive changes is recognising the inherent conflicts of interest in SOEs, and an open and frank discussion about possible solutions.

The devil's excrement as social cement: natural resources and political terror, 1980–2002

Indra de Soysa and Helga Malmin Binningsbø

Using a direct measure of repression of dissent, we find ample evidence to suggest that energy and mineral wealth strongly predict higher levels of political terror, results that are both statistically and substantively large. Oil-rich and mineral-rich countries contain higher levels of political terror regardless of the level of autocracy, the incidence of civil and international war and sundry controls. The results are robust to different measures of resource wealth, alternative measures of repression, testing methods and several model specifications. The quality of economic governance, measured as the level of economic freedom, has strong negative effects on political terror and conditions the effects of resource wealth in the direction of more humane governance. Our results suggest several entry points for global and local policy-makers that seek to extirpate the curse of natural wealth.

Natural resource rent-cycling outcomes in Botswana, Indonesia and Venezuela

Richard M. Auty

Autocracies tend to be more successful than democracies in deploying natural resource rent. This renders democratic Botswana's success an anomaly, which Collier and Hoeffler (2006) attribute to strong checks and balances. This chapter assesses this thesis by comparing rent deployment since the 1960s in democratic Botswana with that in democratic Venezuela and in Indonesia's autocracy under Suharto. It draws on Rent-cycling theory, which posits that the higher the ratio of rent/GDP the more likely it is that the political state will pursue rent distribution at the expense of wealth creation; so that rent is cycled through patronage channels at the expense of markets; and, consequently, the economy is distorted. This increases its vulnerability to external shocks and a collapse in growth. The chapter reaches four conclusions. First, a critical determinant of Rent-cycling outcomes is the strength of the incentives for the elite to prioritise wealth creation over rent distribution. Low rent confers such incentives, as do a rent stream that is precarious (Botswana) and a perception of rent exhaustion (Indonesia). Second, effective institutions reflect rather than mould them wealth-creating incentives. Patronage-driven rent cycling tends to corrode institutions, whereas market-channelled rent tends to consolidate them. Third, few governments manage to pursue all four key policies required for effective rent cycling. Finally, Rent-cycling impacts are cumulative and negative circles are difficult to arrest.

Governance strategies to remedy the natural resource curse

Joseph Siegle

Rising commodity prices in recent years have deepened awareness of the paradox of the resource curse – resource-rich countries consistently facing high levels of poverty, corruption and instability. There is relatively less recognition of the autocratic roots underlying much of this curse, however. Resource-rich autocracies, on average, are subject to lower levels of well-being, higher volatility, a greater propensity for conflict and humanitarian crisis, and more corruption than resource-rich countries on a democratic path. The resource curse persists because sharp inequalities of power limit opportunities for corrective action. Recognising the governance root to the natural resource curse dictates that remedial strategies for resource-rich democratisers should differ from those for resource-rich autocracies. In the latter, effective reform strategies must increase the cost of rent-seeking by the privileged minority and improve the capacity for collective action among the disadvantaged majority. While resource-rich autocracies do not rely on international assistance for budgetary support, they generally must tend to reputational and investment concerns. Accordingly, there is an important role for international actors – governmental, civil society

organisations and the private sector – to play in reversing the resource curse.

Budget transparency and development in resource-dependent countries

Paolo de Renzio, Pamela Gomez and James Sheppard

The objective of this chapter is to examine empirically the nature and extent of budget transparency in resource-dependent countries, as a potential foundation for improving governance and development impact. The resource curse hypothesis claims that resource-dependent countries, despite their riches, grow slower than resource-poor countries. Recent research has attributed part of the explanation to the quality of governance and institutions. Based on data drawn from the Open Budget Initiative 2006, we developed an index of budget transparency and accountability for 24 resource-dependent countries. While resource-dependent countries do suffer from a transparency gap, their performance both with regard to budget transparency and to development outcomes varies greatly. While our index and the United Nations Human Development Index are positively correlated, this relationship cannot be interpreted as a causal one. In order to shed light on the links between the two variables we look at three case studies of countries with very different performances: Peru, Vietnam and Angola. Some of the factors that seem to contribute to shape these linkages include the type and degree of dependency on natural resource revenues, the nature of the political regime and the nature of budget institutions, and the existence of an active civil society.

Before the peak: impacts of oil shortages on the developing world

Ben W. Ebenhack and Daniel M. Martínez

We explore the generally ignored reality that the petroleum shortage will occur before oil peaks, when the rate of growth falls below the rate of the growth of demand. This underscores the fact that the shortage with concomitant price increases will occur relatively soon, even if ultimate reserves are found to be more than is currently believed. Indeed, an energy shortage already exists for the half of humanity that lacks access to modern energy. Supply constraints for affluent, industrialised consumers will adversely affect energy imports for developing countries and at the same time increase international pressure on the developing world's resources for the export market. Many resources that have been deemed sub-commercial in these regions will be re-evaluated in light of higher prices. This will offer some opportunity to earn foreign trade, but at the cost of resources that could be tapped for local development. The development community has an opportunity to help those regions achieve energy security through the development of these resources locally by enhancing professional capacity and offering technical expertise.

Social and economic implications of oil policy development in Nigeria

Alexis Rwabizambuga

National oil exploitation policies are generally designed to maximise petroleum revenues. Countries aim to control over domestic oil exploitation to ensure maximum socio-economic benefits from it. However, not all oil-producing countries can afford the same degree of control. Developing countries have historically been over-reliant on commercial stakeholders such as oil corporations and funding agencies to extract and commercialise their oil resources. This dependency often leads to protracted negotiations dominated by these powerful actors at the expense of state interests. With Nigeria as a case study, this chapter argues that the recent dynamics in the global oil industry have restored the influence of the state. The ever-increasing demand for oil has led to stiff competition for access to oil reserves, compelling investors and oil companies to court any potential oil producer, however marginal. The lack of political stability may be the main explanation for developing countries' limited leverage in negotiating extraction agreements and may have

spawn the circumstances in which local institutions are too weak to make any effective use of oil proceeds for socio-economic development.

The public oversight of oil projects in Azerbaijan, 2004–2007

Farda Asadov

Azerbaijan's rich hydrocarbon resources could bring it up to $US200 billion of income. However, the period for exploiting these deposits will be quite short, and after 2011 the returns will gradually decrease. While the government and people are aware that measures are needed to manage these resources effectively, no mechanisms exist for the government to work together with civil society to exploit this resource in the interests of Azerbaijan citizens. The successful application of the Extractive Industries Transparency Initiative (EITI) in Azerbaijan may seem to be a significant achievement but, because of the historical conditions of the country's development, there are basic risks of corruption in Azerbaijan in the expenditure of resources. The Azerbaijan experience of collaborating with civil society is in practice limited to accounting for income within the framework of the EITI. In developing a culture of dialogue with civil society, special significance has been attached to the partnership with British Petroleum to monitor the construction of pipelines. If successful, the development of these initiatives in Azerbaijan can serve as an example to other countries with economies based on processing natural resources.

Energy relations in Russia: administration, politics and security

Andrey Makarychev

This chapter analyses energy relations through a prism of three interlinked concepts: administration, politics and security. This triad describes the basic approaches to questions about technical, politicised and securitised energy. These three concepts are logically linked to one another and represent an elementary matrix; a prism through which different segments of the energy discourse can be analysed. The proposed scheme is of research interest for several reasons. First, it shows that many problems of communication between participants in energy relations arise when these three approaches are combined, whether consciously or unconsciously. Second, practice shows that one and the same country can have several different modes of communication in its arsenal. Third the interconnection between two concepts are important for understanding energy relations that are at first glance opposing, namely, transparency and security.

Doing business with integrity: the experience of AngloGold Ashanti in the Democratic Republic of Congo

Paul Kapelus, Ralph Hamann and Edward O'Keefe

One of the most prominent illustrations of the challenges and complexities faced by companies operating in weak governance zones has been that of AngloGold Ashanti (AGA) in the Democratic Republic of Congo (DRC). A payment made by AGA exploration staff to a rebel group accused of committing extensive human rights abuses was seen by leading non-governmental organisations as an illustration of corporate irresponsibility and was used to argue that companies such as AGA should not be operating in such areas in the first place. The company admitted that a mistake had been made, but argued that the interests of local people and the DRC in general are better served by its remaining in the area. This case study argues that investing and re-entering the DRC during the period of conflict was an incorrect decision and that a more risk-averse approach ought to guide investment decisions in such circumstances. The company's decision to remain in the area is difficult to assess, though there are indications that it is contributing to improved governance by establishing a local multi-stakeholder forum and, at the national level, support for the Extractive Industries Transparency Initiative.

The International Petroleum Industry Environmental Conservation Association social responsibility working group and human rights

Jenny Owens

This chapter describes how the oil and gas industry is responding to one specific challenge to sustainable development – the promotion of human rights. The human rights activities and practices of the industry fall into three categories: direct responsibility, shared responsibility and indirect influence. Specific responses to human rights issues are illustrated through case studies from some of the member companies of the International Petroleum Industry Environmental Conservation Association. The chapter demonstrates that the oil and gas industry has achieved substantial progress in establishing and implementing human rights policies and practices. However, the debate between industry, representatives of civil society and governments over the roles, responsibilities and accountability for human rights of transnational corporations in general, and of the oil and gas industry in particular, continues. While under international law the responsibility to protect human rights rests primarily with governments, companies and others, including non-governmental organisations and multilateral organisations, can support human rights. The industry recognises the need to develop measures to help address human rights challenges and that this effort will require co-operation and shared responsibility among all relevant actors.

As a condition that affects almost half of the world's population, poverty is the single most important obstacle for people to realise fully their potential, and the most widespread threat to human rights and dignity around the world. Poverty has been recognised as a major challenge for the international community to tackle in the coming decades. Eradicating extreme poverty has been made the first of the eight Millennium Development Goals and represents the major target for various other internationally agreed-upon development initiatives.

UNESCO tries to contribute to these global efforts by tackling such major sources of poverty illiteracy, lack of access to quality education, and gender inequalities in education systems. Based on its unique intellectual mandate, UNESCO, and in particular its Social and Human Sciences Sector, has encouraged debates among researchers and scientists on a range of poverty issues in order to enrich national and international policy-making processes. To this end, the *International Social Science Journal*, together with other relevant publications of the Organization, has sought to provide a forum for an in-depth analysis of key issues in the fight against poverty, such as the HIV/AIDS epidemic, women's empowerment and freedom from poverty as a fundamental human right.

This volume continues the debate by focusing on natural resource wealth as a potential source of sustainable economic growth and human development. It brings together social scientists, practitioners and experts from various parts of the world to engage in the debate about how to translate revenues derived from natural resource exploitation into real benefits for citizens of resource-rich countries. The debate is not about a hypothetical question. It is an unfortunate reality that the intuitive understanding that natural riches should translate into economic growth and development has been proven wrong time and again in countries endowed with an abundance of natural wealth.

The paradox of plenty

Today, over 60 per cent of the world's poorest people live in countries rich in natural resources (Oxfam America 2008). Yet, despite the unprecedented high prices of these commodities on the global market, and the ensuing wealth generated by their exploitation and sale, a significant number of resource-rich countries lag behind in their economic and social development. Twelve of the world's 25 most mineral-dependent states and six of the world's 25 most oil-dependent states are classified by the World Bank as "highly indebted poor countries", with some of the world's worst human development indicators (Ross 2001). As the profits of multinational oil companies continue to soar thanks to record-high crude oil prices, so do the rents flowing to the governments of the developing countries that host the significant share of global oil operations, but the people seem to rarely share in the wealth.

Exxon-Mobil broke its own record in 2007 with a 9.3 per cent growth in profit, amounting to US$39.5 billion – the highest profit of any company in history, while the price for a barrel of oil broke the record by going over the $US140 mark during trading at NYMEX in June 2008. And yet, severe poverty and underdevelopment continue to define millions of human lives in these countries. This counter-intuitive phenomenon, commonly known as the "paradox of plenty" or "resource curse" has been a subject of continued interest for economists, historians and political scientists for centuries.

In fact, the historical evidence of windfall profits' corroding influence on the economic and political health of the country significantly predates the industrial exploitation of oil and gas. An often-quoted example is the squandering of the colossal wealth acquired by Spain in the form of gold and other precious metals after the colonisation of the New World, leading to deep debt and series of bankruptcies of the Spanish crown and laying a foundation for a protracted decline in the country's development. As the economic historian David Landes puts it in his analysis of this case, "Easy money is bad for you. It represents short-run gain that will be paid for in immediate distortions and later regrets" (Landes 1999).

Today, in the context of the global fight against poverty, curbing the negative effects of natural resource wealth on development and using the extractive revenues for the benefit of citizens of the resource-rich countries has become an imperative for the international community. A vast amount of academic knowledge has been generated in this field, pointing to the negative effects of natural wealth dependence on economic growth and other measures of human development (Sandbu 2006). Several studies have demonstrated that the growth of countries in the 1970s and 1980s was strongly and negatively affected by their dependence on natural resources, as measured by the share of primary commodities in exports (Sachs and Warner 1995), or by the share of natural resource wealth in the total national wealth (Gylfason 2001).

The explanations of the natural curse phenomenon generally fall into two categories – economic and institutional (political economy factors). Studies of the economic distortions of natural resource dependence focus on over-reliance on a single primary commodity export and its dampening effect on terms of trade and productivity, known as the "Dutch disease" – a term coined by *The Economist* to describe the decline of the Dutch manufacturing sector after the discovery of natural gas in the country's continental shelf in the North Sea.

In the past decade experts have paid increasing attention to the corrupting influence of windfall profits on the quality of a country's governing institutions, thereby shifting focus onto such issues as transparency, the rule of law, accountability and other key aspects of good governance and democratic institutions. These political economy explanations evoke the lesson in the Spanish case cited above – windfall wealth corrupts. Easy money from the sale of natural resources emboldens ruling elites to divert their spending from the legitimate institutional framework into politically important, yet often wasteful projects. As a result, corruption thrives, the friends and allies of the ruling elites grow richer, the average citizen grows poorer and the economic growth of the country stagnates.

From this picture one could easily discern a vicious cycle that keeps the curse in place. As the increasing demand on energy resources drives their prices up and the treasuries of resource-rich states swell, the rulers become more brazen in circumventing the institutional barriers that ensure that profits are properly invested, and less inclined to compromise with the domestic forces pushing for transparency and accountability. This lack of incentives to manage the high profits in the interest of the people corrodes the domestic institutions of a country, while these ineffective institutions in their turn perpetuate corruption and waste.

In fact, in cases where governments are unable to invest profits to achieve sustainable development, countries might be better off if their natural resource endowment is preserved untouched underground: its value will only appreciate as resources become scarcer and prices increase over time. This is the key point in an argument advanced by J.E. Stiglitz

> The extraction of resources lowers the wealth of a country – unless the funds generated are invested in other forms. Extraction in itself makes the country poorer because resources such as oil, gas, or minerals are not renewable. Once they are out of the ground and sold, they cannot be replaced. It is only the subsequent reinvestment into capital (physical or natural) that can offset the loss of this natural wealth and make the country richer. (Stiglitz 2005)

By refining the insights into the relationship between natural resources and economic growth, the authors in this volume contribute to the ongoing debate on ways to lift the curse, and suggest policy interventions to disentangle the vicious cycle. The chapters cover a broad range of topics and employ different methods of inquiry. Some take an empirical approach and use cross-country comparisons to test various hypotheses on the relationship between natural wealth and growth, while others analyse particular resource-rich countries. The authors converge on one point – that the domestic institutions make a significant difference: with good governance the exploitation of resources can generate revenues that will foster growth and reduce poverty.

Lifting the curse

The year 2015 will be an important juncture in the global fight against poverty. It will be the culminating year for the ambitious Millennium Development Goals, and a year for reflecting on the achievements made during the United Nations Decade of Education for Sustainable Development (2005–2014). The year 2015, besides being a judgment day for global development initiatives, will also mark the date when, according to some industry experts, easily accessible supplies of oil and gas will no longer keep up with demand (Van der Veer 2008). However, as Ebenhack and Martínez argue in their chapter, for half the world's population that relies on inefficient and dirty firewood to meet nearly all of their energy needs, the shortage of clean energy resources is already a pressing reality. The chapter explores the effects of the future trends of energy demand and supply on developing countries which are both the producers and increasingly the consumers of hydrocarbon resources.

Drawing on rent-cycling theory, Auty uses the cases of three countries – Botswana, Indonesia and Venezuela – to illustrate how the different constellations of incentives in these countries have led to different outcomes in terms of natural resource-fueled growth. The rent-cycling theory suggests that the higher the share of windfall profits in the gross domestic product, the more likely it is that the ruling elite will cycle these profits through patronage channels rather than use them for broader wealth-generating investments, such as education and infrastructure, to facilitate sustainable human development and ensure stable tax revenues in the future. Rent cycling through political networks distorts the economy and perpetuates underdevelopment. Auty's findings suggest that if the revenue streams from natural resource exploitation are low, precarious, or perceived as finite, the ruling elites will have a stronger incentive to use the profits for wealth creation, rather than to distribute them amongst their patronage networks. The two different patterns of profit distribution have an opposite and durable impact on governing institutions – channelling rents through patronage networks corrodes institutions, while managing them for wealth creation tends to have a consolidating effect.

The proponents of rentier state theories argue that governments of the rentier states – states that derive most of their national revenues from the sale of indigenous resources to external clients, tend to be socio-politically stable, regardless of the quality and type of their governing institutions, because they can simply buy social consent, and therefore avoid the need to violently suppress dissent. This is a serious challenge to the resource curse theory. Not only does it imply that the rulers' access to windfall revenues will lead to a negotiated social stability and peace, but it also considers financial and other scarcities as the conditions that push governments to repress human rights as the only way to check the social discontent. De Soysa and Binningsbø provide empirical evidence to reject these challenges to resource curse arguments, and show that resource-wealthy states are more likely to take repressive measures in terms of seriously violating the human rights of political dissenters. Their findings support the view that the quality of governing institutions does matter, especially in regard to safeguarding private property and well-functioning markets. The chapter hints at several interesting entry points for global and national policy-makers who seek to turn natural wealth from a curse into a positive factor for development.

Another common line of argument directed against the bad governance explanation of the resource curse claims that the failure to fuel growth in resource-rich countries stems from inherently unfair contractual relationships between the governments of developing countries and the powerful extractive corporations. Due to the asymmetric power relations between poor states and commercial stakeholders, the protracted negotiations are inevitably dominated by the latter at the expense of the interests of the former. Two chapters in this volume refute this view after analysing the relations between the commercial enterprises and national governments in two African states – Nigeria and Democratic Republic of Congo.

Using Nigeria as a case study, Rwabizambuga argues that due to the recent dynamics in the global oil industry, the state today is in the driver's seat. The ever-increasing demand for oil has led to stiff competition for access to oil reserves, tempting the commercial agents to court even the most marginal potential oil producers. It is the socio-political stability of the state, according to Rwabizambuga, that determines the degree of policy control that a developing resource-rich country can exercise over its oil resources. In line with most other contributing authors to this volume, he places the responsibility to translate natural resource wealth into sustainable socio-economic development in the hands of the governments.

Supporting this view is the chapter by Kapelus, Hamann and O'Keefe, who use the example of Democratic Republic of Congo to show that the entry of an extractive company into a weak governance zone can have a detrimental effect on the precarious human conditions in the country. Unless a company adheres to strict precautionary principle in making the decision to invest in an environment where the government is unable or unwilling to assume its responsibilities for maintaining the rule of law, the risk of its complicity in human rights violations will be high. The impact of a company's decision to remain in the area is difficult to assess, though there are indications that it can contribute to improved governance by establishing a local multi-stakeholder forum and, at the national level, support the Extractive Industries Transparency Initiative (EITI).

The importance of corporate responsibility in countries that suffer from the failures of governance institutions is hard to overestimate. According to the chapter, 15 per cent of the world's people live in weak governance zones, notably in sub-Saharan Africa.

The extractive industry sector has accumulated significant experience in dealing with one of the key challenges to sustainable human development – the protection and promotion of human rights. A chapter by the International Petroleum Industry Environmental Conservation Association (IPIECA), which represents some of the world's largest extractive corporations, discusses the role of companies in establishing and implementing human rights policies and practices in the countries that host their operations. IPIECA member companies argue that, while it is the role of the private sector to respect human rights and promote them in its spheres of influence, the ultimate responsibility to protect human rights lies with governments. While the case studies focus on good practices, the chapter admits that the extractive industry

needs to further develop measures of effective cooperation with the governments and the civil society in its effort to promote human rights.

While most of the corrupt practices occur in the interactions between two distinct players – the private companies that possess the expertise of oil production and the regulatory authorities in national governments that are the custodians of the wealth under the country's soil, Radon and Thaler focus on a special type of entities – the state-owned enterprises (SOEs), that control approximately 90 per cent of the world's oil reserves. The authors' work brings into the open a largely overlooked conflict of interests that is inherent in the SOEs. The tight political control and lack of independent management in SOEs hamper optimal usage of resources and thereby dampen a country's prospects of natural wealth-fueled growth.

The first law of petropolitics

Thomas Friedman has coined the first law of petropolitics: the price of oil and the pace of freedom tend to move in opposite directions in countries that are rich in oil (Friedman 2006). The chapter by Siegle empirically substantiates this law. It analyses some of the distinguishing effects of governance on the resource curse, contrasting developmental outcomes, such as per capita income growth rates, infant mortality rates, and improvements in cereal yields, between autocratic and democratic states. The comparisons indicate that the form of governance is the primary factor that determines whether natural resource wealth is a curse or a blessing. Recognising that the resource-rich autocracies often have no incentive to conform to foreign aid conditionalities, Siegel proposes a different approach for external influence: establishing and promoting legal and normative principles of transparency and accountability at the international level, and supporting key stakeholders – governmental, civil society organisations and the private sector – to implement these norms at the domestic level. Acknowledging the EITI as the central global multi-stakeholder forum for addressing transparency concerns, Siegel proposes going beyond the voluntary arrangement to enshrine the principle of citizen ownership of natural resource revenues in a UN-sanctioned forum with penalties for non-compliance.

Several authors emphasise that the principle of transparency is indispensable for achieving sustainable human development in resource-rich countries. It is regarded as a necessary condition for empowering people to exert pressure on authorities for proper management of revenues. As such, it is a central theme of the chapter by De Renzio, Gomez and Sheppard, which uses data drawn from the Open Budget Initiative and the Human Development Index to examine empirically the relationship between budget transparency and the resource curse. While they find a positive correlation between the degree of budget openness and human development in situations of resource abundance, the authors are cautious not to interpret it this as a causal relationship. Instead, comparing the experiences of Peru, Vietnam and Angola, the chapter argues that the extent to which transparency affects human development in resource-rich countries depends on such factors as the degree of dependence on natural resource revenues, the nature of the political regime and the existence of an active civil society.

Transparency and EITI

The EITI figures prominently in this volume as a major international mechanism for promoting transparency of revenues from the extractive industries. The initiative was launched by British Prime Minister Tony Blair at the 2002 World Summit for Sustainable Development in Johannesburg, as an effort to lift the resource curse and help the developing resource-rich nations to use their extractive revenues for the benefit of their people. As a growing coalition of governments, companies, civil society groups, investors and international organisations guided by the common principles (see insert), the EITI represents a global standard-setting instrument that promotes revenue transparency at the national level.

Box 1: The EITI principles

We share a belief that the prudent use of natural resource wealth should be an important engine for sustainable economic growth that contributes to sustainable development and poverty reduction, but if not managed properly, can create negative economic and social impacts.

We affirm that management of natural resource wealth for the benefit of a country's citizens is in the domain of sovereign governments to be exercised in the interests of their national development.

We recognise that the benefits of resource extraction occur as revenue streams over many years and can be highly price dependent.

We recognise that a public understanding of government revenues and expenditure over time could help public debate and inform choice of appropriate and realistic options for sustainable development.

We underline the importance of transparency by governments and companies in the extractive industries and the need to enhance public financial management and accountability.

We recognise that achievement of greater transparency must be set in the context of respect for contracts and laws.

We recognise the enhanced environment for domestic and foreign direct investment that financial transparency may bring.

We believe in the principle and practice of accountability by government to all citizens for the stewardship of revenue streams and public expenditure.

We are committed to encouraging high standards of transparency and accountability in public life, government operations and in business.

We believe that a broadly consistent and workable approach to the disclosure of payments and revenues is required, which is simple to undertake and to use.

We believe that payments' disclosure in a given country should involve all extractive industry companies operating in that country.

In seeking solutions, we believe that all stakeholders have important and relevant contributions to make – including governments and their agencies, extractive industry companies, service companies, multilateral organisations, financial organisations, investors and non-governmental organisations.

The EITI offers candidacy status to countries that follow through with their commitments to implement a range of activities to strengthen resource revenue transparency. These include the regular, comprehensive and easily accessible publication of all oil, gas and mining payments by companies to governments, as well as the revenues received by governments from companies, under the conditions of a credible, independent audit. These reports on payments and revenues are then reconciled by an independent administrator, who applies international auditing standards and publishes its opinion on the reconciliation, including any discrepancies identified. It is also a necessary candidacy criterion that civil society is actively engaged in the design, monitoring and evaluation of this process.

In order to achieve and maintain compliant candidate status, a country must meet the EITI validation criteria at minimum of every two years. Today, 15 countries are considered candidate countries, and have two years to establish themselves as fully compliant. These are Azerbaijan, Cameroon, Gabon, Ghana, Guinea, Kazakhstan, Kyrgyzstan, Liberia, Mali, Mauritania, Mongolia, Niger, Nigeria, Peru and Yemen. A further group of nine countries is currently being evaluated for a candidate status: Chad, Democratic Republic of Congo, Equatorial Guinea, Madagascar, Republic of Congo, Sao Tome and Principe, Sierra Leone, Trinidad and Tobago, and Timor-Leste.

One of the first countries to publish payment and revenue reports in the EITI framework was Azerbaijan, which is also the country with the oldest oil-production tradition. In fact, accounts of oil commerce there may go as far back as Marco Polo's reports on the regional oil trade (Karen 2007). However, until the country's independence in 1991, oil exploitation and the revenues derived from it were managed not by the national government, but by the Soviet Union's state planning agency, which took over this responsibility from imperial Russia. The chapter by Asadov examines the history of oil revenue management since independence, from the perspective of civil society's efforts to achieve transparency and demand accountability from the government of Azerbaijan. The author points to one of the most serious shortcomings of EITI: while the experience of collaboration among the government, the private industry and the civil society is in practise limited to the sphere of revenue collection, the core risks of corruption in Azerbaijan, due to various historical circumstances tend to concern those institutions and practices that deal with the expenditure of these revenues.

The institutions that misappropriate rents from natural resource exploitation continue to exist because of a complete lack of transparency – citizens are kept in the dark as to where the money goes. One time-tested strategy for governments to keep the accounts from public scrutiny is invoking concerns for national security. Makarychev takes on the security–transparency link in the context of Russian Federation's energy relations to the external world. In the energy resources exploitation policy in Russia, it is becoming ever more difficult to speak of security outside the context of transparency, just as it is to discuss transparency without referring to the concept of security.

The complexity of issues revealed by the chapters in this volume suggests that a silver bullet solution to the resource curse is implausible. No single set of prescriptions is likely to turn natural resources into vehicles for growth and development. However, the chapters provide an insight into the nature of the resource curse and hint at various policy reforms. These, if properly implemented by resource-rich countries and by the key actors in the international community, including the private sector and the countries at the consuming end of natural resource exploitation, could create the conditions for lifting the resource curse and turning these resources into a blessing.

Resolving conflicts of interest in state-owned enterprises

Jenik Radon and Julius Thaler

Introduction

Saudi Aramco of Saudi Arabia, Petróleos Mexicanos of Mexico and other state-owned enterprises (SOEs) control approximately 90 per cent of the world's oil reserves. Other natural resources, as well as a diverse spectrum of other industries, are similarly owned and managed by SOEs, often in the belief that a public institution is better suited to be entrusted with the management of a national or public asset than a private company. However, this belief overlooks the basic, classical powers at the disposal of a government: taxation and regulation, which, if used properly, can deliver the same or even better results than direct operational management. Canada, Australia, the UK and a host of other developed nations exemplify the effectiveness of this approach. This chapter investigates its merits and provides suggestions for delinking or minimising the effects of the inherently conflicting functions of regulating and operating or managing SOEs.

A traditional public–private division creates institutional checks and balances. The private sector operates while the public oversees and supervises. This approach is based on an institutional, as well as a personal division of incentives. The private sector strives to make money, and individual managers and employees seek top compensation. The public sector (the government) regulates the process to ensure that the profits are not achieved at the expense of society, the public and the citizens, whether from an environmental, safety or labour point of view. The ministry officials and its employees focus on climbing the bureaucratic ladder and commanding a respectable pay, fully conscious that it will normally be less than what they might earn in the private sector, and often significantly so. In both the public and private sectors, persons are promoted and rewarded based on how well these basic objectives are achieved.

Admittedly this is an over-simplification on how society and institutions function. Lines do at times cross and individuals' motivations often represent a complex web. Nevertheless, personal and institutional conflicts intensify when these basic divisions become blurred or ignored.

Jenik Radon is an attorney with the international law firm of Radon and Ishizumi in New York. He teaches at Columbia University's School of International and Public Affairs and at the Indira Gandhi Institute for Development Research in Mumbai, India and previously taught at Stanford University's Law and Business Schools. With extensive international advising experience, especially in joint ventures, privatisation and energy, Mr Radon was the key negotiator for the Republic of Georgia for the multi-billion dollar BTC oil and South Caucasus gas pipeline projects. He has advised on drafting foreign investment laws for a number of nations and he was a key advisor to Estonia in crafting its privatisation law. He is presently engaged in the constitutional peace process in Nepal and in a national imaging project concerning Mexico with Monterrey Tech, Queretaro. Email: jr2218@columbia.edu

Julius Thaler is an academic associate with the international law firm of Radon & Ishizumi in New York. He is a lawyer and also holds a master's degree in international affairs from the School of International and Public Affairs at Columbia University. He has worked on human rights, law reform and anti-corruption issues in Africa and Latin America. Email: juliusthaler@radonoffices.com

The structure and nature of SOEs

There is no universally accepted definition of an SOE. The defining or overriding feature is ownership or control by a government. A government, however, need not fully own an entity for it to be an SOE – retaining a stake that ensures management and operational control over a company's affairs will suffice. One example is the golden share model that allows a government to keep control by retaining a deciding share and thereby to outvote any other shareholder in the decision-making process. It is harder to ascertain whether a company in which a government has only a minor, non-controlling share, but still has significant influence due to its position and status, should be considered an SOE.

SOEs such as Petróleo Brasileiro (Petrobras) in Brazil and Petroliam Nasional Berhad in Malaysia are also a source of national pride and prestige, an embodiment of a country's sovereign dreams. SOEs are frequently heralded as national champions, just like the national airlines that bear the national symbol and carry the national flag. But, besides evoking a public spirit and inspiring people, SOEs carry a secret. They invariably suffer from an Achilles' heel – inherent conflicts of interest that may prevent them from fulfilling their nation's dreams and becoming the longed for national corporate champion.

In this chapter we have opted for a broad definition of conflict of interest, namely the existence of diametrically or significantly opposing or competing interests (in this case public and private) in a person, institution or body, including a government, with public decision-making authority, which, at the minimum, raises the ethical dilemma of how to reconcile such interests without personally or institutionally suffering or losing out. Any situation that requires or demands the reconciliation or even prioritising of competing interests potentially creates the same dilemma. Such a situation is not necessarily considered a conflict of interest in the classical sense, where a person or institution has the opportunity to exploit a situation for personal gain. However, this chapter shows that in some cases the interests (public versus private) are so opposed to each other that a conflict of interest exists, notwithstanding the fact that no unlawful or traditionally unethical act (such as direct personal gain) results from it.

The source of the conflict of interest in an SOE is simple. The basic public–private division is ignored or, at best, blurred. By operating an SOE a government simultaneously assumes both the public and the private function. This dual (and contradictory) role, on the one hand, as owner, operator and businessperson, and, on the other hand, as the protector of the public interest and therefore the regulator of the SOE (Radon 2007, p. 94) lies at the heart of the conflict of interest. The role of a regulator is traditional in all governments. It is intrinsic to the purpose and the accepted workings of any government. But the commercial or business role that is at the heart of an SOE is a new addition to the generally accepted functions of a government, with the exception of national companies that stem from crown corporations and the historical property rights of monarchs and sovereigns.

Public–private conflicts of interest are by no means unique to natural-resource related SOEs. They are also evident in other SOEs, whether they are a cement industry or an alcoholic beverage producer. Nevertheless, conflicts of interest figure more prominently within SOEs in the natural resource sector because of their heightened importance in their countries' economies and gross national product, as well as in their extended national, if not global, reach. In some countries government revenue is derived almost exclusively from the sale of natural resources, whether crude oil, gas or precious metals. The result is that political demands on and public expectations of natural resource SOEs are more pronounced than those faced by smaller, less visible, SOEs that contribute less to the national budget and are not as prestigious. But in no case, and under no circumstances, do the conflicts of interest disappear.

Balancing politics and commerce in strategic and operational decision-making is a challenge that purely commercial businesses face only when lobbying for protective or other beneficial legislation or tax concessions. But government managers of an SOE routinely face conflicts. They have to weigh the political demands of their SOE to contribute to the broad social and political policy goals set by the government in response to public expectations against their objective of running and developing the SOE as a commercial enterprise and returning (sustained) profits to its owners, in this case the government.

These competing goals can be observed more visibly with natural resource SOEs because of their economic and psychological importance for a country. Their sheer size makes them a formidable political tool to be used for non-commercial activities. SOEs can all too easily be regarded as an extension of the national budget and, in some cases, simply become an accounting black hole. Moreover, some national oil companies are also entrusted with broad social responsibilities such as community education, employment generation, developing technological capacity and building national infrastructure. Private enterprises in contrast, need to pursue only one goal, which is mandated by corporate law: the maximisation of profit. Private corporations and their management are required to act in the interest of their shareholders and can be held liable under the law for failing to do so. It is true that the emerging fields of corporate philanthropy and corporate responsibility seem to question the validity of mere profit maximisation, but such challenges are not yet embedded in the strictures of law.

At first glance private corporations also seem to be pursuing a wide range of social and environmental goals, just like SOEs. However, this interpretation overlooks the basic motivation of all these non-commercial projects and activities. Private enterprises engage in them to maximise their profits and enhance their competitive position, although they never say so in public statements. For instance, employees are said to be more motivated working for a socially or environmentally responsible company and consumers develop a more favourable perception of such a company and its brand. The goal is still increased profits resulting from an increase in labour productivity and in the demand for the company's goods. Moreover, there is an equally important but less openly observable reason why corporate responsibility in fact can serve the goal to maximise profits. Companies eagerly engage in social projects that are heralded in press releases and in advertising in the hope and expectation of more favourable governmental treatment, especially tax concessions (Radon 2007).

The emotional importance that people often ascribe to SOEs as the embodiment of economic and political independence is a product of historical processes that must be understood in order to appreciate the extent of the conflicts inherent in these institutions. Many SOEs evolved out of an emerging nation's struggles against foreign economic control or colonialism. Accordingly, companies, especially in the natural resource sector, have witnessed a change of ownership from that of the so-called "exploitative" foreign corporate owner to the newly independent nation. These SOEs then became the beacons of national economic hopes and their managers in many respects are national heroes. The role of some SOEs as the national standard-bearer is even enshrined in the constitutions of Mexico and Venezuela, to name a few. Sovereign control over natural resources came to shape and become mixed with national identity.

Today, countries face the need to reconcile these ideological aspirations with the pragmatic considerations of profit maximisation – the raison d'être of private enterprises and also the declared goal of most SOEs. In fact, SOEs increasingly express their desire to operate like commercial entities (Marcel 2006). A number of SOEs are doing so effectively and quite well. Saudi Aramco and Petrobras are notable examples of this (Hoyos 2007).

In an ideal world the competing goals of profit maximisation and achievement of societal aspirations would be balanced by an impartial, independent arbiter. Long-term social and environmental needs would be taken into account as readily as, short-term annual budget requirements. Theoretically, SOEs could generate even greater revenue for their governments because they do not have to pay dividends to their shareholders. SOE profits could be channelled to support social and other non-commercial political ends, while reinvesting enough resources back into the enterprise to ensure that core commercial activities are funded, including investment in innovation, development and exploration.

But a wealth of existing experience shows that, except in certain exceptional cases, ideals and operational demands invariably collide. The Government of Venezuela, for instance, spent two-thirds of Petróleo de Venezuela's (PDVSA) budget on social programmes in 2005; a trend that has even accelerated over the past two years according to industry experts (Hoyos 2007). As a consequence necessary investments in research and exploitation have been neglected. Similarly, Pemex has to shoulder a diverse range of social projects mandated by the Mexican government. As a result Pemex, much like PDVSA, lacks the modern exploration technology useful in the Gulf of Mexico that would enable it to increase its oil production. These outcomes are by no means inevitable. Petrobras, as more fully explained below has evolved into a technological leader in exploration processes, thanks to its sustained investments in research.

The institutional conflict of interest has its origin in a government's dual role as owner–operator and regulator. Simply put, the regulator is also the regulated entity. On the one hand, as the SOE's owner–operator the government (normally through the ministry of economy or energy) is in charge of making strategic decisions with the view to maximise profits that go either directly into the national budget or, if it exists, into a special national resource fund. This ministry also enjoys the power and influence that arise from the responsibility for such profits. On the other hand, another government agency, be it the environment ministry or the department of safety, is tasked with regulating the SOE as if it were a regular private enterprise. In the end, both ministers report to the same head of government. Here lies the fundamental challenge for the head of government: to play the role of a neutral arbiter between the competing interests of the ministries. The nature of political pressures faced by governments around the world make this role implausible, if not impossible.

While setting and achieving long-term policy goals is one of the key mandates of governments, elected politicians are at the same time exposed to the routine and immediate demands and expectations of their constituents, which become more pronounced at election time. In order to be re-elected, or to be a credible candidate for higher office, a politician has to deliver in the short term. A SOE offers a reliable and readily available political answer to such demands, thereby giving rise to the conflict.

Valérie Marcel has noted that politicians increasingly intervene in the management of an SOE to maximise the revenues available to the state in order to ensure their short-term political survival at the expense of the productivity of the SOE. The minister of energy, perhaps with the backing of a head of government who shares her perspective, may favour diverting profits into the national budget to finance short-term political projects at the expense of future higher economic dividends from increased investments in research and development and the achievement of long-term social and environmental goals.

Insufficient funding for research and development and the high-risk activity of exploration, the rewards for which materialise, if at all, only at some future undefined date, is a major challenge for many SOEs. Their lack of adequate funding is a direct consequence of the government's need or preference for immediate revenues. Pemex, for example, has been accused of failing to find new reserves, thereby handicapping Mexican development in times of record-high world oil prices. Critics note that PDVSA is failing to keep up on the technology front and is not spending enough to explore for new reserves as two-thirds of its profits are diverted to social programmes. As a result Venezuela's oil output is actually falling (*The Economist* 14 February 2008).

Another consequence of such a short-term approach is environmental degradation. The Nigerian National Petroleum Corporation (NNPC), together with its foreign partners, became a classical example of environmental degradation in its rush to develop the vast oil fields of Nigeria, notwithstanding the exemplary environmental laws of that country. Natural gas flaring is not restricted to Nigeria, but it is hazardous to the environment and human health wherever it occurs. In fact, every oil-producing country is confronted with this issue as gas flaring is still a necessary by-product of oil production, although its impact can be mitigated.

However, regulatory responses and enforcing the environmental regulation of natural gas flaring vary widely in different countries. The World Bank has concluded that efficient and effective regulations and their enforcement need to be in place to reduce flaring and the necessary technology has been available for some time (World Bank 2004). However, as gas-capturing technology is costly, only regulation can mandate its use. The case of Nigeria, among others,

underscores an unintended but real consequence. When profit-making and regulatory
functions are fused into a single enterprise,
penalties for environment violations are low
and enforcement is lax because profits are simply
given preference.

Conflicts of interest in SOEs, embodied in
the split personality of being businessperson and
regulator at the same time, affect all levels of
government. As no person is trained to be both a
businessperson and a public servant at the same
time, there is no objective guidance as to how
decide in individual cases. But more importantly
these conflicts often remain unarticulated by
policy-makers and academics alike. The issue is
not recognised as a serious impediment to
the successful public management of natural
resource wealth. Existing research on SOEs
reform mainly focuses on the consequences of
conflicts of interest. Studies and policy-makers
alike look at effects such as productivity and
efficiency, rather than the root cause of the
problems SOEs are facing.

The conflict of interest described in this
chapter is in fact an agency problem.[1] The agents
(government-appointed SOE managers) often
tend to follow their own inclinations. It is only
natural for people to try to advance their career
and position, which is often simply a more
prestigious, more influential or powerful job in
the bureaucratic structure of a government.
Conflicts of interest do involve agents in the
private sector (see Stiglitz, 2007, p. 26). A
manager may be more interested in his annual
bonus as a short-term personal gain than in the
long-term growth of the company. However,
there is a basic overlap of interest between an
individual and a company because personal
success ultimately depends on and can be
measured by the commercial success of the
company. The individual and the company both
pursue the goal of profit maximisation. In an
SOE, conflicts of interest are more opaque and
can be unexpected.

The principal–agent problem in an SOE is
multidimensional. Government officials' salaries are normally lower than those of their
private sector counterparts. It is obvious that a
person who is willing to accept lower pay may
also have other motivations, especially as
government positions are not infrequently
viewed as a stepping stone to a lucrative position

in the private sector. Cases of former officials
securing well-paid positions in private equity
firms, investment banks or corporations have
become common in the USA, for example.

Persons working for non-profit organisations, such as non-governmental organisations
(NGOs), for example, frequently act out of the
conviction that the organisation's goal is so
important that they are willing to forgo a higher
salary in the private, or even the public, sector.
In fact, such people choose NGOs that
correspond to their own ideals. Public-sector
employees fall somewhere between NGOs
and commercial enterprises. They accept lower
salaries for a number of reasons. Some are
idealists who want to serve their country.
Others want the acclaim of public office and to
climb the political ladder and please the party
leaders.

Ministers who extract the highest possible
revenue out of an SOE, whether or not this
makes commercial sense, can portray themselves
as successful public servants, politicians, who
have generated increased revenue sources for the
national budget, thereby enabling, for example,
their ministry to spend more on social projects
without raising taxes. But no matter how noble a
minister's objectives, they do not necessarily
coincide with operating an SOE as a competitive and sustainable commercial enterprise,
which invariably requires funding the mainte-
nance of an SOE's infrastructure, technological
research and development, and risky and costly
exploration.

A businessperson takes risks, although a
company executive with a watchful eye on the
market price of the company's stock will seek to,
and is required to, balance the short term with
the long term, even if imperfectly. If public
servant–businesspeople take commercial risks,
they will hardly be rewarded for long-term
sustainable success, while their failure to bring
immediate positive results may lead to loss in
elections or lack of promotion. Risk aversion is
therefore a more rational approach for any
manager in an SOE or for the government
official overseeing the SOE, in which there is less,
if any, incentive to develop long-term risk assessment tools. Governments, whether through
SOEs or otherwise, simply are not – and cannot
easily be – structured to be profit maximisers or
commercial risk takers.

Different ministries, different agendas

Since neither ministers of economy nor their counterpart for the environment can enact regulations alien to their respective ministries' scope of responsibility, how can such conflicts be resolved between ministers in the absence of conflict resolution mechanisms, other than consultations among ministers or the assumption of decision-making power by the head of government? In this latter case, the conflict of interest simply shifts from the ministerial to the top executive level, where the head of government assumes the responsibility to reconcile the competing policy goals. In the more developed economies with an independent and competent judiciary, the conflicting interests may be reconciled through the courts.

The failure for the competing functions of profit-making and regulation to be reconciled at any governmental level is illustrated by the case of illegally flaring natural gas from Nigerian oil wells, where the responsible government agency failed to adequately interfere and influence the SOE. Even though flaring natural gas has been illegal in Nigeria since 1979, the companies extracting oil in the country have used this technique to dispose of the natural gas since production started in the country more than four decades ago. In November 2005 the illegality of gas flaring was confirmed by the Nigerian High Court. Nonetheless, flaring by the NNPC and its international partners continues unabatedly. Besides being an enormous waste of a non-renewable resource, flaring causes huge volumes of greenhouse gases, carbon dioxide and methane to be emitted into the atmosphere, while sulphur dioxide emissions return to the delta as acid rain.

Despite the ministry's awareness of the problem, the only action taken so far has been a minimal tax imposed on the flared gas, a measure that has fallen woefully short of deterring this practice (Flaring gas in Nigeria 2005). At the heart of the issue in Nigeria, as well as in other countries, are the institutional and political barriers preventing the Ministry of the Environment from intervening with NNPC, its international partners and the Ministry of Petroleum Resources. The situation in Nigeria needs only to be contrasted with that of Alberta (Canada), with its effective anti-flaring legislation. In Alberta 96 per cent of the gas is now conserved as a result of the regulatory activity of the Alberta Energy and Utilities Board.

Avoidable versus inevitable conflicts

All governments face the challenge of competing interests. For instance, governments must balance the need for environmental protection with the need to create a policy framework that is conducive to investment and avoids overburdening regulations. When two or more core governmental functions, whether social, health, educational or environmental, compete with each other, an inevitable conflict arises because a government is constitutionally obliged to pursue and further all competing objectives. The only solution is in making a political decision – the responsibility cannot be delegated to the private sector.

Avoidable conflicts can surface in cases where a government assumes functions that lie beyond the scope of its core mandate. Commercial activities, including natural resource exploitation, do not fall into the category of core state functions, despite the fact that in most countries natural resources belong to the state or the public sector. There is no reason why the state as owner of a natural resource should also manage the extracting business. It should be noted that such avoidable conflicts are mainly found in developing countries where national energy companies, either alone or as partners of private companies, are in charge of exploiting natural resources. In developed countries such as Canada or the UK, the state, as a rule, is not now an operator, with the notable exception of Norway, as discussed below.

Conflicts of interest can also be observed in government joint ventures with foreign companies. Governments and their SOEs are interested in joint ventures with foreign companies to benefit from their financial strength and technical expertise. However, private businesses have their own expectations of the government's role in a joint venture (Radon 2007). Businesses view governments as contributing partners and expect them to bring more to the table than just the right to exploit a resource, which is essentially a license. It is not a secret that companies hope to enjoy, through the joint venture, privileged relations with enforcement officials. There is an assumption that the government partner will take care of regulatory matters and facilitate solving potential problems with public authorities. In Nigeria, for example, oil companies benefited from the lax enforcement of environmental regulations, which was the consequence of an unspoken quid pro quo. Another example is Texaco's joint venture in Ecuador. In an ongoing lawsuit against Chevron-Texaco, the latter argues that it cannot be held liable for polluting the environment as the government has absolved the company of any liability (Forero 2003).

In the internal joint-venture decision-making process government representatives are confronted with essentially the same conflict of interest as their counterparts vis-à-vis an SOE. The answers to the question of which goals to pursue and what role their personal ambitions should play are basically the same for government officials in both joint ventures and SOEs. Government officials face the same trade-off of competing policy goals. Government officials are also likely to be motivated by the same personal career goals because serving their governments as a representative in a joint venture may well be their first step up the governmental ladder. Moreover, the preference given to short-term profits over long-term sustained growth can also induce government officials to pressure their private partners to produce more than would be economically viable. In oil production sharing agreements, in particular, governments are tempted to press hard for increased and rapid production because their partners are entitled to recover most of the costs of development before they share their revenue with the government. Therefore, governments are tempted to demand maximum production from the outset, paying little attention to the economic viability of the project.

The inherent conflict of interest in operating, overseeing and managing an SOE or participating in a public–private joint venture must be addressed openly. A government should pursue organisational reform and set up a separate and independent management for the SOE while assigning the regulatory function to an equally separate and independent regulatory body. Unfortunately, successful examples of this are few. Norway and Brazil show the viability of such an approach. The Norwegian oil company, Statoil, and its Brazilian counterpart, Petrobras, have both gone public and are listed on major stock exchanges. The Norwegian and Brazilian governments have thereby themselves created a form of checks and balances to theoretically unfettered government control, and have shielded the industry to some extent from the volatility of changes in governments, followed by changes in political focus and goals. Statoil and Petrobras are therefore accountable not only to their governments but also to their private shareholders. Government interference is now mitigated, tempered by shareholders' rights.

However, this managerial independence can theoretically be revoked, even if it causes an outcry from non-governmental shareholders. If a government has a controlling share, it can simply vote its shares as a shareholder and assume control of the management of an SOE. The road to SOE managerial and commercial independence is not an easy one. Until the 1980s Petrobras subsidised oil and gas prices at the behest of the government and had to forego major investments in exploration and development. The result was that Brazil became dependent on oil imports and thus had to learn from experience.

Petrobras' costs of finding oil are lower than some of its private competitors such as Exxon Mobil. A threefold increase in research and development spending over the past five years helped Petrobras to develop cutting-edge technology that, in turn, has enabled the company to be more successful than its competitors in finding new wells and increasing its reserves. As a result Petrobras has doubled its production over the past decade and increased its reserves by 50 per cent. Progress has been accelerated by setting up an independent board of directors and opening up the Brazilian oil market to private competition, forcing Petrobras to become more productive to keep up with its private foreign rivals (Moffet 2007).

Like Brazil, Norway had to learn from its past mistakes. It took, among other salutory experiences, a major scandal for the Government of Norway to shake up the organisational structure of Statoil in 1987–1988. At that time Statoil was a company under the ownership of the Ministry of Petroleum and Energy, which directly interfered with management. The reforms included securing the managerial independence of Statoil and separating SOE operational and regulatory functions.

The current regulatory situation is the result of lessons learnt. Before the reforms of the late 1980s regulatory and operational functions were not clearly separated (OECD 2003, p. 16). Now the Norwegian Government may "only use its ownership influence by participating and voting in the general meeting" (OECD 2003, p. 12) in publicly listed companies such as Statoil and Norsk Hydro ASA. However, Norway's unique societal and institutional structure makes it difficult to draw immediate inferences from the Norwegian experience for other countries. While Norway's evolution from being one of the poorest to one of the richest European nations is remarkable, it has been an egalitarian and homogenous society for at least the past 140 years.

Norway now ranks first in the Human Development Index. Moreover, it has had one of the lowest income distribution inequalities since 1870, which has remained almost unchanged since the discovery of Norway's oil fields, as measured by the GINI coefficient (for a historical account of income inequality, see Nielsen *et al.* 2005). A sense for egalitarianism and community has been traced back to primordial societies (Eckstein 1966) and has been reflected in its institutions at least since 1814, when Norway passed one of the most progressive constitutions in the world for that time. When the country's oil wealth was discovered, a broad national consensus was immediately established on how to ensure its long-term sustainability. What makes the Norwegian experience so unique is primarily not due to the fact that it was among the first nations to adopt constitutionalism and parliamentarism, but to its traditional societal consensus on the basics; namely, its democratic political system and well-functioning and transparent institutions.

What is to be done?

SOEs are part of the world's economic landscape and will continue to be significant commercial drivers in many nations ranging from Norway to Singapore and China. Privatisation of SOEs will accordingly not be a solution to resolving the conflicts of interest addressed in this chapter. Moreover, studies have demonstrated that successful privatisation depends on the existence of complex political and economic structures and conditions (Stiglitz 2007). In the absence of a functioning legal, regulatory and institutional framework, and an experienced and well-trained bureaucracy, privatisations may negatively impact enterprise performance. Therefore, in order to mitigate the impacts of conflicts of interest, as many assume that eliminating such conflicts will remain an elusive ideal, three principal areas of reform should and can be pursued: positioning, organisation and regulatory reform of the SOE.

Clearly defining the objectives of an SOE would address, if not fully remedy, the dilemma of having to achieve too many goals. A focus on long-term sustainable profitability with adequate funding for research and development would enable SOE managers to pursue a strategy of profit maximisation and to resist ever present political pressures to use the SOE profits for national social spending and pork-barrel projects.

Managerial independence for SOEs needs to be embedded in government policy and institutionally established. Guided by and protected by policy guidelines, the managements of Saudi Aramco and Petrobras are largely insulated from political interference. They are thus able to pursue a coherent long-term strategy with a clear commercial focus. In Saudi Arabia, for example, the government has set energy policy targets but leaves the day-to-day operations of Saudi Aramco to highly skilled technocrats (Hoyos 2007) and in Brazil the government has set up an independent board of directors at Petrobras (Moffet 2007).

A single, independent supervisory agency would further mitigate the inherent conflict of interest which arises from a government's dual role as businessperson and regulator. In Brazil, the Agência Nacional do Petróleo or the National Petroleum Agency regulates the oil industry independently from the Ministry of Mines and Energy. In Korea greater managerial autonomy in the country's SOEs was achieved as a consequence of the government's reduced control over the budget, procurement and, critically, personnel management. Both solutions are anchored or embedded in law.

Nevertheless clear-cut functional divisions, even if they are embedded in law, among the government, the regulatory agency and the management of an SOE is in practice negated by the revolving door syndrome. It is not uncommon for officials to leave their government jobs for a position with the SOE they used to regulate or supervise or vice versa. But the fact that this problem also exists to some degree in non-SOE situations does not mean it need not be addressed. Only an absolute prohibition on such revolving door practices will prevent the confusion of what constitutes government and commercial functions. As a complete prohibition is impractical, a long time period ought to be imposed before a person is allowed to make a switch from the government or regulatory agency to an SOE or vice versa.

Additionally, the incentive system governing employees in most SOEs must be re-evaluated. While it is only natural for people to be guided by their personal aspirations, government officials and government-appointed managers are generally more inclined to pursue non-commercial goals such as promoting their own political careers or social goals that correspond to their political convictions than managers of private businesses. Considering the moral hazard SOE employees are exposed to, the organisational incentive structure needs to be changed.

First, material incentives need to be in place so that managers receive remuneration competitive with private industry. Accordingly, SOE employee compensation should also be more than that paid by sister governmental institutions. Only in this way will the incentive to switch from an SOE to a ministry be blunted. The SOE will also need to have the right, as in any private company, to hire and fire in order to avoid becoming a patronage magnet and centre. The incentive system should not promote climbing up the government ladder or encourage a revolving door between an SOE and a ministry. Ideally, as noted, these principles should be anchored in a law.

Secondly, moral incentives can remedy the moral hazard. Material incentives are not the only factors that motivate individuals. Recogni-

tion, pride, esprit de corps and dedication to public service are also motivational forces (Chang 2007, p. 15), especially if a person works for a national champion with global recognition such as Petrobras. But emotional satisfaction cannot, over time, fully make up for non-competitive compensation packages, which are too often ignored, overlooked or simply wished away.

Thirdly, private company-like management rights must be in place. SOE hiring and staffing needs to be merit based and market driven. By increasing the salaries of employees, a more qualified staff would be attracted, although there will always be the risk that SOE could become a patronage centre. Pemex, for example, has approximately 138,000 employees. This is twice the number of PDVSA in Venezuela, even though both companies have approximately the same output. Moreover, Pemex faces almost insurmountable obstacles in firing any of its unionised employees (Black and Martinez 2008). The management of an SOE must have flexibility and independence in making personnel decisions.

Laws are not immutable and can be changed. Accordingly the reforms suggested can always be annulled, modified or restricted. A recent example is PDVSA in Venezuela. After revoking PDVSA's managerial autonomy, the Venezuelan government effectively assumed nearly complete control over the company's management. The head of PDVSA is now the Minister of Energy and Oil. Even Petrobras is experiencing increased government pressure. The Brazilian government is demanding an increase in local content in Petrobras' purchases (Moffet 2007). The likelihood of such a political about-face is significantly higher in countries where the rule of law is weak and power is concentrated in the hands of a few. The Cameroon–Chad pipeline project illustrates this point. The Government of Chad agreed to use the bulk of its oil revenues for development projects and poverty reduction and enacted this commitment into law. However, in 2006 it revoked the law and the oversight agency's independence and allocated the lion's share of revenues to the military (World Bank). But transparency can at least highlight the problem and alert international pressures to spring into action.

In countries where the rule of law, or a democratic give-and-take is more firmly established, legislative hurdles can be introduced to make such reversals less likely. For instance, requiring a supermajority of 75 per cent or more of the votes in parliament could provide a safeguard against a ruling party's attempt to revoke SOE reforms. Normally a supermajority would require the consent of at least some member of the opposition. It would at least institutionalise some degree of checks and balances.

As these conflicts of interest in SOEs will simply not disappear, the only answer is to formally and continually address this issue. Conflict of interest is an issue that must be openly, transparently and regularly confronted. It must be a permanent item on the government agenda, even more so in nations with weak institutions. It is of equal importance that the international community does not ignore this issue. Openly and publicly confronting it is the necessary first step in developing a culture of conflict of interest mitigation and prevention.

Notes

1. In economic theory, the agency or principal–agent dilemma is analysed as arising when information between the principal and the agent is asymmetric (see Chang 2007, p. 14). However, legal scholars approach the problem differently and address the principal–agent problem as a contractual issue. They are concerned with establishing contractually the right incentives to align an agent's interests or motivations with those of the principal. For a concise overview on the agency problem from a contractual perspective see Johnson (2005).

The devil's excrement as social cement: natural resources and political terror, 1980–2002

Indra de Soysa and Helga Malmin Binningsbø

"I call petroleum the devil's excrement. It brings trouble."
(Juan Pablo Pérez Alfonso, cited in Dell 2004, p. 1)

Some scholars blame human rights violations in poor countries on poverty. Poor governments lack the resources to deal with socio-political problems, which means that repression becomes a viable response to dissent (Poe 2004; Poe et al. 1999). Neo-Malthusian scholars too expect the scarcity of natural resources to hinder socio-political development (Homer-Dixon 2000). In resource-rich states, however, rulers enjoy relative financial autonomy and should be able to cope better with social demands.

This, however, does not seem to be the case. Oil wealth emasculates democracy (Bellin 2004; Jensen and Wantchekon 2004; Karl 1997, 1999; Ross 2001).[1] Many identify a "resource curse" that leads to economic failure (Auty 2001; Papyrakis and Gerlagh 2004; Sachs and Warner 2001), poor governance (Leite and Weidmann 1999; Torvik 2002), weak social capital (Woolcock et al. 2001), and even civil war (Collier and Hoeffler 2004; de Soysa 2002; Fearon and Laitin 2003).

Several recent works provide excellent analyses of the "resource curse" literature (Daunderstädt and

Indra de Soysa is Professor of Political Science at the Norwegian University of Science and Technology (NTNU), Trondheim, Norway. He is an Associate Fellow at the Center for the Study of Civil War at the International Peace Research Institute, Oslo (PRIO). He recently co-edited two books entitled *Energy wealth and governance in the caucasus and central Asia* (Routledge) and *How social norms help or hinder development* (OECD). His articles appear in *International Studies Quarterly, International Organization, Journal of Conflict Resolution, Journal of Peace Research, World Development,* and *Conflict Management and Peace Science,* among others.
Email: indra.de.soysa@svt.ntnu.no

Helga Malmin Binningsbø is currently a PhD candidate in political science (Norwegian University of Science and Technology, 2005–) and Research Associate at the Centre for the Study of Civil War, PRIO (2005–). Her research interests include peace-building, post-conflict power sharing and transitional justice. She has recently published an article in *Population and Environment* on the effects of environmental scarcity on civil war.
Email: helga.binningsbo@svt.ntnu.no

Schildberg 2006; Weinthal and Luong 2006). However, rentier-state theories explain some of the outcomes under conditions of resource extraction as a result of the way in which rulers use revenue to buy consent from society in a perverse "development-versus-social stability" trade-off (Basedau and Lacher 2006; Beblawi 1990; Chaudhry 1997; Smith 2004). In other words, bad socio-economic outcomes can be forgiven if rulers maintain stability – buying social peace, after all, is money well spent.

These arguments, however, do not specify clearly what "social stability" means. Such arguments challenge the resource curse hypotheses by suggesting, on the one hand, that financial autonomy for rulers is valuable for social consent and peace, and on the other, that resources lead to a delicate bargain for peace, not conflict. We probe this issue further by focusing on natural resources and the dissent/repression nexus: asking if leaders of resource-wealthy states are able to buy consent due to their relative financial autonomy, as some rentier-state theories speculate?

The aim of this chapter is twofold. We address the debate on whether finance from resource wealth allows rulers to build stable coalitions for remaining in power and dissuading democracy. To what extent is stability achieved without repression? Is it achieved simply by sharing resources via patronage? Since patronage spending is hard to observe directly, we relied on a measure of the level of societal dissent, proxied by the level of repression, to gauge the extent to which resource wealth predicts the stability of regimes at a level short of civil war. In other words, we examine whether it is true that resource wealth, particularly oil wealth, allows rulers to buy social consent, as some have suggested (Basedau and Lacher 2006; Smith 2004). The issue is not just academic. The stability that resource wealth may allow rulers may simply mean a heavy repression of dissent, not successfully soliciting consent.

Second, we investigated the possibility that good economic governance, proxied by the level of economic freedom, conditions the effects of resource wealth on repression. In other words we assess the degree to which economic and institutional reform, which some have discussed in terms of a political-economic conundrun (Bellin 2004), affect decent governance under resource-wealthy conditions, regardless of political democracy and sundry controls.

Natural resources are the devil's excrement

How much of the political performance of countries can be explained by the relative abundance of natural wealth? This question is so paradoxical that it generally commands gradual and halting attention, with the exception some economists who flag poor economic performance among resource-wealthy countries as "the Dutch disease" (Auty 1990; Sachs and Warner 1995). Extracting natural wealth can reduce growth (Sachs and Warner 1995, 2001). A resource boom raises a country's real exchange rate relative to its trading partners, driving up the prices of exports, which has knock-on effects across the rest of the economy. Quite simply, resource wealth makes you expensive (Sachs and Warner 2001).[2]

Apparently, as a long-term consequence, resource-wealthy countries lose out on "learning by doing" since manufacturing industries cannot expand, and the increased consumption and production booms are invariably followed by periods of bust (Rodríguez and Sachs 1999). The empirical evidence for lower economic growth among resource-wealthy countries relative to their resource-poor counterparts is quite numerous (Dell 2004). This is true in the case of highly sophisticated econometric analyses as well as in careful comparative research based on a case study (Auty 2001; de Soysa 2006; Lal and Mynt 1996; Sala-I-Martin 1997).

Other scholars offer more nuanced stories that consider the type of the resources as well as the forms of policy responses that have led to differing outcomes at different times (Auty 2000). Many suggest that economic problems arising from resources can be handled by sound policy and design (Weinthal and Luong 2006). Apparently, the quality of institutions, particularly economic institutions, regardless of the type of regime (i.e. democracy versus autocracy) matters (Bellin 2004).

The "resource curse" literature challenges models of governance and development that assume that welfare and revenue-maximising politicians are constrained from doing good because they lack financial resources and autonomy (Ross 1999). Rather than autonomy for doing good, natural resource rents, particularly those that are easily captured, such as oil and minerals, create perverse incentives that allow rulers to do badly without facing punishment. High rents dissuade the right policies for competitive industrialisation, which in turn has repercussions for the economy and the society (Auty 2001). In short, access to easy money removes the conditions driving the rise of "developmental states". The effects are apparently both cognitive (generating a spend–consume mentality) and strategic (Ross 1999). Resource rents apparently create factional political states, where rent capture allows politicians to survive by dispensing rents, rather than making hard choices about reform (Torvik 2002). Political survival dictates profligacy and waste, rather than providing public goods (Gylfason 2000). In fact, the "paradox of plenty" is driven by policy failure – human folly and vanity.

Another subtle view of outcomes under resource-wealthy conditions is the so-called rentier state effect. According to this view, easy money leads to bad economic outcomes because rulers buy stability by spreading the largess of resource wealth. The vanguard of democracy, the so-called white collar and middle classes, enjoys no tax burden and is thus bought off by the rulers who control the resource rents (Beblawi 1990; Chaudhry 1997). Economic policy failure, for some scholars, might in fact be rooted in political success (Basedau and Lacher 2006; Smith 2004). Regimes that are resource wealthy have the finances to buy off social consent and stave off violent political conflict. These scholars suggest that there are at least as many stable oil-rich countries as there are unstable ones and the discrepant findings might be due to conceptual and measurement confusion about what resource wealth actually means. They suggest that the best way to measure "abundance" is the per capita value of resources, not the per GDP value (Basedau and Lacher 2006). We use both measurements of resource dependence, or resource wealth, as further detailed below

Yet another view of why natural resources matter for conflict is the mechanism of state capacity. Much depends on the related question of how developed state institutions related to taxation and public goods provision are. When institutions related to taxation are underdeveloped, states are institutionally and bureaucratically weak, which in turn affects the ways in which rulers are able to weather hard times or respond to societal pressures (Fearon and Laitin 2003; Karl 1997, 1999). Such processes also lead to the degeneration of social capital, where people are not connected by concerns over public decisions that affect productivity-enhancing public goods (Woolcock *et al.* 2001) and larger questions of political freedom (Ross 2001). Thus, violent conflict occurs because resource wealth weakens state institutions.

Civil war is also explained through another channel. Violent armed conflict is costly and requires finance. Resource wealth allows groups to overcome financial constraints by accumulating natural wealth on the basis of looting (Collier *et al.* 2003). Whether the exact mechanism driving conflict is looting (the availability of finance), state capacity, or another set of political and social maladies related to poor governance remains to be explored more systematically, both in emprical and theoretical terms

(Collier and Hoeffler 2005), but these explanations pose considerable challenge to rentier-state theories that seem to suggest that stability can be bought by resource-wealthy states, even in bad times (Smith 2004).

Since large-scale conflict, regime change and other forms of political instability may in fact be relatively rare, our study explores the connection between levels of political terror (or one-sided violence) and resource extraction. Beyond discussions about conflict, the issues of natural resource wealth and decent government have enormous normative implications. If rentier-state theories are correct and rulers of resource wealth are able to buy peace without state repression, then even if rentier economies do badly, one might call this successful policy-making, or even good statesmanship. However, if stability is being achieved with high levels of repression – that is, if there is considerable dissent – then one might think of patronage spending as wasted money, both instrumentally and normatively, and rulers that rely on such forms of governance are in fact only fooling themselves, sowing the seeds of state failure and violence.

Previous empirical studies on the repression of physical integrity rights have mostly mentioned scarcity of resources as a problem (Poe 2004; Poe *et al.* 1999). For example, the widely-cited studies of Steven Poe and colleagues interpret the negative effect of income per capita on repression and the positive effect of population size on repression as proxies for scarcity (although natural resources are not specifically mentioned). Such arguments accord with those that suggest that oil wealth allows finance and thereby autonomy for building "robust" coalitions that allow regimes (rulers) to survive – the so called rentier-state thesis (Basedau and Lacher 2006; Smith 2004). Smith finds that resource wealth, particularly oil wealth, is associated with less political instability, measured in terms of regime durability, political protest and civil war, even when controlling for repression measured as the level of democracy (Smith 2004). The implication of Smith's (2004) carefully argued study is that oil can be a source of stability, even when autocracy is taken into account. Smith concludes that "many of these regimes may have had robust social coalitions that went beyond the simple purchase of legitimacy" (2004, p. 242). According to Smith (2004, p. 232) "few of these regimes faced serious challenges" even after the collapse of high rents for patronage spending by more than two-thirds in the mid-1980s.

It is also plausible that resource wealth and the nature of the political states that it spawns relate to the nature of the prize available for capture. Thus, for any level of dissent, resource rulers overreact with repression because giving in to dissent may be seen as a sign of weakness. The logic follows others who offer models of autocracy based on income inequality (Acemoglu and Robinson 2006). Why do political rulers block new technologies, better institutions, well-functioning markets and good legal institutions? As they argue, the answer is the fear of replacement, or the proposition that political elites will block "beneficial economic institutional change when they are afraid that these changes will destabilize the existing system and make it more likely that they will lose political power and future rents" (Acemoglu and Robinson 2006, p. 115). If this is true, then understanding how broad-based institutions conducive to good economic management, such as a measure of economic freedom, condition the effect of resource rents on political outcomes is crucial.

Ross (2001) suggests a direct connection between oil wealth and repression. Unlike those who assume that access to finance allows governments to do good, the argument is that rulers prefer to repress dissident opinions to reforming the state because resource rents are easy finances, unlike taxes that would require rulers to make bargains with society. Ross (2001) operationalises repression as the lack of democracy. However, whether or not full-scale democracy is obtained, civil war breaks out, or chronic instability prevails hinges on the actual level of repression of political activism. States practice such acts against dissenters to prevent any one of these scenarios from occurring.

A more direct measure of dissent/repression can be obtained from those who study human rights violations, measured as the threat to personal integrity, or the level of political terror, which may or may not have much to do with the regime type (Davenport and Armstrong 2004). In fact, many find that repression is lower only at very high levels of democracy on the polity scale (Davenport and Armstrong 2004; de Soysa and

Nordås 2007). Testing the effects of resource wealth on a measure of repression defined as the violent repression of dissent (a form of silent violence short of deaths in battle) allows us to address more cleanly the implications of rentier state theories and those who believe in the resource curse.

The policy conundrum

Knowing that there is a resource curse does not break the spell. Poor countries that are blessed by nature cannot ignore this largesse and "keep it in the ground". Several schemes to manage the curse of resources have been tried over the past decades with rather mixed results (Weinthal and Luong 2006). Weinthal and Luong (2006) review the evidence and offer one solution that they claim may be best – allowing competitive private ownership of resources. With illustrative evidence from Russia, they show that what constrains political rulers from mismanaging wealth is the structure of ownership, so that assigning private ownership of extractive activities leads to a demand for better institutions to manage their transactions. We could not test the ownership-structure argument directly, but we observed instead the actual quality of the economic institutions as measured by an index of economic freedom, which should capture those aspects favourable to the development of a private economy (Gwartney and Lawson 2005). In general, others use this index as a measure of good economic governance and as a measure of neoliberal economic policies (Dreher and Rupprecht 2007).

The empirical evidence supporting the view that the resource curse works largely through state and political variables, particularly corruption, education, openness to trade and level of investment, is quite robust (Auty 2001; Bulte *et al.* 2005; Papyrakis and Gerlagh 2004; Ross 1999). When these factors are controlled, the net effect of natural resource wealth turns out to be positive on economic growth (Papyrakis and Gerlagh 2004). When considering more encompassing indicators of human welfare than growth, such as access to food, the human development index, life expectancy and access to safe water, resource wealth works negatively, largely through the quality of institutions (Bulte *et al.* 2005), a result that seems to be true also for economic sustainability (Dietz *et al.* 2006). Thus, the resource curse is not automatic, but it is largely mediated by the quality of institutions. Does the quality of institutions also allow us to understand other political outcomes under conditions of resource wealth, such as the level of dissent and state repression?

Figuring out the best point of entry for policy – political or economic reform – is a conundrum (Bellin 2004). According to Bellin (2004), at least where the Middle East and North Africa (MENA) are concerned, much of the problem is due to the fact that resources have resulted in inward looking state-led development. As a result, these economies have remained technologically backward, having failed to keep pace with changes in the global market place. Thus, a nationalised resource sector drives the economy in ways that lead to the withering away of all other economic activity. The little foreign direct investment that is allowed trickles only into the petroleum sector, and sectors such as tourism and the high technology required by a modern economy are unavailable. Thus, scholars such as Eva Bellin see greater integration in the global market as one viable solution for the stagnant socio-economic and political world of the MENA region. However, since political elites fear change, the *status quo* prevails. This study explicitly tests whether a connection between resource wealth and repression is conditional on the level of economic freedom, holding constant several other factors.

The dissent/repression nexus

Dissent is the sentiment of non-agreement. Political dissenters disagree with the majority or the ruler of a group or a state. Dissenters are those who do not obey standard operating procedures and may actively engage in making their opposition known. Dissent is the opposite of agreement, consensus and consent. Existing models of human rights violations work on the basis of a state's (ruler's) response to threat (Poe 2004). According to Steven Poe (2004), who uses a basic rational actor model of 'willingness and opportunity' for assessing state behaviour (Most and Starr 1989), states resort to repression when

their capacity to handle threat (their strength) is low relative to the level of dissent (threat). In other words, the balance between threat and capacity predict human rights violations.

Empirical analyses of repression, thus, can gauge factors that increase threat while controlling for factors that gauge state capacity. Surprisingly, despite a wealth of theory on natural resources and bad governance, no empirical studies have addressed the effect of resource wealth on the level of state repression directly. Given the enormous evidence now available on the resource curse, this omission is not trivial.[3] We hope to correct this lacuna.

Method, models and data

We used the political terror scale (PTS), one of the most widely used measures of repression (Gibney and Dalton 1996; Hafner-Burton 2005). In robustness checks, we also used the CIRI data, which are generated from similar sources, but scaled in such a way that they capture the patterns and sequence of the severity of repression, freeing the researcher from making a priori assumptions such as whether torture matters more than death and disappearances (Cingranelli and Richards 1999). However, interpreting the results from the nine-point CIRI scale is harder than interpreting results from the five-point PTS scale, since the PTS's cut-off points are much clearer to interpret substantively. Nevertheless, the two measures are highly correlated (r = -0.81).

We used the PTS scale adapted by Emilie Hafner-Burton who defines it as follows (Hafner-Burton 2005, p. 689):

Level 1 If countries are under a secure rule of law, political imprisonment and torture are rare and political murders are extremely rare.

Level 2 If imprisonment for non-violent political activities is limited, torture and beating are exceptional and political murders rare.

Level 3 If political imprisonment is extensive, execution and political murder is common and detention for political views is acceptable.

Level 4   If the practices of level 3 are expanded to a larger segment of population and murders and disappearances are common, but terror affects primarily those who interest themselves in political practices and ideas.

Level 5   If levels of terror affect the whole population and decision-makers do not limit themselves to pursuing private and ideological goals.

Using a basic model described in detail below, we estimated the effects of resource wealth on the political terror scale (PTS) between 1980 and 2002 (we used the US State Department coding, but we also tested the models with the Amnesty coding in checks of robustness (for a detailed examination of the Amnesty and State Department coding, see Poe [2001]). First, we estimated a discrete variable measuring the importance of oil in total GDP, where the variables take the value of 1 if the oil exports are more than one-third of GDP and 0 if not (Fearon and Laitin 2003). Second, we used the World Bank's resource rents data broken up into total resource rents, energy rents (petroleum, coal, natural gas), and mineral rents as a share of GDP (Bolt et al. 2002; Hamilton and Clemens 1999). The rentier argument should work for all "point source" resources that generate high rents, such as oil and minerals. Additionally, we distinguished between resource rents as a share of GDP and resource rents per capita, since this difference should matter in terms of how much actual money (finance) is available per person. The rentier effect is particularly salient in per capita terms as it captures relative abundance (Basedau and Lacher 2006). We tested the rent variables in per GDP and per capita terms.

We followed the initial tests with conditional effects of resource wealth and economic freedom. These data are obtained from the Fraser Institute (Gwartney and Lawson 2005). The Economic freedom in the world data measure the extent to which an economy is free from state interference and allows private economic activity. Economic freedom is judged along 22 criteria, which include both objective indicators, such as the government's share in the economy, trade openness and restrictions on capital controls, and subjective indicators such as the level of independence of the judiciary (for

full details see the Fraser n.d.). These data are presented in quintiles until the year 2000 and yearly for the remaining two years in our analyses. We interpolate between the 5-year intervals from 1980–2000. Since these data change relatively slowly, we think the interpolated values are representative.

Previous empirical literature on the subject of human rights abuse by governments has pointed to several factors that influence the likelihood of state repression. Among the factors that are found to have significant effects on repression are past levels of repression (the human rights legacy), the level of formal democracy, population size, economic standing and the threat of organised violence in the form of involvement in international and civil wars (Carey and Poe 2004). The inclusion of controls for civil war and participation in international wars is based on the existence of real or perceived threats to the leaders' goals (Poe et al. 1999, p. 293) to which the leaders decide to respond by force. If there is an ongoing civil war in the state the threat to the leaders of the state is evident.[4] We used the Uppsala/PRIO dataset on international wars and civil wars with at least 25 battle-related deaths (Gleditsch et al. 2002). We also included the number of years of peace since the last war for both types of war. The peace year variables were calculated using the binary times series cross-section data programme working in Stata (see Beck et al. 1998).

Previous research has explicitly related the effect of political culture to the legal traditions of a state. According to this a British (common law) legal tradition that has independent bureaucracies and court systems constrains arbitrary acts by government (Poe et al. 1999). According to this leftist governments have very little human rights violations compared to other kinds (Poe et al. 1999). Since leftist governments may go in and out of office, we used instead a more permanent measure for a socialist legacy by using a measure for a socialist legal system coded by La Porta et al. (1998). The exact reason why socialist states are prone to respecting human rights is unclear, except that they are less likely to be challenged (dissent is low). Thus, the threat level is low while the capacity to repress is high, particularly because such states often fell outside the western sphere of influence. We used the British legal system and socialist legal systems as dummy variables, as in several other studies of this nature (La Porta *et al.* 1998).

Democracy is an important predictor of respect for human rights, and an important control when estimating the effects of resources on repression (Poe *et al.* 1999). Established democracies have institutionalised means for handling non-violent protest and citizens regularly use the norms of protest, strikes and other civil actions to make demands on government. Authorities that do respond to such action are constrained by how far they can go by the laws of due process and political oversight. Our democracy measure was a dummy variable taking the value 1 if the Polity IV (variable polity2) score was above 6 and 0 if it was below that (Davenport and Armstrong 2004). While some argue there is a non-monotonic effect between democracy and repression, we do not explicitly address this issue since we are interested in capturing full democracy as a check against autocratic conditions under resource wealth (Bueno de Mesquita *et al.* 2005; Regan and Henderson 2002). According to many, democracy might be best defined as a discrete variable (Przeworski 1999). Other find that the level of human rights are positively and significantly predicted only at very high levels of democracy (Davenport and Armstrong 2004).

Economic conditions can affect the likelihood of repression. Poe *et al.* (1999, p. 294) state that "in countries with economies characterised by scarcity, regimes will be more likely to repress domestic threats". Another way of looking at this is that if the country's economy is characterised by abundant resources, such as oil, this might constitute a prize for controlling the state, which is so high that the leaders will be more willing to repress people to stay in power. Henderson's argument is that in more developed states the population will be more content, and thus less repression is needed to keep control (Henderson 1991). We use gross national income per capita in purchasing power parity terms (logged) and the growth rate of income per capita (World Bank 2006).

Scholars argue that states with large populations will be more repressive than countries with small populations (Landman 2005). Theoretically, a large population implies more potential constellations for conflict and a larger number of potential dissidents. A large popula-

tion generally also means a large geographical area, which can be more difficult to control than a small area (Fearon and Laitin 2003). Collier *et al.* (2003) and Fearon and Laitin (2003) find that large populations are at a higher risk of civil war. Poe *et al.* (1999 p. 294) argue that "a large or dense population may increase the occurrence of state terrorism by increasing the number of occasions on which threats and coercive acts can occur", and that large population also affects repression by putting strains on available resources. We use population size (logged), and these data are from the World Bank (2006). We also use the level of ethnic fractionalisation, since population size and ethnicity are related and it might be that repression relates to "governability" under conditions of cultural fractionalisation (Easterly and Levine 1997). Some authors, however, report no effect from higher ethnic and cultural fractionalisation on the level of state repression (Lee *et al.* 2004; Walker and Poe 2002).

A recent history of repression should be another central factor. Bureaucracies may have standard operating procedures that are inert. Therefore, repression one year is likely to lead to repression in the next. This lagged dependent variable (LDV) is highly significant in previous studies. On the one hand, the LDV controls time dependence and serial correlation and it presumably captures factors omitted in the models. On the other, the LDV may soak up so much of the variance that it masks potential causal factors explained by the other X variables (Achen 2000; Kittel and Winner 2005; Plümper *et al.* 2005). We run tests with and without the LDV but only report results excluding the LDV. Finally, we also control for trends over time. Time dummies also take care of any unobserved factors, such as the end of the Cold War or global policy shifts that may affect human rights. The descriptive statistics of all the variables are displayed in the appendix.

We estimate the main models using ordered probit techniques. Pooled data (or cross-section, time series data) are plagued by problems of serial correlation (autocorrelation) and heteroscedasticity (non-spherical errors). We controlled these factors by using the cluster option in the statistical programme Stata (v. 9.2), which assumes that the observations are non-independent within units (countries) but independent across them. The Huber–White robust standard errors computed with the cluster method is robust to serial correlation and heteroscedasticity (Wiggins 1999). In our robustness checks using the CIRI "physical integrity rights" measure, we used linear repression because this nine-point scale is relatively normally distributed (Hamilton 1992). We use ordinary least squares (OLS) with panel corrected standard errors using an AR1 process to control for autocorrelation (Beck and Katz 1995). We estimated our variables of interest in the following basic model:

$$PTS = \beta0 + \beta1(lnincome/pc) + \beta2(growth/pc)$$
$$+ \beta3(democ) + \beta4(lnpop.size)$$
$$+ \beta5(civ\ war) + \beta6(int\ war)$$
$$+ \beta7(civ\ peace\ yrs) + \beta8(int\ peace\ yrs)$$
$$+ \beta9(ethfrac) + \beta10(British\ legal)$$
$$+ \beta11(socialist\ legal\ system)$$

Results

In Table 1, columns 1, 2, 3 and 4 report the results of natural resource wealth on political terror. In column 1, we see that the discrete variable measuring oil exports greater than one-third of GDP has a positive and statistically highly significant effect on the level of political terror (the replication dataset and files will be made available for download upon publication at http://www.svt.ntnu.no/iss/Indra.de.Soysa/default.htm).

In columns 2, 3 and 4 we test the continuous measures of resource, energy, and mineral resource rents per GDP, which also yield positive and statistically highly significant effects on the level of political terror. These results hold when running these models with the PTS based on the Amnesty coding, when we included a lagged dependent variable, when we tested the physical integrity rights data (CIRI data), when using a linear and squared term of democracy, the share of the Muslim population, and a sample of only less developed countries (results can be obtained from the authors).[5] We detected no multicolinearity as the VIF scores were all well below the problematic cut-off of 10 (Rabe-Hesketh and Everitt 2004). Almost all the control

variables yield results similar to those reported by others, except that countries that have recently experienced interstate war seem to have better respect for human rights. This may signify the nature of current interstate wars where democratic coalitions from rich states target violators of civil rights (such as in the First Gulf War and Serbia), or are likely to be partners in UN-sanctioned actions against failed states. Democracy, the British legal system, the population size, civil war and so on are all robustly related to repression with the expected sign.

What is the size of the substantive impact of natural resources on the observed levels of repression? To assess the substantive impact, we computed the marginal effects (or elasticities) of each of our variables of interest, holding all other variables at their mean values. We first computed the predicted probability of the entire model with all variables held at their means for the PTS cut-off point of four and above; the point at which repression of the politically active population becomes widespread (see above). Then we changed the variables of interest by some reasonable quantity and re-compute the predicted probability (We use the mfx function in Stata to compute the marginal effects).

The predicted probability when oil exports is held at 0 and all the others at their mean is 0.0479, but this prediction increases to 0.0976 when oil is at 1 and the controls at their means, an increase of the risk by 104 per cent. The same exercise using democracy (going from 1 to 0) increases the risk of observing the PTS values four and above from 0.0214 to 0.1036, or 384 per cent. The predicted probability at civil war = 0 with the controls at their mean is 0.0365, which increases to 0.21 (the highest effect of all the discrete variables in our model), or an increase in the risk of observing 4 and above on the PTS by 475 per cent. These effects suggest that oil's real effect is probably much greater than reported above, working directly and indirectly through civil war and the lack of democracy (de Soysa 2002; Fearon 2005; Fearon and Laitin 2003; Humphreys 2005; Ross 2001).

In column 5 (Table 1), we test the conditional effect of oil exports and the level of economic freedom on political terror. As seen there, the conditional effect (oil × economic freedom) is negative. Since the oil exports variable is a dummy variable, the interpretation

TABLE 1. Ordered probit regressions of natural resource dependence and political terror, 1980–2002

	Column 1	Column 2	Column 3	Column 4	Column 5
			Political terror scale		
Oil exports > 1/3 GDP (dummy)	0.395				1.036
	(2.62)***				(1.37)
Resource rents/GDP (log)		0.140			
		(3.26)***			
Energy rents/GDP (log)			0.136		
			(3.17)***		
Mineral rents/GDP (log)				0.227	
				(3.1)***	
Economic freedom index					− 0.273
					(− 3.1)***
Oil exports × econ. freedom					− 0.175
					(− 1.3)
Income per capita (log)	− 0.486	− 0.516	− 0.551	− 0.486	− 0.344
	(6.14)***	(6.30)***	(6.43)***	(6.19)***	(− 3.4)***
Income growth per capita	− 0.004	− 0.003	− 0.003	− 0.005	− 0.006
	(0.75)	(0.55)	(0.42)	(0.78)	(− .86)
Democracy (dummy)	− 0.805	− 0.757	− 0.756	− 0.872	− 0.777
	(7.16)***	(6.39)***	(6.35)***	(7.20)***	(− 5.8)***
British legal system (dummy)	− 0.145	− 0.332	− 0.287	− 0.358	− 0.199
	(1.03)	(2.24)**	(1.92)*	(2.49)**	(− 1.2)
Socialist legal system (dummy)	− 0.257	− 0.375	− 0.402	− 0.347	− 0.469
	(1.58)	(2.10)**	(2.24)**	(1.99)**	(− 2.1)**
Ethnic fractionalisation	− 0.706	− 0.667	− 0.716	− 0.669	− 0.64
	(2.50)**	(2.34)**	(2.44)**	(2.38)**	(− 2.0)**
Population size (log)	0.251	0.269	0.259	0.280	0.267
	(5.56)***	(5.63)***	(5.33)***	(6.01)***	(4.9)***
Civil war (dummy)	1.092	1.103	1.115	1.078	1.03
	(7.57)***	(7.55)***	(7.62)***	(7.71)***	(6.4)***
Time since last civil war	− 0.023	− 0.023	− 0.023	− 0.024	− 0.022
	(4.98)***	(4.91)***	(4.96)***	(5.03)***	(− 4.5)***
International war (dummy)	0.366	0.358	0.344	0.413	0.302
	(1.50)	(1.33)	(1.27)	(1.54)	(1.3)
Time since last international war	0.013	0.013	0.014	0.012	0.011
	(3.04)***	(2.97)***	(3.22)***	(2.80)***	(2.3)***
Observations	2674	2412	2412	2412	2151
No. of countries	130	124	124	124	110
Wald χ^2	646.9	582.9	592.3	593.1	554.3
Prob > χ^2	0.00001	0.00001	0.00001	0.00001	0.00001

Robust z-statistics in parentheses. *significance at 10%; **significance at 5%; ***significance at 1%. Year dummies computed in all tests, results not shown. PTS, political terror scale.

of the interaction effect is relatively straightforward (Brambor *et al.* 2006; Braumoeller 2004). The positive effect of oil exports on political repression seems to be moderated at higher levels of economic freedom, holding constant the control variables. This relationship can be seen graphically in Fig. 1.

The solid line from the top left corner represents the interaction between economic freedom and oil exporter, and the dotted line represents the effect of economic freedom when oil takes the value 0. As seen there, the risk of repression among oil exporters decreases as the level of economic freedom increases. The three variables are jointly highly significant (p < 0.00001). In fact, the risk of repression among oil exporters falls below the prediction of economic freedom among non-oil exporters (roughly around the value six on the economic freedom index). The conditional effects between oil exports and economic freedom clearly suggest that resource-wealthy states can avoid facing the dissent–repression nexus through institutional reforms that support markets. These results support those who say that rulers with access to easy money have little incentive to make political and economic reforms that may undermine their hold over society – the political,

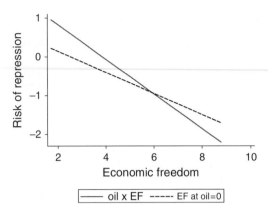

FIGURE 1. Conditional plot of oil exports and the level of economic freedom (EF).

economic conundrum (Acemoglu and Robinson 2000; Bellin 2004).

We have thus far tested only a discrete variable measuring oil exports and resource wealth as rents per GDP. In Table 2 we test the effects of energy and mineral rents per capita, since the per capita measure captures the available finance for patronage spending to a less ambiguous degree than rents per GDP (Basedau and Lacher 2006).

As seen in Table 2, the independent effects of both energy and mineral rents per capita are positive and highly significant. In column 3, we entered an interactive variable as above. Again, the effects of energy rents per capita on repression are unambiguously lower the higher the values of economic freedom. The results remain the same if we use rents per GDP rather than rents per capita.

These results are certainly additional empirical evidence suggesting that resource wealth distorts state society relations in violent and degenerative ways below levels of extreme forms of armed conflict. They also suggest that resource-wealthy states are more likely to take repressive measures in terms of substantial physical violations of personal rights of political dissenters independently of macro-political factors such as regime type. In other words, the stability of oil-wealthy states, even when stability is defined as the absence of organised violence, may come at a rather high price.

Nor does it seem that stability is being bought easily from at least some in the political classes, which suggests that many of the maladies faced by resource wealthy states may be related

to the physical repression that dissuades democracy and other types of good governance (Jensen and Wantchekon 2004; Ross 2001). Easy money for rulers might also mean easy repression, following the logic of the "political replacement" argument, which suggests that rulers will not easily make reforms because of their fear of losing control of future rents (Acemoglu and Robinson 2006). Our results lead us to reject the recent challenge to resource curse arguments, which suggest that resource wealth may allow leaders to use this wealth for effective peace-buying. On the contrary, the quality of institutions seems to matter, above that of income. There is support for the view that state capacity

TABLE 2. Ordered-probit regressions of resource wealth per capita and political terror, 1980–2002

	(1)	(2)	(3)
	Political terror scale		
Energy rents per capita (log)	0.074 (2.81)***		0.337 (2.48)**
Mineral rents per capita (log)		0.119 (2.92)***	
Econ. freedom × energyrentspc			−0.051 (2.24)**
Economic freedom index			−0.164 (1.62)
Income per capita (log)	−0.594 (6.62)***	−0.520 (6.90)***	−0.429 (3.87)***
Income growth per capita	−0.002 (0.29)	−0.004 (0.72)	−0.007 (0.99)
Democracy (dummy)	−0.777 (6.45)***	−0.905 (7.53)***	−0.804 (5.97)***
British legal system (dummy)	−0.298 (1.95)*	−0.369 (2.59)***	−0.179 (1.07)
Socialist legal system (dummy)	−0.355 (2.10)**	−0.311 (1.85)*	−0.593 (2.52)**
Ethnic fractionalisation	−0.726 (2.46)**	−0.662 (2.39)**	−0.772 (2.37)**
Population size (log)	0.255 (5.36)***	0.268 (5.95)***	0.241 (4.33)***
Civil war (dummy)	1.112 (7.53)***	1.078 (7.65)***	1.052 (6.39)***
Time since last civil war	−0.023 (4.97)***	−0.025 (5.17)***	−0.023 (4.65)***
International war (dummy)	0.350 (1.34)	0.428 (1.62)	0.279 (1.16)
Time since last international war	0.014 (3.30)***	0.011 (2.71)***	0.010 (2.16)**
Observations	2430	2430	2050
No. of countries	124	124	101
Wald χ^2	588.4	571.4	513.2
Prob > χ	0.00001	0.00001	0.00001

Robust z-statistics in parentheses. *significant at 10%; **significant at 5%; ***significant at 1%. Year dummies computed in all tests, results not shown. energyrentspc, energy rents per capita.

in resource-wealthy states is affected by good institutions that safeguard private property and well-functioning markets. Our results, taken together, do not support the view that poor governments may resort to repression because they face "scarcities" and lack resources (Poe *et al.* 1999).

We conducted several tests for sensitivity. Since oil wealth is largely concentrated where there are a large number of Muslim populations we entered a variable for the share of such population. This variable is obtained from Fearon and Laitin (2003). Rather than oil wealth, it could be Muslim cultural traits and social institutions that matter (Huntington 1997). Neither the inclusion of religious variables nor regional dummies affected our basic results. In fact, rather than the share of the Muslim population, it was the share of the Catholic population that had the strongest relation of all the religions tested with the level of political terror; a result also reported by others (de Soysa and Nordås 2007). Entering regional dummies for the Middle East, North Africa and sub-Saharan Africa did not change the basic results. We tested all models with the CIRI data on respect for human rights using linear estimating techniques, such as the OLS with panel corrected standard errors, but the basic results obtained with the PTS data hold up. Resource-wealthy countries have an independent effect on repression.

Conclusion

Despite widespread evidence for political failure within countries that rely on resource wealth, some argue that oil-wealthy states can buy social consent and thereby create socio-political stability. In a similar vein, others argue that states repress human rights when they face financial and other scarcities for solving social problems. We demonstrate that natural resource wealth has an independent effect on repression defined as state sanctions against political activism and dissent by citizens. These findings preliminarily suggest that rentier-state arguments about the ability of rulers to buy off dissidents are perhaps only partially true and need qualification: "stability" may be bought at some price. Are socio-political coalitions of governance robust if dissent is widespread and requires repression? Our results point at possible ways in which rulers of resource-wealthy states may be constrained from the outside, and how pressure for democracy can be supported and nourished by aiding those who dissent. Good policy for overcoming the "political Dutch disease" will depend very much on the dynamics shaping the incentives of political actors; a lesson that is easily gleaned from resource-wealthy success cases such as Norway and Botswana.

Our results, taken together, suggest that there is nothing automatic about a poor performance on respect for human rights under conditions of resource wealth. We find in particular that higher quality institutions that support markets, regardless of income and democracy, matter for the way in which governance is affected. Since humans build institutions and devise and implement policies, it is the autonomy allowed of the ruler (individual, group, or class) to access easy money, not scarcity, that matters. How to constrain the incentives that drive bad policies, thus, will be crucial for mitigating the effects of the political Dutch disease in resource-wealthy countries. This would require thinking hard about the constraints that drive rulers in resource-wealthy states to build better institutions. Although we have not addressed it directly, perhaps good institutions emanate from the ownership structures of the resource industry, where better institutions are required for mediating the transaction costs among private actors and the state (Weinthal and Luong 2006). More focused research on this and other mechanisms will allow us to understand better the conditions under which we can escape the resource curse.

Appendix: summary stats

Variable	Obs	Mean	SD	Min	Max
PTS amnesty	2579	2.57	1.12	1	5
PTS state dept	2674	2.41	1.13	1	5
CIRI physint	2536	4.89	2.30	0	8
Oil exporter	2674	0.15	0.35	0	1
Resource rents/GDP (1n)	2412	1.26	1.16	0	5.83
Energy rents/GDP (1n)	2412	0.88	1.22	0	5.83
Mineral rents/GDP (1n)	2412	0.32	0.62	0	3.34
Energy rents per head (1n)	2430	2.32	2.45	0	9.95
Mineral rents per head (1n)	2430	1.15	1.47	0	6.19
Index of economic freedom	2151	5.61	1.24	1.72	8.85
Income per capita (1n)	2674	8.07	1.14	5.80	10.49
Income growth per capita	2674	0.89	5.57	-46.99	37.49
Democracy	2674	0.46	0.49	0	1
British legal system	2674	0.31	0.46	0	1
Socialist legal system	2674	0.12	0.33	0	1
Ethnic fractionalisation	2674	0.42	0.28	0.0041	0.93
Population size (1n)	2674	16.11	1.45	12.79	20.97
Civil war	2674	0.18	0.38	0	1
Civil peace years	2674	20.90	17.60	0	56
Inter-state war	2674	0.031	0.17	0	1
Inter-state peace years	2674	24.79	15.69	0	56

CIRI, Cingranelli and Richards physical integrity rights data; GDP, gross domestic product; PTS, political terror scale.

Notes

1. What we mean by resource wealth and resource dependence is the degree to which states rely on rents from natural wealth relative to other economic activity. The correlation between resource rents per capita (logged) and resource rents per GDP (logged) is very high $r = 0.87$. This is not surprising, since population size is reflected in GDP.

2. The "Dutch disease" refers to the rise in a country's real exchange rate during resource booms, which ultimately hurts exports. The term emanates from the poor performance of the Dutch economy after the discovery of natural gas.

3. The NGO and activist literature highlight a tight connection between oil and human rights violations, particularly when they are castigating oil companies, such as Shell's activities in the Niger delta. See Amnesty International 2005.

4. The justification Poe and associates use for including international war in their models of an intra-state phenomenon such as repression of citizens, is a little vague. Although the causal mechanisms are not fleshed out, they find evidence of increasing repression during involvement in international crisis situations. One possible explanation might be that leaders see an increased need for instituting measures such as states of emergency for fear of internal dissent to the war. However, others fail to verify the finding on international war (Richards *et al.* 2001).

5. The effect of democracy is monotonic; i.e., the more democracy, the more respect for personal integrity rights.

Natural resource rent-cycling outcomes in Botswana, Indonesia and Venezuela

Richard M. Auty

Context

The application of multi-country regressions to test the natural resource curse thesis has reached a stalemate. The resource curse thesis received a boost when Sachs and Warner (1995, 1999) concluded that the disappointing performance of resource-rich governments during 1970–1989 was associated with trade policy closure designed to counter the employment-diminishing effects of Dutch disease. Later econometric analysis suggested, however, that the quality of the institutions inherited from the colonial experience was a more critical determinant of development outcomes than natural resources per se (Acemoglu *et al.* 2001). This finding was in turn challenged by Glaeser *et al.* (2004), who queried the utility of the institutional indices selected and found that human capital accumulation and policy choice determined institutional quality. Subsequently, Collier and Hoeffler (2006) reported that, in the presence of high rent, autocracies outperform democracies in terms of economic growth whereas in the presence of low rent the reverse is true. Most recently, Lederman and Maloney (2007) use estimates of mineral rent to suggest that natural resources have a positive effect on economic growth and that the role of institutions is equivocal at best.

Comparative country case study analysis can revitalise research into the resource curse by identifying the factors that govern rent deployment

Richard Auty, Professor Emeritus of Economic Geography at Lancaster University, has advised many multilateral agencies on economic development issues. He previously taught at Dartmouth College and the University of Guyana. His research interests include industrial policy and rent-cycling theory.
Email: r.auty@lancaster.ac.uk

and by tracing their interaction, thereby setting the econometricians' hyperbolic "silver bullet" explanations in their broader context. As an example, Collier and Hoeffler (2006) suggest that high mineral rent makes it politically more profitable for democratic governments to channel public revenue through patronage networks to secure swing voters, rather than into providing public goods, which confer no electoral edge since they benefit supporters and opponents alike. The successful rent deployment by democratic Botswana is therefore an anomaly, which they attribute to strong institutional checks and balances. This chapter qualifies their hypothesis after comparing rent cycling in Botswana since the late-1960s with that in democratic Venezuela, which experienced a collapse in growth and with Suharto's autocratic Indonesia, which sharply cut poverty during 1967–1997.

The chapter begins by briefly introducing rent-cycling theory. It then sets out, first, the initial conditions of the three case study countries in the early 1970s on the eve of sizeable increases in their mineral rent; and, second, the nature of their subsequent rent streams. In the subsequent sections, rent-cycling theory is applied to explain, respectively, the Venezuelan failure, Botswana's success and the broad-based welfare gains of Suharto's Indonesia. The chapter argues that high rent corrodes institutions when it is cycled via patronage networks but that successful rent cycling owes less to resilient institutions and more to country-specific incentives for the elite to create wealth.

The emerging theory of rent cycling

Rent-cycling theory focuses upon the frequently neglected interaction between politics and the economy in developing countries. It grows out of the fact that the three principal forms of rent (natural resources, geopolitical [foreign aid] and regulatory [from government intervention to change relative prices]), can each comprise a sizeable fraction of GDP in low-income countries (5–20 per cent of GDP), and more in aggregate, which can distort the political economy. Since rent can be detached from the activity that generates it, it elicits political contests to capture it (Krueger et al. 1992). Consequently, rent streams strongly impact both on the incentives of the political state and on the structure of the economy. Since rent from subsoil assets is the theme of this ISSJ monograph, this chapter concentrates on natural resource rent.

The central premise of rent-cycling theory is that the scale of the rent systematically moulds political incentives to vary the degree of an economy's divergence from its optimum development trajectory. Stylised facts models of low-rent and high-rent economies explain why (see Auty 2007 for a detailed description). The low-rent competitive industrialisation model provides a "best practice" counterfactual against which to compare the high-rent staple trap model, which is strongly associated with mineral-driven economies. The model is based on the premise that low rent encourages wealth creation because the principal means for the government to increase its revenue is by taxing an expanding economy. Low rent therefore creates incentives to provide public goods and to maintain efficiency incentives. These incentives favour channelling rent through markets rather than patronage networks. The economy therefore adheres to its comparative advantage, which in a low-rent economy initially lies in exporting labour-intensive manufactured goods. This drives a pair of virtuous economic and social circles.

The low rent economic circle sees rapid export-oriented industrialisation quickly absorb surplus rural labour, which drives up wages and triggers competitive diversification of the economy into more productive activity. Early industrialisation also advances urbanisation, which accelerates the demographic cycle so population growth slows and the dependency : worker ratio falls. This lifts the saving and investment rates while competitive diversification maintains investment efficiency to sustain rapid per capita GDP growth. The virtuous low-rent social circle limits income inequality because labour scarcity puts a floor under the wages of the poor while the rapid accumulation of skills through economic diversification puts a ceiling on the skill premium. In addition, sustained rapid per capita GDP growth strengthens three sanctions against anti-social governance to nurture an endogenous democratisation that is consensual. Specifically; (a) the rapid diversification of taxation from exports to profits, incomes and expenditure increases pressure for political accountability; (b) market-driven urbanisation strengthens civic voice and (c) the growth of private firms elicits demands to protect profits by strengthening property rights and the rule of law.

In contrast, high rent deflects political and economic agents into rent capture and distribution at the expense of wealth creation because the benefits of rent redistribution are both substantial and immediate, whereas the benefits of wealth creation accrue through the long term and may be captured by successors. This triggers a negative economic circle because it boosts the fraction of rent cycled through patronage channels rather than markets, which reduces investment efficiency so that GDP growth slows even if the rent sustains high investment. A prolonged reliance on primary exports also skips the labour-intensive industrialisation phase of the low-rent model so that surplus rural labour persists and feeds income inequality. Wary of urban unrest, governments deploy rent to create employment that markets will not support, typically by protecting infant industry and over-extending the bureaucracy.

The burgeoning demands of this rent-seeking sector eventually exceed the capacity of the primary sector to meet them due to either ongoing structural change or a negative price shock. Governments must then reform the economy by promoting markets and rationing rent, which rent recipients resist. High-rent governments therefore find it politically expedient to augment the rent by extracting returns to capital and labour from the primary sector, which further undermines its viability. In this way, the high-rent economy becomes locked into a staple trap as an expanding rent-dependent sector corrodes the viability of the primary sector upon which it increasingly depends. In addition, declining investment efficiency slows economic growth and retards competitive restructuring of the economy, undermining its resilience to shocks.

Finally, the high-rent negative social circle is rooted in the rise in income inequality explained above. The resulting social tension is exacerbated when faltering GDP growth necessitates rent rationing. High rent also corrodes institutions by weakening all three sanctions against anti-social governance. First, the rent substitutes sovereign revenue for revenue from income, profits and value added taxes so that pressure for political accountability falls. Second, patronage-driven rent channelling creates a dependent form of social capital. Third, corruptions worsens because businesses increase their returns by lobbying politicians and civil servants for favours rather than by investing productively and pushing for a strengthened rule of law to protect returns to economic risk-taking. The following section now compares initial conditions in the three case study countries and the nature of their subsequent rent streams.

Initial conditions in the early 1970s and subsequent rent shocks

On the eve of the expansion in mineral rent that all three economies experienced through the 1970s and into the 1980s, Botswana and Venezuela were both consensual democracies (that is, with broad agreement on the direction of economic policy). The Botswanan elite had long-evolved forms of consensual governance and in 1965 backed a rural-based political party that won the first election and retained power over four decades, despite rising urbanisation (Acemoglu *et al.* 2003). In Venezuela the

collapse of the Jiminez dictatorship in 1958 ushered in a two-party consensual democracy that deployed oil rent to consolidate its position, initially commanding widespread support and high electoral turnouts (Hausmann 2003). Lastly, Indonesia remained an autocracy as Suharto consolidated army power following the chaotic "guided democracy" of Sukarno (Bevan *et al.* 1999).

The Venezuelan democracy was less healthy than it appeared. The imposition of sizeable income taxes on the multinational oil companies in 1943 established the state's reliance on oil rent to subsidise socio-economic activity and limit non-oil taxation (Karl (1997, pp. 88–89). Private capital and the trade unions captured the import substitution policy in the 1960s to siphon away rent by retaining protection so the infant industries had no incentive to mature (Bourguinon 1988). Consistent with the staple trap model, a moderate GDP growth (of 4.6 per cent) during 1960–1974 masked a fall in investment efficiency and slowing per capita GDP growth (Elias 1978). Rent cycling had already distorted Venezuela's economy by the eve of the 1973 oil shock. Table 1 generates an index of Dutch disease effects by comparing the actual structure of GDP with the predicted structure for a country of Venezuela's per capita income, based on an analysis of market economies (Syrquin and Chenery 1989). The Venezuelan Dutch disease index in 1972 was high at 13.9, because agriculture generated less than half its predicted share of non-mining GDP while manufacturing produced barely two-thirds of its expected share. Yet, high as it is, the index underestimates the Dutch disease effects because most Venezuelan manufacturing and much agriculture required protection from imports.

Botswana achieved independence in 1966 as an impoverished drought-prone country that depended heavily upon foreign aid and cattle herding, although a mining boom was just commencing. The economy was relatively undistorted, however, with a Dutch disease index of 5.4, due more to neglect by the British protectorate than to shrewd economic management. The ruling elite of tribal leaders and large cattle herders was well aware of the economy's fragility. It displayed considerable caution towards macro-policy and fashionable interventionist policies and showed no haste to replace

TABLE 1. Economic structure in 1972 and structural change for 1972–1981 (Venezuela and Indonesia) and 1972–1996 (Botswana)

	Venezuela Actual	Venezuela Syrquin norm	Indonesia Actual	Indonesia Syrquin norm	Botswana Actual	Botswana Syrquin norm
Share of NM GDP 1972 (%)						
Agriculture	7.6	14	45.1	46	36.9	37
Manufacturing	19.5	27	11.0	11	6.6	12
Construction	6.0	7	4.3	3	12.4	11
Services	66.9	52	39.7	40	44.1	40
Share of mining GDP 1972 (%)	20.5	1	12.1	6	5.8	6
Annual change in share of NM GDP (%)	1972–1981		1972–1981		1972–1996	
Agriculture	− 0.10	− 0.32	− 1.50	− 1.31	− 1.19	− 0.75
Manufacturing	− 0.04	0.06	0.77	0.34	0.04	0.42
Construction	0.02	0.03	0.26	0.10	0.00	0.24
Services	0.13	0.24	0.48	0.86	1.25	0.12
DDI 1972	− 13.9	0	− 0.9	0	− 5.2	0
DDI change 1972–1981	− 1.3	0	− 2.4	0		
DDI change 1972–1996	n.a.	n.a.	n.a.	n.a.	− 20.0	0

DDI, Dutch disease index; NM, non-mining. The norm refers to the mean share of GDP for all countries at a similar level of economic development.
Source: Gelb 1988, p. 88. Author's calculations for Botswana.

expatriate civil servants. The elite maintained property rights, open trade and limited expansion of state-owned enterprises, all of which promoted wealth creation. All this was also initially true for the elites in Kenya and Côte d'Ivoire, which closed their economies during the 1970s, but this was not the case for Botswana, as further explained below.

Suharto also promoted broad-based wealth creation for reasons explained below. To achieve this his government vested responsibility for macro management in able technocrats and controlled (but by no means eliminated) rent-seeking (MacIntyre 2000). In addition, mindful that the downfall of his predecessor owed much to rural neglect Suharto ensured that rent reached the majority poor in rural Java (Timmer 2007), a policy that supported broad-based growth. Despite decades of oil extraction, the Indonesian economy was minimally distorted in the early 1970s: the share of tradeables in non-mining GDP was barely 1 per cent less than expected and the economy was recovering strongly from its nadir in the 1960s.

Turning to the subsequent rent streams: the two oil exporters experienced several strong price shocks, both positive and negative, whereas Botswana's rent stream was stable. Gelb and Associates (1988) provide a measure of the scale of the 1974–1978 and 1979–1981 oil

windfalls by projecting the pre-shock trend and measuring the actual departure from it expressed in terms of non-oil GDP (Table 2). By this measure, the 1974–1978 rent windfall was equivalent to an extra 16 per cent of non-oil income per annum for Indonesia and 11 per cent extra for Venezuela whereas the 1979–1981 windfall added 23 per cent and 9 per cent of non-mining GDP respectively. Hausmann (1999) estimates the scale of the negative oil price shock of 1983–1985 at the loss of 7 per cent of GDP annually in Venezuela and the 1986 price fall lopped off another 7 per cent. Indonesian oil rent was around 10 per cent of GDP annually lower through 1985–1989 than the previous five years, according to World Bank estimates of oil depletion shown in Table 3.

Table 3 also traces the shift in the terms of trade, which from the mid-1970s exhibit greater amplitude for the two oil exporters than Botswana. The total rent stream of Botswana was even steadier because the price stability conferred by the diamond cartel was complemented by the fact that the expansion of diamond rent offset a decline of initially generous aid (Table 3). Copper and nickel rent expanded ahead of diamonds and peaked at 4.9 per cent of gross national income during 1975–1979 before slowly tapering off as diamonds came to dominate the rent stream. The World

TABLE 2. Oil windfall deployment 1974–1981 for Indonesia and Venezuela (% non-mining GDP)

	Indonesia 1974–1978	Indonesia 1979–1981	Venezuela 1974–1978	Venezuela 1979–1981
Domestic oil windfall/year	15.9	22.7	10.8	8.7
Real	1.6	− 2.5	− 20.5	− 28.0
Price effect	14.3	25.2	31.3	36.6
Absorption effects				
Trade and non-factor service	5.3	9.6	− 1.0	1.1
Current balance	4.8	6.1	3.9	7.0
Non-oil growth effects	− 2.4	− 3.5	5.9	− 6.6
Real allocation + growth effect				
Private consumption	− 1.5	7.7	1.9	20.0
Public consumption	1.5	3.0	1.6	− 0.7
Private investment	− 3.4	7.9	3.3	− 6.0
Public investment	7.9	n.a.	4.9	n.a.

The table is based on a counterfactual of the outcome in the absence of the oil windfall and makes four key assumptions:
1. Relative price deflators remain constant at their average 1970–1972 "base period" ratio.
2. The ratio of real mining output to non-mining GDP is constant.
3. The ratio of total absorption to output is constant.
4. Consumption and investment change their share of absorption as per capita income rises in line with their "normal" shares (derived from Syrquin and Chenery [1989]).
The windfalls and their uses are derived as deviations of actual supply and demand shares from the projections and expressed relative to non-mining GDP to aid comparison. It then becomes possible to distinguish the contribution of volume changes and price changes, and also to adjust for any acceleration or slow-down in the growth of non-mining GDP (assumed attributable to windfall absorption) compared with the base period (See Gelb 1988, pp. 56–59).
Source: Gelb 1988, pp. 62–65

TABLE 3. Rent stream indices 1965–2004 for Botswana, Venezuela and Indonesia

	1965– 1969	1970– 1974	1975– 1979	1980– 1984	1985– 1989	1990– 1994	1995– 1999	2000– 2004
Botswana								
Aid (% GNI)	23.8	14.7	11.9	9.3	7.8	3.0	1.8	0.5
Ore depletion (% GNI)	n.a.	0.1	4.3	2.8	3.9	1.0	0.7	0.5
Diamond depletion (% GNI)[1]	n.a.	7.0	8.7	17.4	18.5	25.9	21.4	18.9
Net barter terms of trade[2]	n.a.	128.6	89.4	71.4	91.6	91.8	96.3	96.9
Venezuela								
Aid (% GNI)	0.2	0.1	0.0	0.0	0.0	0.1	0.0	0.1
Oil output (mbpd)[3]	3.6	3.4	2.4	2.0	1.9	2.5	3.2	3.0
Oil depletion (% GDP)	n.a.	15.7	29.3	36.4	24.2	28.7	22.6	29.0
Net barter terms of trade[2]	n.a.	61.0	108.8	151.2	91.0	71.8	65.3	94.8
Indonesia								
Aid (% GNI)	3.9	4.2	1.5	1.0	1.4	1.4	0.9	0.7
Oil output (mbpd)[3]	0.5	1.1	1.5	1.5	1.4	1.6	1.5	1.3
Oil depletion (% GDP)	n.a.	4.5	16.0	21.1	10.4	7.2	5.9	9.6
Net barter terms of trade[2]	n.a.	71.3	124.3	177.5	105.0	89.5	87.1	99.9

[1]Auty and Mikesell (1998)
[2]2000 = 100, with 1970–1979 rebased from World Bank 1989
[3]BP 2007
GNI, gross national income, mbpd, million barrels per day
Source: World Bank 2006a

Bank does not estimate diamond rent due to lack of published statistics, but Harvey and Lewis (1990) calculate Botswana's diamond rent at 50 per cent of export earnings through the 1980s while Auty and Mikesell (1998) estimate the rent from company reports at 60 per cent of export revenue for the early 1990s. Assuming rent comprised 60 per cent of exports from the start of production, the share of diamond rent in GDP steadily expanded to peak at 26 per cent in the early 1990s before commencing a slow relative decline of 1 per cent of GDP annually (Table 3).

Venezuelan rent cycling follows the staple trap model of cumulative deterioration

Venezuela's development since the 1960s is consistent with the staple trap model. With governments electing to diversify the economy by overriding markets in the 1950s and 1960s, the extra rent from the 1974–1978 and 1979–1981 oil booms was used to accelerate the process. In brief, the booms fed patronage entitlements that absorbed the rent too rapidly, and further distorted the economy and eroded institutions. Subsequent policies to ration rent were inadequate so that stabilisation failed. This discouraged investment in economic restructuring, which prolonged the growth collapse and increased income inequality that polarised the electorate.

More specifically, although half the 1974–1978 windfall was earmarked to a long-term saving fund to limit Dutch disease effects, parliamentary scrutiny was weakened when the fund was placed under presidential discretion to speed decision-making. The windfall was absorbed too rapidly so that, far from saving rent during the booms, Venezuela accumulated foreign debt. The boom also added two rent-seeking constituencies, consumers and state enterprises, to the existing duo of private capital and unions. Table 2 indicates that the 1974–1978 windfall boosted consumption by an extra 16 per cent of non-mining GDP annually compared to the pre-boom trend, mainly through subsidised prices and lower taxes on income and expenditure. Investment increased by half as much as consumption, mostly to diversify the economy by expanding the Orinoco metal complex. Steel and aluminium are capital intensive, however, and require large investments that state enterprises undertook. They accounted for 70 per cent of manufacturing investment but created few jobs, so additional rent was cycled to boost public sector employment more generally (Karl 1997, p. 104).

Consumption dominated domestic absorption during the 1979–1981 oil boom. Instead of cooling the overheating economy by cutting current public consumption, the government resorted to price controls and subsidies. The policy failed because it squeezed producer margins, which cut supply so domestic prices

rose and strengthened the real effective exchange rate by 20 per cent during 1982–1983 (Gelb and Associates 1988, p. 79). Efforts to slow public investment also failed because the state enterprises substituted inadequately monitored overseas finance for domestic capital. Worse, poor project implementation delayed the start-up of the metal plants and rendered them uncompetitive so they were unable to service their debt. Little non-oil tradeable activity was competitive by 1981, so that Table 1 grossly underestimates the Dutch disease effects. The economy depended on oil for 94 per cent of exports and two-thirds of government revenue when the 1983–1986 negative oil shocks struck.

Failure to ration the rent when oil prices fell broke Venezuela's consensual democracy (Karl 1997, pp. 179–88). Cuts were required in social spending and support for loss-making state enterprises, but opposition from state enterprise unions and management shifted expenditure cuts on the more diffuse and weaker consumer lobby (Marquez 1995). Public expenditure still remained excessive, however, and the electoral cycle further undermined stabilisation policies. In 1982 a newly elected government attempted to grow out of recession by reflating the economy instead of cutting the fiscal deficit. Similar electoral concerns launched another populist boom in 1986 when a sharp fall in oil prices required fiscal tightening. Sachs (1989) analysed Latin America's populist booms: they collapse within four years leaving the economy worse off than when the boom started. Finally, in 1989 a left-leaning government sprang market reforms on an unsuspecting electorate, cutting GDP by almost 10 per cent and spiking inflation to 80 per cent (Hausmann 2003, p. 270). Labour was inadequately cushioned against the policy, which the government diluted in 1992 after two failed coups.

The failure of successive Venezuelan governments to ration rent and stabilise the economy caused the real exchange rate to fluctuate sharply. This discouraged domestic investment to replace the lost output, revenue and exports that oil had previously generated. Private sector investment slumped from almost 25 per cent of GDP in the 1970s to 11 per cent in the 1980s and then to 7 per cent in the 1990s. Massive capital flight combined with low economy-wide investment efficiency to perpetuate

TABLE 4. Economic growth indices 1965–2004 for Botswana, Venezuela and Indonesia

	1965–1969	1970–1974	1975–1979	1980–1984	1985–1989	1990–1994	1995–1999	2000–2004
Botswana								
Per capita GDP (US$2,000)	302.2	581.0	904.7	1328.4	1876.9	2468.7	2894.1	3912.1
Population growth (% per yr)	2.8	3.2	3.4	3.3	3.0	2.6	1.9	0.4
GDP (% per yr)	8.7	19.9	11.5	11.0	11.9	4.5	7.6	6.2
Per capita GDP (% per yr)	5.8	16.1	7.8	7.3	8.7	1.9	5.6	5.9
Crop output index[1]	70.0	88.7	96.2	81.3	91.2	98.7	103.5	108.0
Venezuela								
Per capita GDP (US$2000)	n.a.	n.a.	7379.2	6309.2	5969.4	6122.5	6027.4	5411.7
Population growth (% per yr)	3.3	3.4	3.5	3.0	2.5	2.2	2.0	1.8
GDP (% per yr)	3.3	3.9	4.0	− 1.9	1.5	4.1	0.9	1.7
Per capita GDP (% per yr)	− 0.1	0.5	0.5	− 4.7	− 2.3	1.7	− 1.1	− 0.1
Crop output index[1]	45.6	51.6	58.7	60.9	74.6	79.7	89.9	98.4
Indonesia								
Per capita GDP (US$2000)	203.5	261.3	335.3	429.0	516.9	692.7	832.1	848.1
Population growth (% per yr)	2.3	2.4	2.3	1.9	1.8	1.6	1.4	1.3
GDP (% per yr)	4.9	8.2	7.4	6.7	6.1	8.0	1.7	4.6
Per capita GDP (% per yr)	2.5	5.6	5.0	4.7	4.2	6.2	0.3	3.2
Crop output index[1]	31.2	38.2	43.7	56.8	70.6	85.0	96.5	108.1

Note [1]1991–2001 = 100
Source: World Bank 2006a

the growth collapse. Relative poverty increased from 39 per cent of the population to 48 per cent during 1986–1995 (Marquez 1995, p. 411) and through 2000–2004 mean per capita income was less than three-quarters of its peak in 1975–1979 (Table 4). Income inequality rose sharply as the share of wages and salaries in GDP slumped to 36 per cent after averaging 47 per cent through 1950–1988. Much of the corresponding gain in the share of capital was held offshore.

The regressive redistribution of income discredited both economic reform and the principal political parties, spawning short-lived political parties under charismatic leaders that pursued specialised interests. In 1998 the democracy polarised when a left-of-centre coalition won power and chose Chávez, the leader of one of the 1992 coups, as president. The positive oil shock of the mid-2000s boosted patronage-driven rent cycling by easing pressure to create wealth by economic reform. Extra-parliamentary protest grew as the middle class sought to prevent the government from cutting the commercial independence of the state oil corporation in order to channel more rent into patronage. In summary, consistent with both rent-cycling theory and Collier and Hoeffler (2006), Venezuela shows how cycling high rent corrodes checks and balances as part of a negative socio-economic spiral.

Botswana's precarious but stable rent has sustained wealth creation, so far

This section argues that although Botswana developed healthy institutions, they remain untested by severe price shocks. Hill and Knight (1999, p. 313) identify just two mild downswings during 1980–1983 and the early 1990s (when markets were briefly over-supplied) and one upswing associated with a major mine expansion in the late 1980s. Rather, Botswana's more successful rent deployment reflects the perpetuation of the initial bias of the elite towards wealth creation. This appears to result from the economy's precarious dependence on a cartel-sustained diamond rent arising from Botswana's strongly skewed natural resource endowment. However, the remarkable stability of the rent stream to date has, along with limited ethnic factionalism and astute leadership, facilitated both macro-economic management and control of rent seeking.

Barely 5 per cent of Botswana's land area is suitable for cultivation and even then rainfall is unreliable. Yet industrial diversification is constrained by the small size of the domestic market, the lacklustre performance of adjacent economies and a land-locked location. Consequently, the expansion of diamond rent to one-quarter of

GDP as a result of an unusually long-lived cartel rendered Botswana's mineral dependence potentially precarious, exerting strong pressure for cautious rent cycling. Although the central role of the government in absorbing the rent pushed public spending to two-thirds of GDP (Harvey and Jefferis 1995) the rent was sensibly transferred to the private sector through public purchases of goods and services rather than by lowering taxes, subsidising prices or protecting infant industrial activity, which all build rent-seeking constituencies and unsustainable entitlements. In addition, the government converted diamond rent into alternative forms of capital by investment in human capital (education and health) and eliminating the backlog in economic infrastructure.

In contrast to most resource-rich countries in sub-Saharan Africa and Latin America, the Botswana elite eschewed import substitution policy, which (as in Venezuela) invariably degenerates into a system for rent extraction that intensifies barriers to trade and heightens economic distortion. The government initially stimulated the rural economy because until the late 1990s the majority resided in rural areas. It supported export-oriented cattle-rearing, which was dominated by the elite, but also boosted rural smallholding through a policy of food self-sufficiency, which was phased out in the 1990s. Some mineral rent was invested in state-owned directly productive activity in the late 1980s but it yielded few profitable projects and the loss-makers were quickly divested (IMF 1999). By minimising protection, Botswana's rent deployment limited rent seeking and the associated corrosion of institutions. Table 5 shows that Botswana compares favourably with the middle-income oil-exporters in terms of its quality of governance, with both a robust civic voice and rule of law, as Collier and Hoeffler (2006) note.

However, the resilience of Botswanan institutions remains to be tested because the unusual stability of diamond prices facilitated both macro-economic management and control of rent-seeking. The absence of unexpected surges in Botswana's rent stream avoided the sudden ignition of political pressure for government spending, while price stability avoided abrupt and draconian rent rationing. Moreover,

TABLE 5. Per capita GDP and institutional quality 2005: selected high-rent mineral economies

Country	Per capita GDP (US$PPP 2005)	Voice+ accountability	Political stability	Effective governance	Regulation burden	Rule of law	Control of graft	Aggregate index
Nigeria	1,113	−0.65	−1.48	−1.02	−1.26	−1.44	−1.11	−6.96
Sudan	2,151	−1.84	−2.05	−1.30	−1.29	−1.48	−1.40	−9.36
Angola	2,425	−1.02	−0.95	−1.14	−1.40	−1.33	−1.12	−6.96
Indonesia	3,843	−0.21	−1.42	−0.47	−0.45	−0.87	−0.86	−4.28
Ecuador	4,272	−0.19	−0.83	−0.85	−0.60	−0.71	−0.75	−3.93
Azerbaijan	5,607	−0.97	−1.52	−0.81	−0.57	−0.85	−1.04	−5.76
Libya	6,400[1]	−1.79	−0.02	−0.73	−1.52	−0.65	−0.91	−5.59
Venezuela	6,531	−0.46	−1.10	−0.96	−1.24	−1.10	−0.94	−5.80
Algeria	7,111	−0.91	−1.42	−0.46	−0.93	−0.73	−0.49	−4.94
Iran	7,979	−1.36	−0.91	−0.66	−1.33	−0.83	−0.59	−5.68
Kazakhstan	8,515	−1.21	−0.11	−0.63	−0.89	−0.98	−1.10	−4.92
Mexico	10,209	+0.36	−0.13	−0.02	+0.55	−0.26	−0.27	+0.23
Botswana	10,790	+0.68	+0.94	+0.79	+0.76	+0.70	+1.10	+4.97
Russia	10,897	−0.81	−0.85	−0.21	−0.51	−0.70	−0.72	−3.80
Trinidad & Tobago	13,758	+ 0.49	+0.04	+0.47	+0.61	+0.17	+0.02	+1.80
Saudi Arabia	14,729	−1.63	−0.60	−0.06	−0.34	+0.20	+0.15	−2.27
Oman	15,260[1]	−0.90	+0.76	+0.91	+0.43	+0.98	+0.78	+0.49
Kuwait	21,534[1]	−0.48	+0.29	+0.55	+0.10	+0.65	+0.71	+1.82
UAE	24,056[1]	−1.01	+0.91	+1.20	+0.95	+0.85	+1.23	+4.13
Qatar	26,000	−0.75	+0.83	+0.55	+0.20	+0.87	+0.82	+2.52
Norway	40,199	+1.53	+1.53	+1.97	+1.33	+1.95	+2.11	+10.42

Note [1]2004
The six index scores each range from 2.5 to − 2.5 and are based on several surveys in each country. PPP, purchasing power parity.
Source: World Bank 2006b

the government cushioned against rent volatility by establishing saving funds in 1972, which typically allocated two-fifths of the rent to offshore investments that pushed financial reserves to 125 per cent of GDP by 1998 (IMF 1999). Unlike Venezuela, Botswana responded promptly when mineral prices briefly faltered in the early 1980s and executed a 20 per cent depreciation of the real exchange rate, lifted interest rates, made modest cuts in public investment and postponed public sector pay rises.

Controlled rent-seeking and cautious macro-economic management were part of a positive economic circle that drove the economy at similar rates to the East Asian dragon economies during 1972–1990 and contrived a slow deceleration thereafter (Table 4). The sustained per capita GDP growth raised all boats and although income distribution was skewed the GINI coefficient remained stable, unlike Venezuela, at around 0.51 (Sarraf and Jiwanji 2003: 15). This in turn helped the ruling party to consistently retain a majority of the seats in parliament whereas its largest opponent only once captured one-third of the seats and typically garnered one-sixth. The ruling party maintained its parliamentary majority despite the relative decline of its bedrock rural constituency by accommodating social pressure rather than repressing it or buying it off with subsidies. For example, the loss of seats in the 1969 election prompted an acceleration of rural development while electoral setbacks in 1996 led to an extension of the franchise to 18-year olds and to nationals resident outside the country.

The economy remained largely mineral-driven during 1995–2004 as the diamond rent went into a relative decline (Bank of Botswana 2006) and the government struggled to maintain economic growth and employment. Table 1 shows that the diamond expansion pushed Botswana's Dutch disease index up fivefold to 25.1 per cent of non-mining GDP by 1996. This departure from the projected norm reflects in equal measure the rapid demise of agriculture and the slow growth in manufacturing (Lange and Wright 2004). Progress with competitive diversification of the economy lagged, due more to the geographical constraints on agriculture and manufacturing than, as in Venezuela, to maladroit rent cycling.

Overall, Botswana's rent deployment to date has postponed a growth collapse rather than eliminated the threat. Somewhat ominously, the government responded to the recent mining slowdown by raising public expenditure in an unsustainable manner. It expanded public sector employment which, in combination with rising expenditures to combat HIV/AIDS, swelled the public sector deficit (IMF 2005, p. 16). The financial reserves declined from 125 per cent of GDP in 1998 to 75 per cent in 2005 (Bank of Botswana 2006). The prospect of ever-tighter rent rationing will provide a sterner test of the country's institutions than has occurred hitherto.

Natural resource exhaustion explains autocratic Indonesia's economic gain

The Suharto government shared with its Botswana counterpart the aim to create wealth. The anticipated depletion of the Indonesian oil reserves and mounting rural population pressure in densely settled Java engendered a bias for caution from the outset which, as in Botswana, led to policies to control rent seeking and prioritise macro-economic management. In addition, learning from its predecessor, the Suharto regime allocated rent to boost the welfare of the majority poor in a sustainable manner as part of a strategy to competitively diversify the economy. These three policies underpinned three decades of successful rent deployment, but the regime was eventually undone by its failure to maintain its pro-growth political constituency.

Although some rent was deployed as patronage to maintain political support, which spawned "crony capitalism", the Suharto regime exerted sufficient control on rent seeking to limit its adverse economic effects (MacIntyre 2000). This outcome conferred two benefits. First, it facilitated macro-economic management in contrast to Venezuela, which lost control of rent absorption. Second, it enabled Indonesian firms to plan for rent obligations and benefits, whereas their counterparts in, for example, the Commonwealth of Independent States economies, experienced arbitrary rent extraction that greatly heightened risk (Jones-Luong 2004). In addition, Indonesian rent cycling built a dualistic manufacturing sector

TABLE 6. Changing export composition 1965–2004 for Botswana, Venezuela and Indonesia (% total)

	1965–1969	1970–1974	1975–1979	1980–1984	1985–1989	1990–1994	1995–1999	2000–2004
Botswana								
Agriculture	n.a.	n.a.	n.a.	n.a.	n.a.	n.a.	n.a.	3.3
Fuel	n.a.	n.a.	n.a.	n.a.	n.a.	n.a.	n.a.	0.1
Ore[1]	n.a.	n.a.	n.a.	n.a.	n.a.	n.a.	n.a.	89.4
Manufacturing	n.a.	n.a.	n.a.	n.a.	n.a.	n.a.	n.a.	7.0
Venezuela								
Agriculture	1.2	1.5	0.9	0.6	2.1	2.7	3.1	1.5
Fuel	92.9	92.2	93.6	94.1	81.9	79.4	77.9	83.3
Ore	4.6	4.7	3.9	3.0	7.2	6.4	5.0	3.4
Manufacturing	1.2	1.5	1.5	2.3	7.4	11.6	14.0	11.7
Indonesia								
Agriculture	50.5	43.7	31.2	15.0	21.0	16.1	22.6	15.3
Fuel	41.3	48.9	63.5	76.4	50.0	34.1	23.6	23.7
Ore	6.6	6.0	3.5	3.5	5.2	4.1	5.1	5.7
Manufacturing	1.6	1.4	1.8	5.1	23.8	45.7	48.7	55.3

Note [1]Ore comprised 1.3% of exports in 1968, 43.6% in 1972, 52.7% in 1977, 81.4% in 1980 and 84.1% in 1986, according to Harvey and Lewis (1990, p. 110)
Source: World Bank (2006a)

in which state enterprises and some private firms took the rent in terms of reduced levels of efficiency, passing the costs on to domestic consumers in terms of prices above world levels, whereas other private firms, mostly Chinese-owned, strove for efficiency and took the rent in terms of higher profits that they reinvested. This dualism spawned dynamic competitive firms alongside sluggish protected ones. When oil prices fell in the mid-1980s and the technocrats depreciated the real exchange rate to help stabilise the economy, dynamic domestic firms along with new Japanese investors expanded rapidly into global markets (Timmer 2007). Within 15 years the Indonesian economy restructured from oil dependence to competitive manufacturing (Table 6), helping to sustain rapid per capita GDP growth until the 1997 financial shock (Table 4).

Sound macro-economic management was the second policy behind successful rent cycling in Indonesia. During the 1974–1978 oil boom the technocrats sterilised 40 per cent of the oil revenue in a largely successful attempt to slow the rate of domestic rent absorption and limit Dutch disease effects. They had also begun to rein in public expenditure and to depreciate the real exchange rate in response to softening oil prices prior to the 1979 price shock. As in most oil-rich countries, a laxer fiscal stance was adopted during the 1979–1981 boom (Table 2, column 2) and the economy exhibited modest

Dutch disease effects. By 1981 the tradeables share of non-mining GDP was an additional 2.4 per cent smaller than the norms predict (leaving the index at a still modest 3.4), due mainly to a slightly faster rate of decline in the share of agriculture (Table 3). Unlike Venezuela, however, the mid-1980s oil price collapse was promptly met by sharp depreciation of the real exchange rate, the opening of trade policy and public expenditure cuts, which stimulated manufacturing exports and revived agriculture (Table 6).

The third key policy was to channel rent to the majority poor, which in Indonesia meant rural communities, mainly in Java. This was achieved by expanding infrastructure, notably rural roads to improve farmers' access to markets, and by diffusing green revolution techniques. The resulting expansion in labour-intensive agriculture helped drive Indonesia's remarkably rapid per capita GDP growth during 1967–1997 (Table 4), maintain the GINI coefficient around 0.34 and cut the headcount poverty index from two-thirds of the population to one-eighth (Timmer 2007). Incomes rose because high productivity growth in manufacturing and agriculture spilled over into a demand for goods and services from the rural informal economy, which still employed 45 per cent of the workforce in the 1990s. Neither Botswana nor Venezuela succeeded in drawing such a high fraction of workers into unsubsidised market activity.

In achieving control of rent-seeking, a sound macro-economic policy and the absorption of surplus labour Indonesia conforms to the low-rent model. However, the low-rent model predicts broadening of the pro-growth political constituency, whereas in response to pressure to ration rent in the mid-1980s the Suharto regime narrowed it. The regime concentrated the reduced rent on cronies at the expense of the army and the main political party, Golkar. The neglected groups continued to support the regime as long as it sustained rapid GDP growth but they increasingly resented the elite (Timmer 2007). They swiftly withdrew support during the East Asian financial crisis when the elite pressured the ageing Suharto to tailor macro-economic policy to defend their rents and shift the costs of a 14 per cent contraction in GDP in 1998 onto the majority.

Conclusions

This chapter reaches four principal conclusions that can inform econometric analyses of the resource curse and strengthen rent-cycling policies. First, the strength of the incentives for the elite to prioritise wealth creation over rent distribution is a critical determinant of rent-cycling outcomes. Rent-cycling theory explains why low rent encourages wealth creation, but this chapter shows that pro-growth incentives can also be conferred through reliance on a precarious rent stream, as in the case of Botswana, or concern for resource exhaustion, which motivated the Suharto regime to promote economic growth to ease poverty in densely settled Java. (Although it is not demonstrated here, regression studies should note that elites may also be motivated to create wealth by targeted geopolitical rent and external security threats). In contrast to Botswana and Indonesia, Venezuelan governments expected the country's vast size and rich and diversified natural resource endowment to transform a small and underpopulated mid-income import substitution economic enclave into a large, high-income diversified economy. To this effect, Massachusetts Institute of Technology planners were commissioned in the 1960s to draft a growth pole strategy to develop a metallurgical complex based on exploitation of the water and ore

resources of the Orinoco. This was expected to generate capital to reduce reliance on oil rent and construct further generations of growth poles to open up the southern two-thirds of the country that remained virtually empty (Friedmann 1966).

The second conclusion is that patronage-driven rent cycling tends to corrode institutions, whereas market-driven development tends to consolidate them. The quality of institutions is positively related to per capita income but high-rent economies tend to have poorer institutions than the mean for their per capita income peers. Venezuela exemplifies institutional corrosion, which deteriorated from policy capture during the 1960s into the establishment of unsustainable rent entitlements during the 1973–1981 oil booms. The quality of institutions weakened further as failure to ration rent destabilised the economy and prompted first extra-parliamentary protest and then populist authoritarianism. In contrast, the expansion of diamond rent to offset the withdrawal of geopolitical rent in Botswana sustained a remarkably stable rent stream that helped the wealth-creating elite to sustain a positive circle so that the country's institutions have yet to be severely tested by rent shocks. In Suharto's Indonesia, the co-existence of crony capitalism and effective macro-economic management also cautions against ascribing a dominant role to institutions which, contrary to some parsimonious explanations produced by regression studies, appear to reflect rent-cycling incentives rather than to shape them.

Third, the case studies underline the cumulative impact of rent deployment, whether negative or positive. Venezuela illustrates the negative spiral associated with the high-rent staple trap model. Over-rapid absorption of the oil windfalls further weakened constraints on the rent-seeking that had emerged in the 1960s. Successive governments repressed markets in a counter-productive attempt to sustain growth, expand employment, diversify the non-oil economy and curb Dutch disease effects. Subsequently, the inertia of rent-seeking prevented the political parties from crafting a coalition to ration rent so that the Venezuelan economy could be stabilised and investment in economic restructuring could occur. The negative spiral cumulated further as the prolonged growth collapse amplified asset inequality and polarised the electorate, which empowered a populist government that cycled the mid-2000s' windfall rent through patronage networks.

In contrast, wealth-creating elites in Botswana and Indonesia espoused policies of timely macro-economic management and control of rent seeking that triggered positive cumulative circles. However, the fourth conclusion is that two additional policies characterise sustained successful rent deployment. These are effectively targeting rent at the poorest and building a pro-growth political coalition. Indonesia deployed rent to lift the incomes of the majority rural poor in a sustainable fashion, which replicated a key feature of the low-rent competitive industrialisation model that facilitated competitive diversification of the economy. However, Suharto rationed rent in the mid-1980s to favour the elite and lost support when the financial crisis cut GDP by 14 per cent in 1998. Botswana to date has successfully adapted its pro-growth political coalition to the declining importance of the rural population, but competitive diversification has lagged due to a landlocked location and an arid environment so that decelerating mineral expansion will test the resilience of its institutions.

Rent-cycling theory cautions against silver bullet diagnoses. Development requires many things to "come right", not all of which are easily controlled, so that it is unsurprising that developing countries struggle to grow or that sustained growth spells are relatively rare. However, more nuanced policy prescriptions based on the emerging theory of rent cycling that is grounded in accumulated country experience can improve the prospects of positive outcomes.

Governance strategies to remedy the natural resource curse

Joseph Siegle

A predictable outcome

The natural resource curse represents "a perfect storm" of influences detrimental to citizens' well-being and stability. Resource-rich countries typically develop more slowly, are less diversified, more corrupt, less transparent, subject to greater economic volatility, more oppressive and more prone to internal conflict than non-endowed countries at similar income levels. Meanwhile, the outsized revenues available to resource-rich governments allow them to pursue more belligerent and radical policies than they would otherwise be able to support. The pernicious ripple effects generated by these states, in turn, consumes a disproportionate share of global time and resources.

Despite the growing attention to the phenomenon, strategies for remedying the resource curse remain poorly understood and compartmentalised. This is, in part, due to an under-appreciation of the multi-dimensional nature of the resource curse. It is not solely an economic distortion (or "Dutch disease") due to over-reliance on a single primary commodity export and the dampening effect this has on terms of trade and productivity. Nor is it wholly a matter of inadequate transparency and the resulting corruption made easier by the large sums of easily consolidated revenues. And the higher levels of political instability cannot be attributed solely to the fact

Joseph Siegle is the Director of Research for the Africa Centre for Strategic Studies at the National Defence University and a Senior Research Scholar with the Centre for International and Security Studies at the University of Maryland. The views expressed in this article are his own. Dr Siegle is a leading authority on the political economy of development as well as the economic and security implications of democratisation. He is co-author of *The democracy advantage: how democracies promote prosperity and peace*, Routledge, 2004 (2nd edition forthcoming). Email: sieglej@ndu.edu

that resource-rich countries have more to fight over. Each of these considerations is important but they are insufficient on their own to base an effective reform strategy.

Often overlooked in this discussion is the distinguishing feature that governance type plays in the resource curse. Over 70 per cent of all hydrocarbon-rich countries are autocracies. Nearly 40 per cent of autocracies are resource-rich. These patterns are not a coincidence but central pieces to understanding the resource-curse puzzle. Autocracies survive, by definition, on exclusive structures of power. The revenues at their disposal are committed to sustaining this narrow power base – typically consisting of patronage networks, the military and ethnic group allegiances. Development, defined in its broadest sense, suffers. Low accountability coupled with intimidation allows the inequity to persist. When resource revenues are added to the mix the effects are even more lopsided: greater inequality, corruption, coercion and underdevelopment. The seemingly paradoxical outcome of resource-rich countries being development-poor is, in fact, quite predictable.

Historically high resource prices, especially oil, have tightened the grip on power of many resource-rich autocracies. The upsurge in their revenues has also fundamentally changed the relationship between these governments and the broader international community. Resource-rich autocracies have little need for the aid on which many reform initiatives are conditioned. Accordingly, alternative reform strategies are required.

This chapter analyses the distinguishing effects of governance on the resource curse. It then lays out some of the governance challenges that perpetuate the resource curse. Focusing on these challenges, the remainder of the chapter offers a series of recommendations for ameliorating the resource curse.

Governance distinctions in the natural resource curse

Thirty-six countries are considered to be hydrocarbon rich according to the International Monetary Fund (IMF) (see Table 1).[1] An additional 16 qualify as mineral rich. Two countries, Indonesia and Uzbekistan, meet the criteria on both lists. While these resources are often considered together, important differences between the two exist. First, the median per capita income in hydrocarbon-rich countries is significantly higher than in mineral-rich countries – US$1,978 versus US$563. Next, while roughly 70 per cent of all hydrocarbon-rich countries are autocracies,[2] less than a fifth of mineral-rich states fall into this category. Conversely, only five of the 36 hydrocarbon-rich countries qualify as democracies, compared with eight of the 18 mineral-rich nations. Stated differently, on a democracy scale of 0–10, the median score for hydrocarbon-rich countries is zero. Among mineral-rich countries it is seven – matching the global median. To illustrate these differences, Table 1 lists the respective hydrocarbon-rich and mineral-rich countries according to their regime classification – autocracy, mixed and democracy.

Not coincidentally, the two categories of resource-rich countries also have distinctive geographic distributions. Nearly 40 per cent of the hydrocarbon-endowed countries are in the Middle East (12), 25 per cent are in sub-Saharan Africa (nine), and 15 per cent are each located in the former Soviet Union and Latin America (five each). In contrast, 10 of 18 mineral-rich countries are located in sub-Saharan Africa.

TABLE 1. Resource-rich countries by governance category, 2007

Hydrocarbon-rich autocracies	Mineral-rich autocracies
Angola	Guinea
Azerbaijan	Jordan
Bahrain	Uzbekistan
Brunei	
Cameroon	
Chad	
Congo, Republic of	
Equatorial Guinea	
Gabon	
Iran	
Iraq	
Kazakhstan	
Kuwait	
Libya	
Oman	
Qatar	
Saudi Arabia	
Sudan	
Syria	
Turkmenistan	
United Arab Emirates	
Uzbekistan	
Vietnam	
Yemen	

Hydrocarbon-rich mixed regimes	Mineral-rich mixed regimes
Algeria	Democratic Republic of Congo
Colombia	Kyrgyzstan
Ecuador	Liberia
Nigeria	Mauritania
Russia	Namibia
Timor Leste	Sierra Leone
Venezuela	Zambia

Hydrocarbon-rich democracies	Mineral-rich democracies
Indonesia	Botswana
Mexico	Chile
Norway	Ghana
São Tomé and Principe	Indonesia
Trinidad and Tobago	Mongolia
	Papua New Guinea
	Peru
	South Africa

Resource-rich categorisations compiled from IMF (2007). Governance ratings derived from Freedom House and Polity IV.

Three are in East Asia, and two each in the former Soviet Union and Latin America. Only one mineral-rich country is in the Middle East.

The run-up in prices of certain natural resource commodities in recent years, particularly oil, has provided a substantial boost to growth rates (and government revenues) in resource-rich states. Indeed, between 2000 and 2005, median per capita incomes in oil-rich and mineral-rich countries expanded by 17.5 per cent and 15.2 per cent, respectively. This compares to the global average of 5.8 per cent. When broken down by regime type, little variation in these growth rates is observed among oil-rich countries. Among mineral-rich countries, however, mixed regimes and democracies realised distinctly higher rates of growth during this five-year period – over 16 per cent compared to the median rate for autocracies – 5.7 per cent.

Growth figures in all natural resource-rich countries need to be interpreted with caution, however. The stimulus for the growth typically comes from externally driven factors (that is, demand for resource commodities) rather than from improvements in productive capacity. Growth in resource-rich countries is also much more subject to volatility. In fact, a standard measure of volatility, the coefficient of variation, shows that resource-rich countries experience 60 per cent greater volatility in their growth than the global norm. Growth volatility in resource-rich mixed regimes and democracies more closely resembles the global average, experiencing half the levels of volatility that is seen in resource-rich autocracies. (This also helps to explain the governance-based growth differences among mineral-rich countries). Notably, greater volatility is a characteristic of autocratic growth regardless of resource wealth. As an illustration of this, between 1996–2005 autocracies were more than twice as likely to experience an annual contraction in GDP of more than 5 per cent as were democracies. These are non-trivial differences for people already living at the margin in these societies.

Another important difference between governance types is how growth is translated into improved living conditions. For example, despite the rapid income growth of recent years, improvements in infant mortality rates among resource-rich countries between 2000 and 2005 have lagged behind the global norm. Hydrocarbon- and mineral-rich countries saw median levels of infant deaths drop by 8.4 per cent and 3.4 per cent, respectively, during this five-year period. The global norm was 11.9 per cent.

(These patterns are consistent controlling for income). Again, however, there are significant differences in rates of progress seen between governance types. Among hydrocarbon-rich countries, autocracies saw levels of infant mortality rates drop by 4.2 per cent. Mixed regimes and democracies were apparently able to do more with their resource booms, showing median improvements of 15.3 per cent and 18 per cent, respectively. Similar, though more modest differences are observed among mineral-rich countries. Between 2000 and 2005 autocracies experienced a median decline in infant deaths of 2.3 per cent compared to a decline in infant deaths of 5.7 per cent and 13.6 per cent for mixed regimes and democracies, respectively. This was the case even though resource-rich autocracies were starting from a higher level of infant deaths, making marginal gains relatively easier. For example, the median infant mortality rate in hydrocarbon-rich autocracies in 2005 was 44 per 1,000 live births, compared to 19 per 1,000 live births in democracies.

Improvements in cereal yields provide another illustration of changes in levels of well-being linked to governance. This is all the more important in that the rural sector represents 70 per cent of employment in most developing societies, where the natural resource curse is most pernicious. Globally, cereal yields improved by 4.9 per cent on average from 2000 to 2005. This exceeded the median rate of improvements seen in hydrocarbon-rich autocracies (2.0 per cent) and mineral-rich autocracies (3.1 per cent). In comparison, mixed regimes and democracies in hydrocarbon-rich countries saw cereal productivity improve by upwards of 12 per cent. In mineral-rich democracies and mixed regimes the median rate was 13.5 per cent. In short, the deficiency in development performance of resource-rich countries is most closely linked to those that are autocratically governed. Similar divergences by governance type show up on other measures of well-being, such as healthcare spending, life expectancy and educational attainment.

The below par development performance of resource-rich autocracies coincides with their regularly inferior corruption ratings. The global median score on Transparency International's annual corruption perceptions index in 2007 was 3.2 (out of 10). The median for hydrocarbon-rich

autocracies was 2.6 and for mineral-rich autocracies 2.2. In comparison scores for democracies in both resource categories were 3.5.

Resource-rich autocracies are also more
conflict prone. Of the 22 internal conflicts taking
place in 2005, eight (35 per cent) were in natural
resource-rich countries (seven of these eight were
hydrocarbon rich). Fuel exports as a share of
GDP a statistically significant in predicting civil
conflict since 1995, controlling for income and
other factors. Consequently, the probability of
hydrocarbon-rich countries experiencing civil
conflict is double the norm. Unsurprisingly,
then, hydrocarbon countries are often the locus
of humanitarian crises. Five of the top 10
countries generating internally displaced people
are hydrocarbon-rich autocracies. If autocratically governed mineral-rich countries were
added, the total would be seven of these top 10
countries. Similar patterns are observed for
refugee outflows. The destabilising effects of
the natural resource curse, in short, are not
confined within the borders where the instability
originates.

These comparisons indicate that governance type is a defining feature in determining
whether resource riches are curses or blessings.
Yet, while resource-rich autocracies are more
prone to the resource curse, it should be recognised that this is a two-way effect. Bountiful
natural resource holdings have a corrosive effect
on political institutions. In fact, fuel exports as a
share of GDP are a statistically significant negative predictor of democracy, controlling for income. Similarly, a rapid rise in natural resource
revenues in young democratisers can cause a
weakening of their nascent accountability structures. Therefore, while the prospects of avoiding
the curse of resource wealth are far greater if a
country has already established democratic
institutions prior to the inflow of resource-
generated revenues, this is not a guarantee of
immunity.

To summarise, there is a strong political
economy aspect to the resource curse. Benefits
from these resources generally flow to a relative
few. While booming commodity prices expand
GDP, these proceeds are not reinvested in
productive capacity, especially in resource-rich
autocracies. Instead resource booms are typically accompanied by the flight of capital (as
beneficiaries transfer their assets abroad for safe

keeping). As a result inequality grows and
development lags. Those benefiting under the
exclusive arrangement vigorously resist efforts
that would reduce the rents they are capturing.
While most people would gain by a more
equitable revenue-sharing arrangement, the
costs of informing, organising and mobilising
them, particularly in repressive environments,
are prohibitive.

The upshot is that the reasonable assumption that natural resource wealth is automatically a boon for development is unfounded. This
conclusion is counter-intuitive. Who, after all,
would want to shun the billions of dollars in
additional revenues these resources typically
represent? Surely these resources must have
some positive social benefit. Experience shows,
however, this is the exception rather than the
rule. It is much more frequent to observe lagging
development among resource-rich autocracies.

Looking at the positive, resource wealth
need not condemn a society to poverty and
instability. Resource-rich democracies and democratisers have done a relatively better job of
transforming these riches into sustained development gains while avoiding the scourges of the
resource curse. Norway, Botswana, Ghana,
Chile, Mexico, South Africa, Namibia and
Trinidad and Tobago are among the handful
of resource-rich countries that have benefited
developmentally from their resource endowments. Recognising this reality provides a
valuable starting point for any strategy aiming
to redress the natural resource curse: the
transparency, accountability and policy inclu-
siveness needed to overcome the oil curse are
much more likely under democratic political
systems.

Recommendations: reshaping the legal landscape

The natural resource curse is fundamentally
about unfairness. A privileged minority benefits
extravagantly from their insider status at the
expense of the majority. This inequity persists
because those in power are able to take
advantage of a lack of public scrutiny to conceal
from the public the degree to which they are
profiting from these national endowments.

Control of these revenues, in turn, funds the capacity of autocratic governments to suppress resistance. The incentives that autocratic political leaders face to stay in power, meanwhile, reinforce the pattern of using these revenues for patronage. A political monopoly facilitates an economic monopoly and vice versa. Checks and balances, already weak, are further emasculated by this concentration of power, facilitating ever greater abuses of authority.

At its root, then, the natural resource curse is a classic challenge to collective action propelled by unaccountable governance. Accordingly, remedial action entails both reshaping the incentives these political leaders face as well as informing and mobilising the disadvantaged majority so that they can assert their claims for a more equitable distribution of these resources.

A starting point is establishing a broad-based international legal framework that criminalises the diversion of natural resource revenues. The United Nations Convention against Corruption (UNCAC) lays the foundation for such a framework. Since December 2005 the Convention has obliged ratifying countries to help trace, freeze and confiscate the proceeds of corruption, as well as help in the repatriation of the stolen assets. Complementing this Convention, a joint UN–World Bank programme, the Stolen Asset Recovery initiative, was launched in 2007 to help build global partnerships, strengthen national institutional capacity and provide technical assistance to facilitate the recovery of stolen assets. Such an international commitment is required since industrialised countries with large financial centres have historically been the main havens for diverted assets. As of December 2008, 140 countries have signed the Convention and 129 have ratified it into law. However, of the G8 countries Germany, Italy and Japan have not yet ratified the Convention, and neither have the major financial centres of Liechtenstein, Singapore and Switzerland.

A top priority in remedying the natural resource curse is to expand the number of countries that have ratified this emerging global legal framework – thereby limiting the havens for ill-gotten natural resource revenue diversions. This international legal framework could be further strengthened if citizens of countries subject to asset diversions were recognised as aggrieved parties and incorporated into the UNCAC process. Currently, only states are party to the Convention – and this is the basis of cooperation for asset recovery. While this arrangement works when a new reformist government is attempting to recover assets stolen by a previous regime, it does not permit action in countries where leaders of a corrupt government remain in power and are actively diverting natural resource wealth.

Complementing the initiative to criminalise natural resource diversions should be an effort to establish the normative principle that natural resource revenues belong to all citizens of the endowed country. Since this is a public resource the general population has a right to know the financial details of any revenues such as royalties, fees and exploration licenses generated from these resources. Access to this information, in turn, will facilitate a public dialogue on the appropriate uses and oversight of these resources. The Extractive Industry Transparency Initiative (EITI) established in 2002 has taken important steps in this direction with its lists of principles and criteria upholding the view that revenues generated from natural resource wealth should contribute to development and poverty alleviation. Since then over 20 resource-rich developing countries have signed the EITI, though they have made varied levels of progress toward publishing revenue and payments data.

Other stakeholders in EITI include donors, international financial institutions such as the World Bank and the IMF, private sector extractive firms, investors and civil society organisations. Accordingly, the EITI has emerged as the central global forum for addressing natural resource transparency concerns. However, this is a voluntary protocol. Enshrining the principle of citizen ownership of natural resource revenues in legally binding conventions such as UNCAC and in national legislation would go further in establishing this as a legal tenet with penalties for non-compliance. It would also oblige greater support from all member states as well as financial institutions.

Other strategies for remedying the resource curse focus on improving the tools by which the voice of the majority and the accountability of the leadership can be strengthened. This will necessarily entail targeting issues such as transparency, freedom of speech, an independent media, shared power, civil society advocacy, political competition and the responsibility of government to serve all citizens. Accordingly, the scope for undertaking these reforms will differ markedly depending on the type of political system currently in place. Countries on a democratic path have already accepted the principle of checks and balances. That is, they have a political framework in place amenable to corrective action. Reforms in resource-rich autocracies, on the other hand, must be aimed, at least initially, at the more fundamental challenge of establishing the political space in which citizens can begin to make demands for transparency and the oversight of their government.

Democratisers

Resource-rich countries that are already engaged on the road to democratic reform (such as Nigeria, Indonesia and Zambia) represent a vital opportunity to break the resource curse. Accordingly, these countries merit energetic international support so that they can reset their institutional incentives away from the unaccountable norms they have inherited. Leaders in these democratising states have already made the hard decisions by accepting the principles of political competition, popular participation and the oversight of public officials. Entrenched patterns of self-serving behaviour die hard, however. There are many powerful impulses and counter-pressures for officials in these governments to revert to established practices.

The governance trajectories of these resource-rich democratisers, therefore, are uncertain. For this reason this transition period is a pivotal, though finite, window of opportunity. Domestic and international reformers can contribute to a positive outcome by maintaining high expectations for full revenue and budget transparency, while helping to strengthen what are still weak democratic checks and balances. They should also be persistent, since long-established norms will not change overnight. To illustrate, contemporary democratisers Nigeria, Indonesia, and Zambia have averaged 28 years of autocratic rule since 1960.

Natural resource-rich countries that are just emerging from conflict such as Liberia, Sierra Leone, the Democratic Republic of Congo and south Sudan present another time-sensitive window of opportunity to establish incentives for accountability. Establishing a transparent revenue-sharing formula with multiple layers of checks and balances early on in the post-conflict process should be a top priority and, arguably, a condition for international funding. At the least such a framework should be in place before these revenues start to flow to a new government. To be sure, institution-building in the turbulence of a post-conflict environment is very difficult. Nonetheless, a context without dominant autocratic actors – and one possibly with reformist elements – constitutes an opening for change that may not exist once the political die has cast.

In some cases conflict has been so devastating or prolonged that new institutions will effectively have to be created. While it is a daunting undertaking, this challenge has certain advantages for introducing international best practices on a clean institutional slate. Capacity deficiencies and still nascent democratic instincts among government officials of these new states oblige adopting practical implementation strategies that can be managed and sustained by the young governments. Coupled with the strong personal temptation for leaders of these new authorities to take the path of self-enrichment, close international engagement at each stage of this process will be required. Sovereignty claims are likely to be invoked by some government leaders who will chafe at the transparency and oversight mechanisms that emerge from this process and who have a self-interest in maintaining some opaqueness around these revenue flows. This argument must be addressed head on. Sovereignty is indeed a priority – but it is the sovereignty of the citizens that should be upheld.

In line with treating natural resources as a public resource, the norm that all natural resource contracts must be ratified by democratic legislatures should be instituted. The full disclosure of the financial and in-kind conditions of the contract would provide an invaluable starting point for citizen supervision and tracking the ways in which the flows of revenues are being used. In many resource-rich countries, these revenues are "off the books" altogether. Requiring a parliamentary sign-off on all natural resource contracts would introduce an initial layer of checks and balances and move away from the current norm of contracts being negotiated on opaque terms solely with the executive branch. This stipulation would also formally interject citizen interests over these national resources, if only symbolically in some cases, into the decision-making process with the aim of making this part of an ongoing national dialogue.

International actors should complement their transparency-raising and accountability-strengthening initiatives in resource-rich democratisers with development support. Since the extractive sector generates relatively few jobs, a key priority would be to foster economic diversification. Development initiatives that stimulate more employment would help balance some of the inequities that fuel the social instability so common in resource-rich societies. It will also help to reduce the country's vulnerability to the distortions, volatility and political monopolisation that plague single resource-dominated economies.

This carrot of development investment should be contingent on resource-rich governments agreeing to EITI transparency standards towards royalties and other revenues generated from their natural resource sectors. As part of this commitment to transparency, all political leaders in democratising natural resource-rich societies should establish and maintain the precedent of fully disclosing the source of their personal finances on an annual basis. Governments that are unwilling to comply with these basic transparency standards should be deemed ineligible for new development aid.

A complementary standards-raising strategy to the EITI protocols would be to mandate the IMF to conduct bi-annual "report cards" of all natural resource-rich countries. The IMF has developed a 73-page guide on resource revenue transparency that lays out the best practices for ensuring natural resource revenues are accounted for and allocated in a transparent manner that enhances economic performance (IMF 2007). Countries would be rated on how well they adhered to these practices. This technical review would then serve as a template for dialogue and reform between the government, internal watchdog groups and international actors. It would also be a means by which comparisons between countries could be made and relative progress assessed.

Other development investments that should be a priority for international actors include building the capacity of civil society watchdog organisations in the accounting and budget analysis sectors so that they can engage in effective oversight of the revenues generated from natural resources. This would include skills development in forensic accounting in order to investigate fiscal and budgetary inconsistencies. Along these lines, specialised media training should be promoted so that investigative journalists can gain an understanding of the financial management of the extractive sector and its link to government revenues. This capacity building would contribute to empowering key representatives of the excluded majority with information and analyses that would facilitate their mobilisation and, ultimately, a fairer distribution of natural resource revenues.

Certain economically motivated reforms such as reducing government subsidies of the hydrocarbon sector (which keep fuel prices artificially low and introduce distortions in other parts of the economy) and cutting back the often massive, centrally managed line ministries that control large parts of the government budget will also have clear governance benefits by reducing key opportunities for corruption and patronage that sustain the resource curse.

A common point of tension in resource-rich democratisers is the extent to which these resources should be considered a national versus a local endowment. There are valid arguments to be made on both sides of this debate. However, seen from the perspective of the state-building enterprise in which many resource-rich countries are engaged, there are compelling reasons to treat these as national revenues with provisions for certain local taxes, royalties and defined infrastructural improvements. This approach removes a combustible source of friction between jurisdictions while creating incentives for stronger ties between regions and national unity more generally. Allocating these revenues at the national level also offers the flexibility to forge the necessary compromises between competing interests as part of the social compacts on which democracies rely. Similarly, it increases the potential contributions of resources to greater geographical and group equity rather than amplifying disparities. To reiterate, the national collection and allocation of natural resource revenues will work only if the national government is subject to democratic checks and balances and the transparency in reporting and civil society supervision this entails. Otherwise, national level consolidation of these resources is highly susceptible to the logic of exclusion underlying the resource curse.

A complementary dimension of this resource-sharing dialogue is to require all resource extraction contracts to specify development investments that would be made in regions where the resource extraction is occurring. This will help to mitigate the perceived lack of tangible social and economic benefits and sense of exploitation among citizens in these regions that breed the resentment and the instability so often seen. Given that the private extractive sector typically generates relatively few local jobs, developmental benefits to the local jurisdiction from these extraction activities cannot simply be assumed. The development elements in these contracts would also be subject to parliamentary debates and approval.

Another means by which international actors can strengthen incentives for natural resource transparency is to make membership in elective international bodies espousing principles of good governance such as the EU, the New Partnership for African Development (NEPAD), the Commonwealth and the Community of Democracies, among others, contingent on adherence to international transparency norms. Similarly, this should be an explicit criterion for eligibility to the US Millennium Challenge Account, which deems that qualifying countries are ruling justly and democratically, fostering economic rights and investing in their citizens. The eligibility requirements to these bodies have already been shown to stimulate reform among countries seeking this legitimation.

Autocracies

Reshaping the incentives of oil-rich autocracies also entails a series of sticks and carrots. While it is commonly assumed that resource-rich autocracies are immune from outside pressures, this is a fallacy, especially in an increasingly globalised world. Most leaders, regardless of how insulated they may seem, care about their international reputations. These leaders want to be seen as meeting minimally accepted norms of legitimacy, human rights and respect for the rule of law. Challenging resource-rich autocracies to meet international standards in these areas, therefore, is an initial point of dialogue for reform. Governments falling below these norms, meanwhile, must increasingly answer to international public opinion – and assume the direct economic effects this entails.

Comparative indices that score every country in the world on their provision of these rights and measures of well-being provide an independent basis for identifying those governments with substandard records. Advocacy groups can take these ratings and shine the spotlight of global attention on those with deficiencies. Officials from organisations that conduct or use such surveys in the allocation of resources – such as Freedom House, the World Bank, the Millennium Challenge Corporation, Transparency International, and Global Integrity – report that such rankings matter. These groups are regularly approached by autocratic governments on how to improve their scores. While their goal may not be to become an open, democratic society, these governments want to avoid being scored at the bottom of any governance measuring programme, considering the negative reputational effects this would generate. In short, comparative rankings – and the unwanted attention this may bring – can be a meaningful incentive for expanding space for citizen supervision. In the process they can help redress some of the information and public mobilisation constraints that allow the inequities of the natural resource curse to persist.

Another point of intervention is for international development organisations to come to terms with the counter-intuitive reality that the massive revenue flows generated by natural resources in countries with autocratic governments do not typically lead to widespread improvements in levels of well-being. Accordingly, international financial institutions, especially the World Bank and regional development banks, should stop lending autocracies money for resource extraction.

This "do no harm" lending philosophy would help these organisations avoid inadvertently entrenching the dysfunctionality at play in most resource-rich autocracies. Resources controlled by governments without checks and balances are far more likely to reinforce the existing inequitable power structure than to advance development. Compelling economic arguments of the need to take advantage of a nation's natural comparative advantage are simply trumped by the political economy dynamics that dominate these societies. In some cases private capital may step in with additional resources to fill the gap. But these firms know they face a risk premium for their investments, which is a primary reason why the resource-rich state seeks international public sector support in the first place.

Furthermore, officials in resource rich autocracies often rely on international banks to safeguard and manage the revenues they are siphoning off. This is because the economic and financial volatility typical of autocratically governed economies means that domestically held assets are inherently vulnerable. This augments the leverage that UNCAC can bring to bear on these governments. Accordingly, foreign governments should come under greater scrutiny to freeze the assets of political leaders and their families in natural resource-rich countries that were generated from these resources. The recent willingness of Swiss banks, long-renowned financial safe havens, to cooperate in the exposure and seizure of ill-gotten wealth is a hopeful development in this regard. These efforts can be further accentuated by simultaneously ensuring additional funding support for non-governmental oganisations and OECD government ministries tasked with tracing these assets.

Development investment in resource-rich autocracies should be held out as a carrot for reforms. However, as with democratisers, this should be strictly contingent on autocratic governments meeting minimum standards of transparency on the reporting of resource revenue. Otherwise, international development agencies risk perpetually absorbing the costs of autocratic governments' anti-developmental policies. Funding civil society actors, strengthening the capacity of watchdog groups and facilitating information access and exchange would remain a priority in any case.

Similarly, opportunities for expanding trade and private sector investment should be held out as tangible incentives to resource-rich autocracies for opening up to reform. OECD governments can encourage or discourage such investment by signalling to capital markets and political risk-rating agencies when genuine steps toward more accountable governance and the rule of law are being made. OECD governments could further encourage such investment by engaging in public–private partnerships reducing some of the risk faced by private investors. The investment pursued in these contexts would be aimed at the non-extractive sector – with the intention of contributing to economic diversification, job creation and strengthening the private sector.

Private sector

The private extractive sector also has an important role to play in remedying the natural resource curse. In an era of globalised communications extractive sector firms are increasingly under the glare of international public opinion for their perceived role in contributing to the underdevelopment, corruption, human rights abuses and instability associated with resource extraction. They more and more frequently feel the brunt of resentment from restive local populations who blame them for their enduring poverty. Recognising the potential effects these perceptions will have on their bottom line, a number of large extractive sector firms have welcomed the efforts by EITI and others to establish international standards of conduct. However, any firm that attempts to apply minimum transparency, human rights, labour, environmental, health or development standards on its own places itself at a competitive disadvantage. Firms with fewer qualms working in such contexts (and typically based in more insulated environments) are quick to step in. Consequently, there is a lowest common denominator effect where, if even only a few extractive firms are unwilling to adhere to minimum standards, the dynamics of the natural resource curse are reinforced.

In consultation with extractive sector firms, accordingly, the EITI and the IMF through its revenue transparency report cards should also rate countries on how strenuously they apply labour, environmental and health standards for extractive operations. Such standards, in turn, would be written into all future natural resource contracts negotiated between governments and extractive firms. The aim of setting these standards would be to minimise the scope for less socially responsible firms to gain a competitive advantage at the expense of the health and well-being of local people. In the process, standards for extractive operations globally would be raised. Establishing such standards would also provide extractive firms with greater clarity about the operating environment in which they are competing, while reducing the risk to their investment from social and political instability.

Making all such contingencies of a natural resource extraction contract public would put pressure on national governments to make deals only with firms that maintain strong records of social responsibility. Engaging locally affected populations in the decision-making process would also garner greater support for the project. Along the same lines, locally elected community leaders should have a seat at the negotiating table when extractive agreements are being crafted. This would institute a channel of two-way communication early on in the relationship between an extractive firm and society. Obtaining the endorsement of local leaders, in turn, would be in the financial, public relations, and social stability interests of both the private extractive firm and the national government.

These contracts would also stipulate specific development initiatives that private investors would sponsor in the district(s) where the extractive activity would take place. In the process a local community supervisory committee would be established to meet regularly with the extractive firm to ascertain progress and proactively discuss problems. Annual reviews of the performance of the extractive firm with local leaders and communities as well as national stakeholders would be required. This would introduce greater local accountability into these agreements and provide a specific, transparent forum where adherence to the health, environmental and labour standards can be reviewed and grievances proactively aired. It would also provide a discrete platform to assess whether the development strategies outlined in the contract have contributed to economic and social progress in the targeted district(s) over time. Moreover, it would provide a series of meaningful opportunities for private firms to enter into dialogue with local people, ensuring they are aware of the developmental benefits these investments have made while clarifying any points of misinformation. These standards and procedures are aimed not at making the extractive process more onerous for socially responsible firms but to expose and pressure those who are undercutting the reforms aimed at reining in the damaging effects of the natural resource curse.

Adopting a baseline code of conduct in the international extractive sector will require enforcement mechanisms and penalties for non-compliance if these standards are to be meaningful. In other words, if the goal is to reverse the "race to the bottom" dynamic current in place, firms that undercut global norms need to be penalised. This is especially relevant, given that the costs to the public interest are so high. Penalties would differentiate between firms that were actively subverting these transparency protocols and those that were participating, but had fallen short on certain measures.

The non-complying transgressors would be subject to a name and shame campaign. Drawing on EITI and IMF reports, non-governmental organisation watchdog groups like Global Witness, Revenue Watch and the Publish What You Pay coalition could publish a monthly bulletin of the major firms and financial sponsors that are skirting transparency, health, environmental, labour, or developmental standards. Meanwhile, firms scoring in the bottom 10 per cent of the IMF revenue transparency rankings for more than two years running would be barred from competing for contracts and raising assets from capital markets in EITI signatory countries. The United Nations Office on Drugs and Crime (UNODC), which is the lead agency responsible for implementing UNCAC would issue démarches to the UN ambassadors of state-owned or state-financed firms that were involved in these undermining actions. These censures would be widely publicised to draw international attention to companies that are effectively sponsoring the corrupt, counter-developmental and destabilising rule of resource-cursed states. Firms that are playing by the established rules, conversely, would derive reputational benefits by scoring on the positive end of these monitoring ledgers.

Firms that sign up to the EITI standards, though not meeting some of the health, environmental, labour or developmental goals as determined via their annual reviews, would be required to submit their plans for remedial action to local and national stakeholders. Persistent shortfalls would be referred first to national political leaders and then to the EITI and UNODC secretariats.

Conclusion

The natural resource curse is a global curse. The instability, corruption, confrontational govern-ance and poverty it fosters are at the heart of regional and international development and security challenges. Resource-cursed states, non-coincidentally, are also overwhelmingly auto-cratic. Political monopolisation fosters economic monopolisation. The easily consolidated nature of hydrocarbon extraction makes petroleum-rich states particularly susceptible and resistant to the transparency, accountability and supervision that are needed to ensure the revenues generated benefit most people. At its heart, then, the natural resource curse is a problem of political govern-ance. Curbing this accordingly, is linked to advancing accountable, democratic institutions.

The natural resource curse is also about unfairness – a few, politically well-connected people can profit at the expense of the many. Remedies, therefore, must focus on raising the costs to rent-seekers while empowering the majority. Prospects for doing so are greatly facilitated in societies that have already taken the first steps towards democratic systems of governance. They should, therefore, receive maximum support from the interna-tional community lest leaders in these democra-tisers slip back into the powerful gravitational pull of self-interest before natural resource reporting norms and institutional checks and balances can gain traction. While the challenges to reform in resource-rich autocracies are more difficult, reputational and investment interests in these governments – connected as they are to the global economy – still provide considerable leverage to help shape incentives toward a more productive use of these resources.

Notes

1. Countries are considered hydrocarbon-rich or mineral-rich if their (a) average share of hydrocarbon or mineral fiscal revenues exceeds 25 per cent of total fiscal revenue during the period 2000–2005 or (b) the average share of hydrocarbon or mineral export proceeds was greater than 25 per cent during this period (IMF 2007). Hydrocarbons include coal, crude oil and natural gas. Minerals include tin, gold, lead, zinc, iron, copper, nickel, silver, bauxite and phosphate.

2. Political categorisations are based on annual scores for two independent measures of democracy: the Polity IV governance index issues annual democracy scores for every country with a population over 500,000 based on the establishment of institutions for the selection of their political leaders, opportunities for popular participation in the political process and checks on the chief executive (Gurr *et al.* 1990; Marshall and Jaggers 2000). Freedom House conducts an annual survey of political rights and civil liberties, based on independent analysts' assessments of 25 questions for all countries in the world. This generates a 2–14 composite score. For our purposes, countries scoring in the top third of each scale, respectively, are considered democracies; those in the bottom third are treated as autocracies. Mixed regimes containing certain elements of democratic and autocratic systems, score in the middle tier of these indices. Democratisers are countries that have made and sustained a two-point improvement on the Polity IV democracy scale (a three- point gain on the Freedom House index).

Budget transparency and development in resource-dependent countries

Paolo de Renzio, Pamela Gomez and James Sheppard

Introduction

A considerable number of developing countries, while endowed with large amounts of natural resources, are still trapped in a vicious cycle of poverty and stagnation. Over the past decade and more recently due to the global boom in commodity prices this contradiction has become the focus of increasing interest. Some past research has highlighted how natural resource abundance is often linked to slower growth rates (Auty 2001), and actually seems to increase the likelihood that resource-dependent countries will experience negative economic, political and social outcomes. This phenomenon has been commonly referred to as the resource curse or the paradox of plenty (Karl 1997; Sachs and Warner 2001). Sachs and Warner use cross-sectional data on resource exports between 1970 and 1989 to demonstrate the resource curse hypothesis, claiming that it might be due to the high price structure that characterises resource-abundant countries, causing them to miss out on export-led growth. Collier and

Pamela Gomez was project leader of the Open Budget Initiative at the International Budget Project at the time of writing this chapter. She has written extensively on new oil and gas development and human rights in the former Soviet Union for Human Rights Watch and the Economist Intelligence Unit. She covered global financial markets, including commodities and foreign exchange markets for AP-Dow Jones News Services, as well as fiscal and tax policy issues for several specialty publications.

Paolo de Renzio is a doctoral candidate at the Department of Politics and International Relations at the University of Oxford, a Fellow at the London School of Economics and a Research Associate of the Overseas Development Institute. His research focuses on the interplay between aid policies and modalities and public finance management systems in developing countries. Previously, Paolo worked as an economist and policy advisor in Papua New Guinea's Ministry of Finance, and as a UNDP public sector specialist, lecturer and independent consultant in Mozambique.
Email: p.derenzio@odi.org.uk

James Sheppard holds a Masters degree in Public Administration from the London School of Economics and Political Science and the Lee Kuan Yew School of Public Policy.
Email: jsheppard1@gmail.com

Goderis (2007) confirm the existence of a resource curse with richer time-series data, finding that commodity booms have positive short-term but adverse long-term effects on output. A substantial part of the explanation for this, they claim, lies in high consumption and low investment rates and in an overvalued exchange rate.

Some of this literature has emphasised economic factors underlying the resource curse, citing the Dutch disease effect – the pinch on the manufacturing sector caused by the currency appreciation driven by resource exports. In addition, other studies have demonstrated some of the political consequences of resource dependency, including authoritarian government and the onset of civil war (Collier et al. 2003; Wantchekon 1999). Expanding the resource-growth contradiction to issues of human welfare, Bulte et al. (2005) find that resource-dependent countries tend to suffer lower levels of human development. Their main explanation, however, posits an indirect link through the quality of institutions.

In other words, bad governance and poor institutions are the main factor causing the poor performance of resource-dependent countries. This claim seems to be supported by the fact that not all countries blessed with abundance of natural resources experience economic failure. Botswana, for example, is one exception: a resource-rich country demonstrating strong economic growth averaging growth rates of 7.8 per cent since the 1980s (40 per cent of which is due to mining) and characterised by good governance, political stability and strong fiscal discipline (Iimi 2007).

The growing weight and explanatory power attributed to issues linked to politics, governance and economic management (see also Ross 1999) highlights the limitations of more economistic, technical approaches, and is part of a growing trend among economists and development practitioners to eschew the technocratic approaches that minimise or ignore political factors. In the words of Eifert *et al.* (2003) such technical approaches "often confront the reality of opaque, highly politicised fiscal systems that lack the checks and balances needed to ensure that resources are well employed and to provide the fiscal flexibility needed to adjust spending in line with changes in resources" (p. 86). In an attempt to deconstruct critically the political factors underlying the resource curse and its influence on policy, Rosser (2006) presents five perspectives: behaviouralist, rational-actor, state-centred, historico-structuralist, and social-capital.

The behaviouralist and rational-actor explanations both emphasise the role of political elites in poor economic policy and institutional deterioration. However, while the former perspective highlights in particular loose expenditure policies based on the over-collateralisation of commodity resources in state borrowing, the latter emphasises the voracity effect of predatory rent-seeking and the inefficient redistribution of economic rents which ensues. The state-centred view, on the other hand, argues that responsibility for policy errors stems from the lack of political accountability common in rentier states, arguing that both the abundant resource rents and the redistributive policies undermine political accountability and the development of more market-oriented institutions. Looking beyond government, historico-structuralist and social-capital explanations focus upon differences in economic and political power, as well as upon social cohesion between different socioeconomic groups within the economy. They argue that the concentration of wealth favours the policies of specific business groups, with negative consequences for economic reforms.

Rosser (2006) contends, however, that these explanations ignore a country's specific background and initial conditions, as well as the role and mediating effect of external and domestic social forces. External factors have become increasingly important, mostly because of the broadening and deepening of economic interdependence faced by all countries, including resource-dependent ones. In this area, increasing civil society involvement in campaigning against corruption and human rights violations linked to the relationships between multinational extractive industry companies and governments of resource-dependent countries has played an important part.

In recent years a number of international initiatives have been launched in response to these governance challenges. For example, the IMF has introduced special guidelines on resource revenue transparency to complement its focus on fiscal transparency (IMF 2007a). The Extractive Industry Transparency Initiative (EITI) and the Publish What You Pay campaign have encouraged the publication of payments made by extractive industry companies to governments (EITI 2005). The Revenue Watch Institute and the International Budget Project (IBP) have focused instead on developing independent domestic capacity to monitor government earnings and expenditures (Shultz 2005). Shedding light on some of the domestic social forces at play will potentially provide some insight into the mechanisms through which domestic actors with power come to support, or even advocate, institutional change (Dietsche 2007).

Issues of transparency, accountability and civil society involvement in the budget process have therefore increasingly come to the fore as one of the main governance challenges that resource-dependent countries need to face in order to correct the distortions at the heart of the resource curse. The objective of this chapter is to examine empirically the nature and extent of budget transparency in resource-dependent countries as a potential foundation for improving governance and development impact. Budget transparency is here defined as "the full disclosure of all relevant fiscal information in a timely and systematic manner" (OECD 2001, p. 1). Transparency is viewed as a means of improving economic governance through a combination of mechanisms, strengthening accountability and legitimacy as well as facilitating policy consistency and predictability and promoting the better functioning of government (Heald 2003). The linkage between transparency, governance, policies and development outcomes, however, is not automatic, but is achieved through the interaction of various actors, including government, multinational extractive industries and civil society (Hameed 2006). Transparency enables understanding and participation in policy decisions by the public and serves to build trust in government (IBP 2006; Ramkumar and Krafchik 2007).

Although civil society would seem to offer considerable long-term potential for bringing about a sustainable strengthening of domestic institutions for more accountable and effective fiscal management (Petrie 2003), its increased role in promoting fiscal transparency – alongside that of other accountability institutions such as legislatures and audit institutions is quite recent. The limited research that exists on the role of civil society and its impact (see, for example, de Renzio and Krafchik 2007, Robinson 2006) shows that while access to budget information is one of the major hurdles that civil society organisations face, groups in various countries have played a vital role in interpreting and disseminating budget information, in fostering debate to improve transparency and accountability and in significant instances of improving budget policies and outcomes.

This first section of this chapter introduced the discourse on the resource curse and budget transparency, and the relationship between the two for economic governance. The second section develops an index of budget transparency and accountability for resource-dependent countries using data from the IBP's Open Budget Initiative (OBI), and compares these scores with the UN Human Development Index (HDI) for each country, using it as a proxy for development outcomes. The third section

provides a more in-depth discussion of the nature of linkages between resource dependency, budget transparency and development outcomes in Peru, Vietnam and Angola. The final section offers a summary of the main findings and arguments, as well as suggestions for future research.

Measuring budget transparency in resource-dependent countries

Starting in 2002 the IBP aimed to develop a survey instrument that could provide an independent evaluation of budget transparency across countries. Over a three-year period, the "Open budget questionnaire" was designed to collect comparative data on the public availability of budget information and other budgeting practices. The questionnaire contains a total of 122 questions based on generally accepted good practice related to public financial management.[1] The responses to 91 of these, focusing on the content and timeliness of the seven key budget documents that all countries should issue, were averaged to form the Open Budget Index, scoring countries on a 0–100 scale. A country's score on the Index reflects the quantity of publicly available budget information, but not the quality or credibility of such information. For example, the questions do not evaluate whether information about government expenditures, revenues, or debt may have been deliberately omitted, withheld or diverted from government accounts. They do not consider either the credibility of macroeconomic forecasting or economic assumptions used in estimates in a country's budget.[2]

Table 1 summarises the overall results for the Open Budget Index 2006, which covered 59 countries. As expected, there is great variation across countries on the extent to which governments produce and publish budget information. France and the UK achieved the highest scores (89 and 88 respectively) while Vietnam and Angola were at the bottom of the ranking (with scores of 2 and 4).

According to Table 1 of these 59 countries, 24 are resource dependent.[3] The resource-dependent countries (set in bold) also vary

TABLE 1. Open Budget Index 2006

OBI score	Countries
Provides extensive information to citizens (81–100)	France, New Zealand, Slovenia, **South Africa**, UK, USA
Provides significant information to citizens (61–80)	**Botswana**, Brazil, Czech Republic, **Norway**, **Peru**, Poland, Romania, South Korea, Sweden
Provides some information to citizens (41–60)	Bulgaria, **Colombia**, Costa Rica, Croatia, **Ghana**, Guatemala, India, **Indonesia**, **Jordan**, **Kazakhstan**, Kenya, Malawi, **Mexico**, **Namibia**, Pakistan, **Papua New Guinea**, Philippines, **Russia**, Sri Lanka, Tanzania, Turkey
Provides minimal information to citizens (21–40)	Albania, **Algeria**, Argentina, **Azerbaijan**, Bangladesh, **Cameroon**, **Ecuador**, El Salvador, Georgia, Honduras, Nepal, Uganda, **Zambia**
Provides scant or no information to citizens (0–20)	**Angola**, **Bolivia**, Burkina Faso, **Chad**, Egypt, **Mongolia**, Morocco, Nicaragua, **Nigeria**, **Vietnam**

OBI, Open Index Budget
Source: Adapted from International Budget Project (2006). Resource-dependent countries are marked in bold

greatly in their budget transparency scores, with South Africa, Botswana and Norway ranking among the best performers, while a significant number, (Nigeria and Chad, for instance) still provide scant or no information to their citizens. Only four of these countries provide extensive or significant budget information to their citizens through the publication of various budget documents. This highlights the existence of a significant transparency gap that characterises resource-dependent countries. This gap can also be noticed by analysing average scores across the two groups. Countries that are not resource dependent fare considerably better (in that they have have more transparent budget systems) than resource-dependent ones. For the first group the average OBI score is 49.9, while the latter scored on average 39.7. Assuming that budget transparency is a reliable proxy for good economic governance, this seems to indicate that resource-dependent countries suffer from a governance deficit and are characterised by unaccountable governments that are able to divert resource rents from productive uses, fuelling waste and corruption.

Yet the variation in performances within the group of resource-dependent countries calls for a more detailed analysis. In order to arrive at a more precise assessment of budget transparency issues linked to resource dependency we developed a separate index based on a sub-set of questions from the Open Budget questionnaire which are more directly linked to issues likely to be relevant for resource-dependent countries. This index, focusing on budget transparency and

accountability in resource-dependent countries, targets three main areas:

Revenue transparency

A first set of questions assesses the degree to which governments produce and publish information on revenue collection in different phases of the budget cycle. While resource revenues may not be separately accounted for within the budget, the general management of government revenues is here used as a proxy.

General budget transparency

This part of the index covers certain issues related to the macroeconomic framework, debt and expenditure. Medium-term projections of revenue streams based on credible forecasts, the use of resource revenues to back government borrowing and the use of resource wealth are all important factors shaping the potential impact of resource rents.

Budget accountability

Here we focused on some of the additional questions that assess the degree of oversight carried out by the legislature, supreme audit institutions and the public. Opportunities for external scrutiny and debate on executive action on budget matters are important in holding governments accountable for the collection and use of revenues from the extractive sector.

TABLE 2. Transparency and accountability index for resource-dependent countries

Country	Hydr/min	Revenue transparency	General budget transparency	Budget account	Total	HDI (2005)
South Africa	Min	95	83	85	88	0.921
Norway	Hydr	72	88	85	81	0.968
Peru	Min	95	75	61	77	0.773
Russia	Hydr	79	63	58	66	0.802
Botswana	Min	79	63	49	63	0.654
Colombia	Hydr	50	63	70	61	0.791
Kazakhstan	Hydr	60	40	55	51	0.794
Mexico	Hydr	50	48	55	51	0.829
Jordan	Min	62	46	39	49	0.773
Indonesia	Hydr and Min	38	69	27	45	0.728
Namibia	Min	60	56	18	45	0.650
PNG	Min	69	44	12	42	0.530
Ghana	Hydr	50	40	27	39	0.553
Zambia	Min	38	31	46	38	0.434
Ecuador	Hydr	48	29	18	32	0.772
Bolivia	Hydr	33	29	27	30	0.695
Cameroon	Hydr	38	42	9	30	0.532
Algeria	Hydr	36	40	6	27	0.733
Mongolia	Min	26	10	39	25	0.700
Azerbaijan	Hydr	38	31	6	25	0.746
Nigeria	Hydr	26	27	21	25	0.470
Vietnam	Hydr	5	8	30	14	0.733
Chad	Hydr	7	13	9	10	0.388
Angola	Hydr	5	13	6	8	0.446
Averages	General	48	44	36	43	
	Hydr	40	40	32	37	
	Min	62	53	42	52	

Source: Authors' calculations based on International Budget Project (2006) and UNDP (2007)

About 10–15 questions were selected for each of the three areas, for which we calculated separate and joint averages for resource-dependent countries, following the OBI methodology (see Appendix 1 for a detailed list of the questions used). Table 2 presents the results of this exercise, indicating for each country whether it is dependent on hydrocarbons or minerals, its separate and joint index scores, and the value of its latest HDI in assessing its transformation of resource riches into tangible development outcomes (the HDI is a composite indicator based on income as well as health and education outcomes).

Among the 24 resource-dependent countries, 14 are rich predominantly in hydrocarbon resources, while 10 are predominantly endowed with mineral resources. South Africa and Norway emerge as the countries with higher degrees of transparency and accountability, while Vietnam and Angola remain at the bottom of the table, together with Chad. On average, countries that are dependent on mineral resources score much better (52) than hydrocarbon-dependent countries (37), with the greatest difference being in revenue transparency.[4]

Countries score very differently on the various components of our index. For example, both South Africa and Norway do much better than all countries on budget accountability issues, with Colombia not too far behind. On the other hand, the overall scores of countries such as Peru, Namibia and Cameroon are reduced due to their low budget accountability scores. Along with Vietnam and Indonesia, Norway's position suffers from a lower score on revenue transparency.

Some of the more striking differences, however, can be seen when a country's performance in terms of transparency and accountability is compared with overall development performance, for example, measured through the HDI. Generally speaking, there is a clear correlation between higher values in the transparency and accountability index and human development performance (see Fig. 1). This

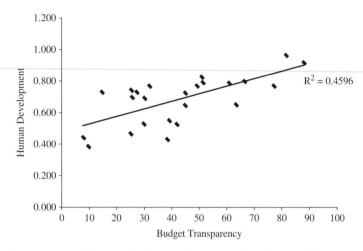

FIGURE 1. Budget transparency and human development in resource-dependent countries

cannot be interpreted as indicating causality, that is, that more transparency brings better development outcomes. Yet this clear statistical association deserves further attention. One way of trying to disentangle the possible linkages between budget transparency and development outcomes is to look at specific countries for which the relationship between the two variables is less obvious.

Short tales of three countries: Peru, Vietnam and Angola

In order to examine in greater depth the relationship between budget transparency and development in resource-dependent countries, we analysed three countries that performed very differently both with regard to transparency and to development outcomes. Peru combines high degrees of budget transparency with high human development results. Vietnam has an HDI score similar to Peru, but a much lower degree of budget transparency. Finally, Angola scores very low in both areas. The three country summaries presented in Table 3 derived from limited desk-based research, aim to assess to what extent factors such as the type and degree of resource dependency, the nature of the political regime and of budget institutions and the existence, strength and role of civil society activism were instrumental in forging such striking differences in performance.

Peru: Increased budget transparency and an active civil society

Peru's resource wealth lies mostly in mineral resources, although the country is also a natural gas producer. It is the world's fifth largest producer of gold and copper and the second largest producer of silver, and ranks highly in its output of lead and zinc. A key characteristic of Peru's resource revenue profile is that the government enjoys diversified sources of revenues. This includes revenues from several types of mineral extraction and from hydrocarbons as well as significant revenues from economic activities that are not associated with the extractive industries. Between 2000 and 2005 minerals constituted 50 per cent of the country's export earnings. Nonetheless, their growth was softened by strong increases in non-traditional exports over the same period. Mineral rents, therefore, comprise a relatively small share of Peru's fiscal revenue (see Table 3).

Peru's key budget documents were made publicly available (see Table 4) as part of an effort to increase transparency in public finances during the mid-1990s. In 2003 laws on fiscal prudence and transparency as well as transparency and access to public information required detailed multi-year economic and fiscal information to be published within specific time limits, as well as government compliance reports at the end of each semester (IMF 2004). The move towards transparency was a continuation of fiscal stabilisation, liberalisation and structural

TABLE 3. Overview of case studies as at 2005

Country	Natural resources[a]	Natural resources (2000–2005)				OBI score	HDI[b] (2005)	Gini coeff[c] (2005)	Polity IV[d] (2005)	Free press[e] (2005)
		% of fiscal revenue	% of GDP	% of export earnings	% of GDP					
Peru	Gold, copper, silver, (oil, gas)	3.3	1.5	50.8	8.1	77	0.773	0.52	9	Partially free
Vietnam	Oil, gas	31.2	7.4	21.3	11	14	0.733	0.34	− 7	Not free
Angola	Oil, (diamonds)	79.8	33.4	91.8	68	8	0.446	0.61	− 2	Not free

[a]See IMF (2007a). Resources indicated in parenthesis are not included in IMF calculations of natural resource wealth. Some caveats on the IMF definition of resource dependency are presented in note 3 at the end of this chapter.
[b]The Human Development Index (HDI) is a summary composite index that measures a country's average achievements in three basic aspects of human development: health (measured by life expectancy); knowledge (adult literacy rate and the combined primary, secondary and tertiary gross enrolment ratio); and a decent standard of living (GDP per capita in purchasing power parity $US) (UNDPa n.d.)
[c]The Gini coefficient is a statistical measure of income distribution. Values range between 0 (complete equality) and 1 (complete inequality). For Peru (UNDP, n.d.), for Vietnam (UNDP, n.d.) and for Angola, World Bank (2007a)
[d]Polity IV (2005) focuses specifically on the institutionalised authority patterns that characterise states. The Polity IV combined polity score measures the relative institutionalised democratic and autocratic elements in each country. Its scale ranges from + 10 (strongly democratic) to − 10 (strongly autocratic). See website: www.cidcm.umd.edu/polity/ Accessed 1 December 2007.
[e]Degree to which each country permits the free flow of news and information. Classification ranges from free, partly free, to not free. See Freedom House (n.d.) homepage

TABLE 4. Peru's budget documents

Pre-budget statement	Exec. budget proposal	Supporting documents	Enacted budget	In-year reports	Mid-year report	Year-end report	Audit report
P D	P D	P D	P D	P D	P D	P D	P D

D, distributed to public; P, produced
Source: International Budget Project (2006)

reform measures and followed a financial crisis between 1988 and 1992. It offered a means to address the country's economic problems, which were rooted in the shift to state-led development in the 1960s and in an over-reliance on external borrowing, weak state organisations and poor ties with organised societal interests (Wise 1994).

Although it has been labelled an oligarchic state with predatory tendencies in the past (Auty 2001), Peru returned to democracy in 1993. Constitutional reforms in 2000 increased the independence of the judiciary and the media, as well as congressional checks on the executive. However, Santiso and Belgrano (2004) note that the contribution of the Peruvian legislature to budget supervision has been inhibited by both external and internal structural factors, including formal and informal rules shaping executive–legislative relations, a fragmented political party

system, the procedures of legislative budgeting and organisation, and resources capacity. Similar constraints in expertise and resources have been noted for the Office of the Comptroller General (IMF 2004) and are important in its ability to complete audit reports for the legislature and monitor the follow up of its recommendations.

Through the emergence of a number of civil society organisations (CSOs), social supervision complements the role played by the legislative and audit bodies. A number of CSOs focus specifically on budget oversight such as Propuesta Ciudadana, Ciudadanos al Dia, and Centro de Investigación de la Universidad del Pacífico. Collaboration also exists between different CSOs – for instance, the formation of the Asociación Civil Transparencia in 2001, the embryo of Proetica and the Peruvian Chapter of Transparency International in 2003.

Vietnam: limited oversight in a developmental context

Vietnam's mining sector is dominated by the oil and gas industry – South-East Asia's third largest, which constitutes a considerable portion of fiscal revenues and export earnings (see Table 3). The development of this resource sector has been linked to the country's *doi moi* (renovation) and economic liberalisation in the mid-1980s to late-1980s. Of the US$20 billion in foreign direct investment Vietnam targeted for 1994–2000, US$8 billion was earmarked for the oil and gas sector (Anon 1994). Foreign direct investment has fuelled growth and facilitated the introduction of advanced technology through joint ventures (Mai 2003). Despite Vietnam's impressive recent growth performance, some doubts exist over its sustainability, due to macroeconomic risks and vulnerability to external shocks (IMF 2007b).

Some information on the central government budget started to be published in 1998 with the 1997 accounts in the wake of the Asian financial crisis. This crisis represented the first stalling of the economy since the adoption of *doi moi*, which can be linked, at least in part, to a lack of fiscal transparency (Thayer 2000). Further disclosure of budgetary policies, supporting data and materials, as well as information on the budget process, came into effect in 2004 as mandated by the 2002 State Budget Law. However, the dissemination of the budget and year-end reports serves more for notification than for policy debate, and is limited to the enacted budget and year-end reports (see Table 5).

Policy and legal changes over the last five years have resulted in a limited expansion of the role of the National Assembly. The 2002 Budget Law, for example, increased the role of the National Assembly in approving overall budget allocations and underlying macroeconomic figures. However, as part of its socialist legacy, the Constitution continues to concentrate power, including on budgetary matters, in the hands of a few very powerful individuals in the legislature's Standing Committee whose membership consists of members of the Communist Party of Vietnam. In fact, the National Assembly is somewhat disempowered by the fact that it meets rarely and the Standing Committee is granted all decision-making powers when it is not in session. As characterised by Salomon (2007, p. 215), the relationship between the executive and legislative powers therefore "must not be considered in terms of opposition or confrontation but in terms of cooperation, ... but [is] generally limited to more technical problems".

Structural constraints also exist for the State Audit Vietnam (SAV), which is not fully independent from the executive and reports to the Standing Committee rather than the full National Assembly. Its responsibilities overlap with those of the Government Inspectorate and the Ministry of Finance, its capacity to enforce auditing recommendations is weak, and there is little evidence that the government acts on SAV reports.

While many forms of CSOs exist in Vietnam, none is independent. The state regulates their activities and the avenues they have to engage in decision-making and supervisory functions. Increased numbers of CSOs – mass organisations, professional associations, Vietnamese non-governmental organisations (NGOs) and community-based organisations – now engage in local community development and poverty reduction (Nørlund 2007). Information is published at the commune level and in government services with the publication of specific budget information (World Bank 2007a), but little exists in relation to the budget at a larger scale, and specifically in relation to revenue. Generally speaking, therefore, weak

TABLE 5. Vietnam's budget documents

Pre-budget statement	Exec. budget proposal	Supporting documents	Enacted budget	In-year reports	Mid-year report	Year-end report	Audit report
P I	P I	P I	P D	P I	P I	P D	P I

D, distributed to the public; P, produced; I, for internal purposes only
Source: International Budget Project (2006)

policy advocacy has been compounded by a lack of information about policies, laws and regulations, and socioeconomic development strategies (Bach 2001).

Angola: low transparency and a predatory regime

The Angolan government is highly dependent on a single commodity – oil – for its revenues. Angola's oil sector, the second largest producer in Africa after Nigeria, accounts for 90 per cent of its export earnings and 80 per cent of government fiscal revenues. Originally a large agricultural exporter before the 1970s, Angola achieved high oil production levels in the early 1980s. Even with its oil and diamonds, the country's second largest export, the resource sector accounts for less than 1 per cent of the workforce and most of the economy subsists in the informal sector (Economist Intelligence Unit 2007). Its offshore location meant that production could continue to boom and remain undisrupted while the country was affected by war, macroeconomic instability and poor policy choices.

Little information is available to the public in Angola about the state budget, with the exception of the enacted budget (see Table 6). Documents are primarily produced for internal purposes but sometimes they are not, for lack of adequate capacity, as in the case of in-year reports or audited accounts. Increased transparency has been a key condition for cooperation with the IMF since the mid-1990s, but the government has often been unwilling to release information (Human Rights Watch 2004). A 2002 "Oil diagnostic", part of the government's efforts to reform the country's public financial management system, found major discrepancies in incoming oil revenues, receipts of taxes and royalties and the accounts of state-oil company SONANGOL, as well as government

expenditures not accounted for, poor record-keeping and missing data (Human Rights Watch 2004). Budgets submitted to parliament are seldom opposed, highlighting the limited role of parliamentary oversight. A Court of Accounts with strong legal powers became operational in 2001, but suffers from serious limitations and has yet to produce an audit report (World Bank 2007b) There is no anti-corruption commission in Angola and the statistics agency is weak (Isaksen *et al.* 2007).

Constitutional amendments in 1992 allowed for NGO registration. This change has seen a growth in the number of active NGOs – over 100 international NGOs and 350 local NGOs (US Department of State in Amudsen and Abreu 2006, p. 1). However, with a few exceptions, such as the Angolan Catholic University and *Associação Fiscal*, civil society groups are not actively engaged in public finance issues. The situation stems from the weak capacity to analyse policy and from government restrictions. As stated by Amudsen and Abreu (2006, p. 41), "the more directly CSOs work on issues of central government accountability and transparency, public financial management and budgeting, the smaller, weaker and less legitimate … the organizations tend to be viewed" by government.

Discussion and conclusions

This chapter attempted to bring together different strands of evidence linking issues of budget transparency, resource dependency and development performance across the world. Recent research has increasingly focused on the importance of poor governance and weak institutions as a key factor behind the resource curse. Based on data drawn from the IBP (2006) we found that resource-dependent countries do, indeed, suffer from a significant transparency gap in their budget systems. Moreover, we

TABLE 6. Angola's budget documents

Pre-budget statement	Exec. budget proposal	Supporting documents	Enacted budget	In-year reports	Mid-year report	Year-end report	Audit report
P I	P I	P A	P D	NP	N P	P A	N P

A, available on request; D, distributed to the public; NP, not produced, P, produced; I, for internal purposes only
Source: International Budget Project (2006)

TABLE 7. Overview of case study findings

Country	Resource dependency	Political regime	Civil society
Peru	Heavy dependence for export earnings only; diversified economy	Democratic regime with increasing transparency and strengthening accountability	Strong (domestic/international)
Vietnam	Medium dependence for both fiscal revenues and export earnings; diversified economy	Undemocratic regime with limited transparency and accountability	Weak (domestic/international)
Angola	Heavy dependence for both fiscal revenues and export earnings; undiversified economy	Predatory regime with low transparency and underdeveloped accountability	Weak (domestic) Strong (international)

developed an index rating the transparency and accountability of budget systems in 24 resource-dependent countries, showing not only that resource-dependent countries are characterised by very different degrees of budget transparency and accountability, but that they also differ in their levels of human development. While the numbers show that our index and the HDI are positively correlated, this relationship cannot be assumed to imply causation in either direction.

In order to try and shed some light on the linkages between budget transparency and accountability on one side and human development outcomes on the other, we looked at countries with extremely different performances on both: Peru, Vietnam and Angola. The short, desk-based case studies are not in any way exhaustive, but they nonetheless highlight a series of factors that contribute to shape these linkages. These include, first, the type and degree of dependency on natural resource revenues, and whether the economy as a whole is diversified and integrated with the global economy. They also include the nature of the political regime – whether it is democratic or autocratic, developmental or predatory – and the nature of budget institutions, including the process through which they were reformed to increase transparency and accountability. Third, they include the existence of an active civil society that is interested and engaged in issues of fiscal transparency and oversight. These factors are not independent from each other, and in some cases they are heavily interrelated.

Table 7 summarises the case study findings. Peru's reliance on mineral resources rather than hydrocarbons and its diversified economy may have been combined with deepening democratisation, increasing degrees of fiscal transparency and growing civil society involvement to deliver better development results. In Vietnam's case, successful growth-oriented policies were coupled with timid attempts at improving transparency and encouraging participation, given the autocratic – but developmental – nature of the state. Growth and development outcomes were achieved despite weak transparency and accountability, but these may not be sustained in the future. Angola remains locked in a vicious cycle of poverty and poor governance, with limited domestic accountability and mobilisation, despite increasing international pressure and scrutiny.

While none of these findings gives a clear and uncontroversial answer to the question of how budget transparency can contribute to improved governance and development impact, and what the role of civil society might be, we hope that this chapter has contributed interesting data and ideas to the ongoing debate around the resource curse. But the limited evidence garnered in the three desk-based case studies calls for further investigation and different uses and combinations of the rich information generated by the Open Budget Index, in combination with other data sources, in an effort to contribute to a better understanding of the linkages between governance and development in resource-dependent countries.

Appendix 1. OBI questions used in index

Category	Question	OBI No.
Revenue transparency	Does the executive's budget or any supporting budget documentation identify the different sources of tax revenue (such as income tax or VAT) for the budget year?	7
	Does the executive's budget or any supporting budget documentation identify the different sources of non-tax revenue (such as grants, property income, and sales of goods and services) for the budget year?	8
	In the executive's budget or any supporting budget documentation, are estimates of the aggregate level of revenue presented for a multi-year period (at least two years beyond the budget year)?	9
	In the executive's budget or any supporting budget documentation, is more detail than just the aggregate level presented for revenue estimates that cover a multi-year period (for at least two years beyond the budget year)?	10
	Does the executive's budget or any supporting budget documentation present information for at least the budget year that show how policy proposals in the budget as distinct from existing policies, affect revenues?	17
	In the executive's budget or any supporting budget documentation, what is the most recent year presented for which all revenues reflect actual outcomes?	32
	Does the executive's budget or any supporting budget documentation present information for at least the budget year on tax expenditures?	45
	Does the executive's budget or any supporting budget documentation identify all earmarked revenues?	46
	Does the executive make available to the public a description of the tax rate or fee schedule for all revenue sources?	56
	How often does the executive release to the public in-year reports on actual revenue collections by source of revenue?	87
	What share of revenue is covered by the in-year reports on actual revenue collections?	88
	Do the in-year reports released to the public compare actual year-to-date revenue collections with either the original estimate for that period (based on the enacted budget) or the same period in the previous year?	89
	Does the executive release to the public a mid-year review of the budget that includes updated revenue estimates for the budget year underway?	96
	Does the year-end report, or another document released to the public by the executive (please specify below), explain the difference between the enacted levels (including in-year changes approved by the legislature) and the actual outcome for revenues?	106
General transparency	Does the executive's budget or any supporting budget documentation present the macroeconomic forecast upon which the budget projections are based?	14
	Does the executive's budget or any supporting budget documentation show the impact of different macroeconomic assumptions (i.e., sensitivity analysis) on the budget (including expenditures, revenues, and debt)?	15

Does the executive release to the public a mid-year review of the budget that discusses the changes in economic outlook since the budget was enacted?	93
Does the year-end report, or another document released to the public by the executive (please specify below), explain the difference between the original macroeconomic forecast for the fiscal year and the actual outcome for that year?	107
In the executive's budget or any supporting budget documentation, are estimates of the aggregate level of expenditure presented for a multi-year period (at least two years beyond the budget year)?	5
Does the executive's budget or any supporting budget documentation present information for at least the budget year that shows how policy proposals in the budget, as distinct from existing policies, affect expenditures?	16
Does the executive's budget or any supporting budget documentation present information for at least the budget year on extra-budgetary funds?	35
Does the executive's budget or any supporting budget documentation present information for at least the budget year on transfers to public corporations?	37
Does the executive's budget or any supporting budget documentation present information for at least the budget year on quasi-fiscal activities?	38
Does the executive's budget or any supporting budget documentation explain how the proposed budget is linked to government's stated policy goals, by administrative unit (or functional category), for the budget year?	48
Does the executive release to the public a mid-year review of updated expenditure estimates for the budget year underway?	94
How long after the end of the budget year does the executive release to the public a year-end report or another document that discusses the budget's actual outcome for the year?	102
Does the year-end report, or another document released to the public by the executive (please specify below), present the actual outcome for extra- budgetary funds?	111
Does the executive's budget or any supporting budget documentation present data on the total government debt outstanding for the budget year?	11
Does the executive's budget or any supporting budget documentation present interest payments on the debt for the budget year?	12
Does the executive's budget or any supporting budget documentation present information related to the composition of government debt (such as interest rates on the debt, maturity profile of the debt, currency denomination of the debt, or whether it is domestic and external debt) for the budget year?	13

Accountability	Does the executive publish a "citizens budget" or some non-technical presentation intended for a wide audience that describes the budget and its proposals?	61
	Do citizens have the right in law to access government information, including budget information?	64
	Are citizens able in practice to obtain financial information on expenditures for individual programs in a format that is more highly	65

OBI, Open Index Budget
Source: International Budget Project (2005)

Notes

1. Most of the criteria used are similar to those developed by multilateral organisations, such as the International Monetary Fund's *Code of good practices on fiscal transparency* and the *Lima declaration of guidelines on auditing precepts* issued by the United Nations International Organization of Supreme Auditing Institutions.

2. For further details on the background and methodology, see IBP 2005 and the International Open Budget Initiative (2006).

3. In identifying resource-dependent countries, this chapter adopts the IMF's definition that distinguishes between countries rich in hydrocarbons (oil and gas) and those rich in minerals (such as gold, silver, diamonds and platinum). Resource dependency is defined as either an average share of resource revenues in total fiscal revenues of at least 25 per cent during the previous three years, or an average share of hydrocarbon and/or mineral export proceeds in total export proceeds of at least 25 per cent during the previous five years (IMF 2007a). Two important caveats to the IMF definition are that it examines hydrocarbon and mineral data separately and does not capture countries where collective measures of hydrocarbon and mineral revenues/exports are above the dependency threshold. Additionally, the definition is based on current production and does not examine reserves or potential future production.

4. The reasons for this difference are not entirely clear. It might be due to the fact that hydrocarbons are more commonly under state control because of high capital-intensity and technology, and therefore are more prone to opacity. Or it could be due to distortions in the the data, given the small sample size. This is an area that requires further research.

Before the peak: impacts of oil shortages on the developing world

Ben W. Ebenhack and Daniel M. Martínez

Introduction

The notion of an impending oil shortage is quite misunderstood and misrepresented, especially as it is contextualised, with the developing world seen as exporters of the resource, but not as consumers of it. It has often been discussed as "running out of oil" and this concept seems to have shaped many people's opinions. It creates the image of depleting the world's petroleum reserves much like water swirling down a large drain – it is there one second, and utterly gone the next. Petroleum depletion will be nothing like this. Instead, it will be a long process, transitioning from sustained exponential growth to slower growth, then a broad peak and, probably, a long and slow decline. Petroleum is likely to be a valuable commodity, contributing significantly to energy demands, well into the twenty-second century.

Some pundits point out that it was not a shortage of typewriters that led to their demise, but their displacement by a superior technology – computers. This analogy, while oversimplified, speaks truthfully to the final transition away from petroleum. It will not occur because the last drops of oil have been drawn out of the world's reserves. Petroleum production will some day cease because it is no longer needed in the face of newer, ultimately better energy technologies and organic chemical

Ben W. Ebenhack is the founder and Chairman of the Board of AHEAD Energy Corporation in Rochester, NY. He is also a senior lecturer in the Chemical Engineering Department at the University of Rochester.
Email: benw@mail.rochester.edu
Daniel M. Martínez is an AHEAD researcher and an University of Rochester Postdoctoral Fellow. AHEAD works with energy-poor communities to assemble resources needed to develop local energy services that improve lives and livelihoods in ways that safeguard the natural environment.
Email: daniel.m.martinez@aheadenergy.org.

feedstocks. But that transition in the relatively distant future is not the real problem. A real crisis looms in the much nearer future when petroleum production is still continuing to grow, but is no longer able to grow as rapidly as the world's demand for it. This will be exacerbated by emerging markets and their growing thirst for this resource.

Additionally, half of humanity still relies on extremely inefficient and dirty firewood to meet nearly all of its energy needs. This is linked to a myriad of health and social problems (UNDP 2005). Indeed, the more a nation depends on firewood for all needs, the more likely the quality of life of its people is substantially reduced.[1] Whereas the industrialised world is expected to increase its exploration activities of fields in developing nations previously deemed sub-commercial for export, these developing nations (as well as the development agencies that can assist with the professional and technical capacity to develop those resources) should seriously consider the benefits of utilising the resource for their own internal projects. Such internal development projects appear more likely to improve the quality of life for the people in developing nations, as opposed to accumulating wealth from exports that does not directly translate to the same improvement.

In this chapter we present a brief history of the Hubbert peak, the likely differences between his observations and predictions of North American fields and world fields, the impacts a global crisis will have on the developing world, and the roles industry and humanitarian aid organisations can play to provide local, cost-effective services to benefit those that still require access to them.

Peak oil

Geologist King Hubbert launched an ongoing line of inquiry with one of the first and most famous scientific approaches to predicting the future of oil production. He analysed geological potential, drilling activity and discovery success ratios in sedimentary basins throughout the world in order to estimate the ultimate potential world petroleum production and overlaid a smooth, nominally bell-shaped, Gaussian curve on the growth trend of petroleum production. This curve has become the very emblem of the discussions about running out of oil. Books and chapters written about it always show a symmetrical rise and fall of petroleum, with a peak – Hubbert's peak – occurring when approximately half the world's oil has been produced. Interestingly, this symmetry is not really part of Hubbert's original work. His seminal article published in 1949 actually showed asymmetrical trends (Hubbert 1949). In fact, the director of the Hubbert Centre notes: "Hubbert wrote virtually nothing about the decline side of his Hubbert Curve. The decline side of the curve does not have to be symmetrical with the ascending side; it is just easier to draw it as such" (Ivanhoe 1997).

Hubbert's analyses are being carried forward by a host of modern researchers, many of whom seem to view his model almost as an inviolable law of nature, with a focus on a symmetrical shape, and the peak itself as a crisis point (Smil 2005, p. 212). While Hubbert's work presented an original scientific approach to evaluating petroleum's future and advanced a comprehensible image of how its production will ultimately decline, certain aspects of the phenomenon deserve to be revisited. The current research continuing Hubbert's work neglects two important factors: that the sweeping global petroleum shortage will not occur at the peak, but before it, and that half of the world already suffers from an energy shortage. These analyses also neglect the economic and technological factors that will tend to make the decline shallower than the growth side of the curve – a possibility which Hubert himself did not discount.

The character of the peak

One of the great strengths of Hubbert's work was demonstrating the relatively gradual nature of the transition from growth to decline. The climb up to Hubbert's peak has been controlled by the growth of demand – a purely marketplace-driven phenomenon. Essentially, oil has been available in excess of demand throughout its history (barring a few price spikes associated with demand growing faster than supply in the very early days, and more sustained market disruptions associated with international political conflict, such as those seen in the 1970s). The ready availability of energy allowed for new industries and economic opportunities that have fuelled exponential growth in energy demand across the globe. While an exponential growth in population has also made a contribution, even in nations currently approaching zero population growth levels the demand for new goods and services derived from energy continues to provide upward pressure on the demand for even more energy. Considering that most of the world's inhabitants have yet to reap the benefits of cheap, abundant energy, there will certainly be a need for continued economic and social service growth, with an attendant need for additional energy supplies.

As the path up to the peak begins to level off, it will signal the transition from a demand-dominated regime to one controlled by physical limits. During the exponential growth phase of petroleum surplus production capacity permitted demand to control production rates. This also means that there has been a nominal steady-state balance between reserves extracted by production and new reserve additions to offset the extraction. At some point, global reserve additions will fail to keep pace with extraction and the surplus production capacity will dwindle away. Once surplus production capacity is gone the world will enter this new phase of a

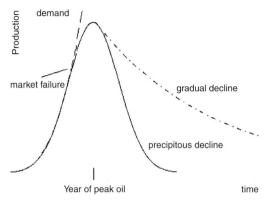

FIGURE 1. The peak oil phenomenon. The solid line of the Gaussian curve follows the commonly cited representation of M. King Hubbert's calculations of production and decline. The dashed curve represents an exponential increase in demand on the growth side of the curve. The dash-dotted curve represents a more likely gradual decline in production spurred on by enhanced exploration and recovery. Market failure occurs when the demand curve and the production curve separate, some time before the actual peak in production. This will be exacerbated by rising global energy demands.

production that is limited by physical constraints.

Numerous authors have correctly championed Hubbert's legacy by highlighting that running out of oil in the absolute sense is not the problem. Rather, they argue, it is when the world reaches half of the total recoverable oil, assuming a purely Gaussian-shaped rise and decline. This movement has also been commonly referred to as "peak oil", depicted (as the solid, Gaussian curve) in Fig. 1.[2] One large over-simplification of most of the peak oil authors is their presumption of a relatively precipitous decline. We suggest that there is considerable evidence to indicate that the decline may be quite shallow, especially as technology and conservation become more important in the recovery (Ebenhack 2005).

Most peak oil proponents assume that the decline will be a mirror image of the growth side of the petroleum production curve. Whether or not they personally hold this view as a necessary condition of the phenomenon, public sentiment has overwhelmingly been shaped to believe just that. While symmetry may have been a fairly reasonable simplifying assumption for Hubbert to make in the 1940s and 1950s, in more recent times there is no good reason to believe that the

decline rate will match the growth rate. Indeed, there are good reasons to expect the decline to be much more gradual than the growth was. Most notable among these reasons is price. When a shortage occurs the clearest and most immediate outcome to expect is an increase in price. If demand moderates quickly, or if alternatives are readily available, the price increase should not be very high.

It is the character of the gradually diminishing growth rate for petroleum, followed by a broad (and doubtless irregular) peak, followed in turn by a long, gradual decline, also represented in Fig. 1 (dash-dotted line curve), that we believe is important. Since the transition will be gradual, not instantaneous, only looking back at it many years later will define clearly the date of the absolute peak. It is easy to imagine that crossing the peak and beginning the long decline will generate shortages. Yet, in light of the numerous factors that will continue to drive demand upward, the gradual bending over of the growth side of the curve will represent a shortage. Thus, a long crisis will actually begin at the point of inflection, where the curve begins to bend. By our best estimates, it could begin at least a decade before the peak. This will create a deficit between demand and supply that will represent an economic market failure and a global crisis.

Market failure

Global energy demand has been rising exponentially for more than 100 years. A number of factors will drive continued growth in the global thirst for oil. Not the least of these is the reality that half the world's population has essentially no access to modern energy sources and services. Thus far, global petroleum production has been able to keep pace. Notice also in Fig. 1 the departure from exponential demand growth to declining production growth rates before peak oil actually occurs. At this point the hypothetical demand curve exceeds the real supply. Economists refer to this as a market failure.

A clear departure between an extrapolation of the growth curve and the actual expected production curve will represent a real shortage of energy in the market-place. Rapidly rising consumption of energy in China and India illustrates the energy gap that already exists.

Indeed, there is and has been an unmet need for modern energy in the developing world. This need becomes reflected as a demand in the market-place only when a country's ability to pay grows to an adequate level. As long as people do not have adequate energy to meet their basic needs reliably there will always be some unmet demand.

At this point, the market-place will seek to correct. Shortages will push prices higher. The higher prices will provide an incentive for oil companies both large and small to expand their exploration efforts. The higher prices will extend the lives of existing fields. Some wells that are closed down or abandoned will be reviewed, reworked and returned to production under the new higher prices. Some fields in which wells have been plugged and abandoned will be redrilled. Reserves will be re-adjusted, as prices rise.

Note that reserves are calculated for individual fields based on their own production declines and economic limits. These limits represent the points at which revenue from oil sales drops below the operating expenses for the wells or fields. Therefore, any increase in the sales price of the oil automatically lowers these economic limits. Thus, higher prices generate revised reserves estimates, which in turn bring new reserves into play. This has and will continue to help bolster production rates at the time. Enhanced incentives for exploration will bring new production online, but its impact will take longer to feel. In general, the supply side will see a number of reserve additions that in turn will create a more gradual transition.

The demand curve may be able to respond more quickly, with higher prices suppressing some discretionary consumption. In the most energy consumptive nations, there will be some relatively prompt response. In the USA, for example, there is a significant portion of purely discretionary consumption that can be relatively easy to displace. Using private automobiles for extremely short excursions and personal pleasure are two conspicuous examples of this. However, most of the conservation potential will not be realised quickly. New consumer demand for more efficient vehicles will not instantly result in the disappearance of wasteful vehicles from the roadways. There will be an even longer, slower shift in the real estate

markets. People will have an increased incentive to live closer to their work, but this will not create a sudden migration from expensive out-lying suburbs back into decaying urban centres.

Although the rising prices will support more investment in exploration and production technologies, which will add new reserves, ultimately there will not be enough production to maintain surplus capacity. Moreover, the reserve additions will result from the increased activity that follows the price increases prompted by shortages. While some reserve additions will be the immediate result of lowered economic limits, they will not add to current production, but merely extend the lives of existing fields. Only new drilling and the implementation of enhanced recovery projects will add new production, but neither of these will occur quickly. Therefore, reserve additions resulting from increased prices will not serve to delay the peak, but only to make the decline shallower. There will be some market failure associated with the inability of production to meet demand. The market already fails to provide necessary energy for the needs of the some 3 billion people who lack the ability to pay. Price increases and market failure will only exacerbate this problem.

Overarching impacts on the developing world

Taking a broad, global view, for half of humanity the energy shortage is already here. Most people in the developing world lack access to modern energy and rely on firewood and charcoal to meet their essential survival energy needs. This absolutely limits development opportunities. Neither industry, nor medicine, nor education can be built on firewood and charcoal-produced energy. Furthermore, in the face of modern population levels, the firewood and charcoal are themselves used unsustainably. In many urban areas in the developing world wood fuels are not really goods gathered by house-holders, but are imported to cities by the truckload by firewood and charcoal marketers. This activity can impoverish the local environment, while miring the people in poverty and poor health.

Thus a vicious cycle is promoted in which poor people must deplete their natural environments to support their most basic energy needs. Without the ability to develop new kinds of enterprises, using different kinds of resources, they have little opportunity to move away from an unsustainable dependence on firewood. The deprivation of the local environments directly impairs the economic activities of agrarian families. The often significant financial burden on them to buy firewood or charcoal just for cooking, undercuts the economic opportunities of urban households (Energy Sector Management Assistance Program 2006, p. 53).

This destructive cycle, though, is not inevitable. Other energy resources, including fossil fuels, are present in many developing countries. A part of the problem is that the fossil fuels are generally developed only by foreign entities to be exported to the affluent industrialised world. However, as the industrialised world begins to experience the global energy crisis that already exists, the developing world will once again be a focal point for the extraction of now cost-effective fossil resources, while simultaneously impairing their current low-level imports in these same regions.[3] Thus, major themes that will affect the developing world and its relationships with international entities will be opportunities from untapped fossil resources; promoting energy's role in sustainable development and expanding capacity and infrastructure for self-reliance and energy security.

Untapped fossil resources

What makes an oil and gas project commercial or sub-commercial? The context plays a role in this, that is, whether an energy development project is situated in the developed or the developing world. This commonly produces two different orders of magnitude in the minimum threshold for commercial oil and gas discoveries.

Consider that the average oil well in the USA barely produces 10 barrels of oil per day, while the average well in Africa produces over 1,000 barrels per day. It is not likely that this is because the USA is endowed with many small oil and gas accumulations, while the African continent has a very different distribution of very few, very large reservoirs. First, it is a matter of being close to centres of consumption.[4] Even

markets in the capital cities of developing nations are tiny in comparison with the markets of affluent developed nations. The developing world's markets are largely also of limited appeal due to perceptions of their political instability, the attendant risk of resources being nationalised, and the likelihood of soft unstable local currencies. Multinational corporations therefore are very rarely interested in developing oil and gas prospects for local use in these unstable markets. They prospect internationally with the intention of exporting oil and gas to the large well-developed markets of the industrialised world. The most noteworthy exception to those are the rapidly growing markets of China and India.

International oil companies bring expatriate workforces to find and produce oil and gas resources for export. The export preference also produces a preference for offshore operations. Offshore drilling and production is much more expensive than onshore, but it eliminates the need for large, (even more) expensive pipeline projects in order to get the product to the coast, where it can be loaded onto tankers.

Reliance on expatriate workforces also increases the economic scale. The workers are often paid a substantial hardship bonus. They fly first class, travelling between their corporate office and their overseas assignment. The multinational companies build small cities to house their expatriate workforce, their families, their children's teachers and their nurses and doctors. All of these people are extremely well-paid and given significant vacation and travel benefits. Corporate managers and senior technical experts also travel several times a year to meet and advise their expatriate staff. A single, brief trip for a single technical expert to consult with resident staff is likely to cost more than US$10,000. And where there is a major oil and gas development expatriate workers from support and service companies set up camp as well such as Schlumberger, Halliburton, Baker and others. The prices they charge for their contract services are also a function of their costs.

Thus, everything about operating in a developing country becomes expensive for the multinational. Consequently, when drilling a single rank wildcat (an exploratory well that is not near any established production), the company wants to get as much information about the area from that single multimillion dollar well as possible. So the geologists and geophysicists recommend the deepest plausible horizon which might contain significant oil or gas and that sets the target depth for the wildcat. Upper-level management does not want to spend US$10 million drilling one unsuccessful well and three years later entertain a proposal from their staff to drill another well in the same location, seeking a deeper target. The choice to evaluate the deepest possible horizon naturally means that each exploratory well is very expensive. If it is, in fact, a rank wildcat in a totally new province, a commercial success necessarily demands building the new camp for a new expatriate workforce and probably developing a new deep-water port or tanker facility.

All this means that the odds of commercial success for international rank wildcats are quite low. Some years ago the success ratio for this high-stake gamble was commonly considered to be approximately one in 17 – a little better than the odds of the roulette wheel, but you don't have to bet US$10 million on every spin of the roulette wheel. Some authors suggest that exploratory success has grown dramatically thanks to new and improved technologies. It is suggested that such improvements provide the basis for considerable optimism and will serve to forestall any oil shortage indefinitely (Deming 2003; Simon 1996, pp. 162–181; Tippee 1993, p. 129). This is a dubious claim, in large part because the relatively depressed petroleum prices of the 20 year period from 1981 to 2001 also curtailed true rank wildcat exploration. The data for improved success ratios are more likely to reflect a shift toward lower risk exploration in proven producing provinces.

Opportunity or penalty?

As we approach the real crisis point before the peak, higher prices for oil will reinvigorate exploration activities. As companies begin gambling their enhanced profits on higher risk projects, the success ratio can be expected to fall. This will put more pressure than ever before on unutilised resources in developing nations. Of particular concern will be the focus on Africa for these resources. Unlike Latin America and Asia, in which foreign investment focuses on the utilisation of cheap local labour for industry

(and more recently, information technology), foreign investment in Africa is mainly directed at the production of raw materials for export. Mineral extraction, in particular, has been a major source of foreign investment. In fact, much controversy exists around the way in which mineral extraction occurs.

Since fossil fuels will continue to be a strongly sought after commodity, it would seem obvious that any developing country with substantial fossil reserves should begin exporting them to bring in foreign investment. Indeed, capital is one leverage point that can theoretically be used for development. However, considering the way in which foreign investment often occurs, specifically in regards to oil and gas development, this raises serious questions about exploitation and corruption and challenges notions of true foreign investment.

For example, Ferguson suggests that investments in petroleum production are commonly "socially thin" (Ferguson 2006, p. 197). Consider that the Organization for Economic Cooperation and Development found that between 1994 and 1996, the five top recipients of foreign investment were countries that fell into the study's most risky category (Ferguson 2006, p. 196), including Angola, the Democratic Republic of Congo and Equatorial Guinea. These countries, along with Sudan and Nigeria, are hotbeds of political unrest, yet they continue to receive some of the highest levels of foreign investment.

Furthermore, foreign investment in oil and gas development almost exclusively goes towards production for export, as opposed to domestic use. While contracts may entitle local governments to some royalties for the oil or gas produced, little accountability exists for foreign companies to follow through. For example, recent violence in Nigeria directed towards oil and gas companies stems from this very dispute. These nations are almost completely dependent on thecompanies operating within their borders. Nigeria, the highest petroleum-producing sub-Saharan African country, has a per capita GDP of US$1,400. However, 95 per cent of its foreign exchange earnings and 20 per cent of its GDP come directly from petroleum exports. Angola's per capita GDP is US$3,200 (CIA 2007), however, over two-thirds of the population live on under US$1 dollar a day. Oil accounts for 40 per cent of the GDP and 90 per cent of its exports (Energy information Administration 2006). "The Angolan government currently receives something in the order of $8 billion of oil revenue each year ... Angolans today are among the most desperately poor people on the planet" (Ferguson 2006, p. 198).

In addition to the disparity between oil wealth and the standard of living, a serious disconnect exists between the oil companies and the local socio-economic communities. "Today, enclaves of mineral-extracting investment in Africa are usually tightly integrated with the head offices of multinational corporations and metropolitan centres but sharply walled off from their own national societies (often literally walled off with bricks, razor wire, and security guards)" (Ferguson 2006, p. 36). In Angola, fewer than 10,000 nationals work for oil and gas companies (the petroleum industry is not particularly labour intensive, which exacerbates their limited potential for job creation). Additionally, most oil production facilities operate offshore.

The correlation between petroleum-producing nations and corruption on the African continent challenges the notion that foreign investment in the energy sector for export is always a desirable to the local community. In fact, the previous examples, though extreme, may not be as abnormal as many would like to think. Mozambique, for example, has far less corruption compared to the aforementioned nations and lacks complete dependency on foreign energy firms. An enhancement of an energy market would further diversify the Mozambican economy. However, as energy projects in Mozambique move forward, often at the urging of neighbouring countries desperate to import more energy from nearby and accessible resources, past experiences with mineral extraction on the continent may become apparent.

This is not limited to oil and gas – electricity can be exported as well. In cases such as the production and export of hydroelectricity from Cahora Bassa dam in Mozambique, they may even purchase their own product back from importers. Modern energy purchases create balance of trade deficits, while still not providing enough modern energy to reach most of the population. Economics consideration alone will always urge the exportation of the goods, but this is more than an economic problem. Negative externalities associated with export must be accounted for. If they are they are likely to reveal that all these factors contribute to an energy export penalty akin to the oil curse and may support the use of the resources for internal development projects first.

Energy and sustainable development

The most pervasive goal of development is sustainability, defined by the Brundtland Commission for sustainable development as "development that meets the needs of the present without compromising the ability of future generations to meet their own needs" (World Commission on Environment and Development, 1987). It would seem that the very development context of this definition (and of the Commission itself) has an implicit goal to support improved living conditions for the world's less affluent peoples, and is related to a concern for some form of social justice or equity. Unfortunately, the implicit concern for the well-being of the world's poor in this generation is sometimes lost in the focus on sustaining the environment and resources for future generations. We argue that neither justice for future nor present generations can be adequately addressed while ignoring the other. A sustainable world must be one with some reasonable level of equitable access to essential resources – now.

Energy is at the very crux of this issue and at some minimal level energy is critical to survival itself. Beyond that, it is an essential building block for all kinds of industrial, economic and social enterprises. No development is possible without energy and without development one cannot have sustainable development. Therefore, a transition towards a more sustainable society demand increased access to modern energy for much of the world. At the same time, all that we consume or even desire in affluent, industrialised societies is based on significant energy consumption; energy that is abundant and cheap. Sustaining the benefits of modern affluent society will require continued access to abundant energy supplies, though it will soon probably cease to be cheap energy. Abundance, then, will also have to be reassessed. What gains are we really getting from the energy we consume?

Continued exponential growth in energy demand is not physically sustainable. The resources on which the world currently relies (primarily oil, gas, and coal) will begin to decline in the coming few decades. As energy shortages begin they will drive prices higher and increase competition for the resources. At the same time the larger unmet demand for energy in the developing world must be addressed. Transitions to more sustainable energy systems cannot be viewed as simple transitions to renewable energy. The fossil fuels will and must continue to play a substantial role for some time – even for many decades after their peak productions have been reached and their declines have begun. There is no alternative energy system ready to take a large market share in the time-frame that peak oil is likely to dictate. In fact, one of the most serious problems the fossil fuels raise is the sheer magnitude of consumption their abundance has facilitated. This raises the level at which renewable energy production will have to compete.

Environmental arguments are growing louder in their demands for the developing world to develop with only renewable resources and technologies. This problematic viewpoint unfortunately neglects the fact that fossil resources will nevertheless be developed and exported out of these very regions. If this happens we must consider which activity has a smaller environmental footprint: using the resource locally or exporting it elsewhere to be used anyway. Moreover, it is well-documented that all industrialised nations used fossil fuels and concomitant technology to catalyse their own development. With the knowledge of best practices, fossil fuels can also catalyse and continually support activities in the developing world, with visions for an evolving energy mix and infrastructure that shift the load away from fossils, once established.

The need to expand capacity

The need for expanding professional capacity and the financing of energy infrastructures to support health, education, and trade industries is a critical step (Federal Emergency Management Agency 2007). The work of planning contextually appropriate energy mixes is a highly innovative enterprise. Local access to resources must be well defined in each locality. Current and likely future consumer demands must be characterised. Technologies must be evaluated and adapted to the contexts of resources and needs. Transitions must be planned effectively. This sort of work necessitates collaborative work from a broad range of disciplines: engineering, economics, sociology, policy analysis and probably history as well. Good cohorts of well-trained experienced professionals will be essential. We argue that the best development planning is that directed by people with local knowledge and interest.

Energy projects in developing countries are often hampered by the lack of trained and experienced local energy professionals. Again, focusing on Africa, relatively few citizens have been trained for professions in energy industries because these countries have few institutions of higher education and those that exist may not offer degrees in all the energy-related fields. Even those who have received formal training outside the continent often lack direct industry experience. As pressure mounts to export Africa's rich energy resources to wealthy nations, Africans may be at serious disadvantages when negotiating contracts without the staff needed to verify energy reserves or negotiate favourable terms.

There is then an opportunity for the development community to place seasoned energy professionals with energy agencies in the developing world to assist with efforts to develop modern energy services. In a possible scenario, partner agencies might define their needs and develop position descriptions. Clearing house entities might recruit specialists with 10 years or more of industry or professional experience to serve abroad for three months to two years as unpaid staff with partner agencies. Volunteers would be placed to work on projects that are scalable, economically sustainable, locally controlled, and environmentally conscientious (AHEAD 2007).

While the successful economies of the USA, Canada and Australia are all in former colonies, none of them are cases in which indigenous peoples gained their independence from the colonial powers. Rather, the colonists from the mother country are at the heart of their energy projects. Developing nations, on the other hand, often experienced the flight of trained, professional personnel, largely comprising expatriate colonialists (since professional positions were held almost exclusively by colonialists and relatively limited numbers of indigenous persons had been somewhat officially assimilated into the colonial power structure).

In some cases the departing colonial authorities also deliberately sabotaged much of the physical infrastructure of the country, leaving a newly educated minority in the newly independent nations to struggle with rebuilding their country's infrastructure as well as crafting a nation. Then, the countries that were successful in building a larger base of educated, professionally trained personnel were faced with the difficulty of retaining them as they could earn higher salaries by taking their training to affluent industrialised nations.

This phenomenon, broadly dubbed the brain drain, is a serious challenge to building professional capacity. In the case of energy the problem is exacerbated by issues of scale, since even the indigenous workers who receive professional training and employment opportunities in their own or neighbouring nations are exposed only to the extremely high-level technologies and operations that typify international energy operations. In order to develop local resources effectively for the small, emerging markets of their own economies they need to be able to bring downward scalable technologies and methods.[5]

Conclusions

The challenge of the coming global energy transition is probably one of the greatest faced by today's generation. We must plan technologies and policies to move towards a decreased reliance on depleting fossil fuel resources while expanding access to energy to the half world's population currently mired in energy poverty, and while conscientiously reducing the environmental footprint of our global energy acquisition and consumption activities. A lack of deliberate informed planning is likely to transform this set of challenges into a legitimate crisis. No single technology or policy option is sufficient to meet these triple challenges. We need an array of technologies and policies that are suited to the entire range of contexts in our diverse world.

At the very heart of the challenge is the transition being forced upon us by the imminent decline in petroleum-production rates. Even with an optimistic estimate of the total amount of petroleum that can ultimately be recovered from the earth, it is clear that this will occur considerably before the middle of the twenty-first century, probably sometime in its third decade. Transitions toward a more equitable and sustainable global society demand that we understand the dynamics of a petroleum marketplace that will soon be operating in shortages, and how this relates to the large world population that currently lacks access to modern energy.

Thus, what is really needed is to deliberately plan evolving energy mixes that take advantage of the benefits of finite fossil fuel resources while carefully and prudently increasing the contribution of non-depletable sources over time. In the case of developing countries where no large-scale infrastructure for energy consumption exists it may be feasible to build new modern energy systems that integrate finite and non-depletable resources from the start. It may be possible to design and deploy systems in which new, locally produced fossil fuels can be designed to support variable and lower energy density renewable fuels. In most stand-alone solar or wind systems, fully half of the total capital investment is needed for battery storage. The need for storage in turn dictates nominally doubling the installed production capacity so that during peak production, it can produce enough to charge the batteries and store for the downtimes. Thus, in some cases it could be argued that a hybrid solar or wind with gas or oil system might be as much as four times as cost-effective as a stand-alone system. This could make many of the alternatives more cost competitive sooner. Other non-fossil energy sources can also play the backstop role. Transitions to sustainable systems will be context specific as well as dynamic across time.

Finally, even if the appropriate capital is spent on development projects, without energy it will not be of much use. What is health care without electricity for refrigerating medicines and sterilising surgical tools? What is education without computers for teaching, let alone lights to see? What is industry without energy to deliver goods and services both intra- and extramurally? Development agencies (government agencies, non-governmental organisations, and even oil company charitable foundations) must focus on developing the energy supplies and infrastructure to support real internal development projects.

Acknowledgement

We thank the AHEAD Energy Corporation (501c3) for its continued support of our academic endeavours. We also thank Mr David Ladon for his contributions to the section entitled "opportunity or penalty?" in this chapter. Certain pieces were excerpted or modified from an unpublished report written to fulfil a course requirement at the University of Rochester.

Notes

1. There is a negative correlation between the use of traditional biomass for fuel with a nation's quality of life, as measured by the UN Human Development Index. The more a nation depends on firewood, the more likely is a low Human Development Index value.

2. Since predicting and reporting an actual date for peak oil is troublesome (especially when that date passes by and no peak occurs), we have normalised all analyses and have not set an actual peak-oil year in our visual representation of the phenomenon.

3. The term "re-import" might more aptly describe the practice of extracting the resource and then reselling it to the country that produced it.

4. This is partly because the USA is a very mature oil and gas provider, in which most fields have long been declining, but other factors make these numbers indicative of the economic requirements of scale as well.

5. In the industrialised world technologies are often developed first at the bench scale and then scaled up to the level of a commercial pilot. Only then are they developed to compete fully in the market-place. The ultimate commercial scale up is expected to provide improved profitability through economies of scale. In the developing world, however, especially with respect to energy demands and services, "downward scaleable" technologies and methods may be much more suitable. The irony is that, because of the export orientation of international development, indigenous professionals are exposed only to the very large-scale commercial export operations. As these require economic investments that may be prohibitively costly to the local economies, it will be necessary to find an adequate scaled-down energy mini- to micro-enterprise to meet the demand in local centres.

Social and economic implications of oil policy development in Nigeria

Alexis Rwabizambuga

Introduction

This chapter aims to show that socio-political stability has more significant and durable consequences on the ability of an oil-producing country in the developing world to exercise control over its national oil resources than asymmetric power relations between the state and its commercial stakeholders in the domestic petroleum sector. The chapter argues that the deep causes and spiralling consequences of domestic instability constitute the set of circumstances that undermines the state's ability to maintain firm and consistent oil policy objectives, and impedes their effective use of oil revenues for socio-economic development.

The literature on oil exploitation policies in developing countries has often highlighted their lack of significant policy controls due to structural factors that are mostly related to the lack of access to technology, investment and markets (Fee 1988). It has drawn attention to the asymmetrical power relations that typify state–commercial stakeholder engagement. It has been claimed that an institutionally and financially weak developing nation is unable to withstand the pressure of powerful commercial stakeholders when negotiating the terms of oil exploration and production (Biersteker 1987; Watts 1983). Another strand of literature has concentrated on the way in which the oil proceeds have been used or misused, highlighting the state's failures to

use these capital inflows to spur socio-economic development (Sala-i-Martin and Subrahamanian 2003). Others have explored the mechanisms through which the use or misuse of oil revenues undermines the country's social fabric, giving rise to corruption and rent-seeking behaviour that often threatens public order (Collier and Hoeffler 1998). Few have thoroughly examined socio-political stability as a dependent variable and a major precondition for domestic oil exploitation policy control, in the absence of which there is little safeguard against financial loss. I attempt partly to redress the situation by examining the development of the Nigerian oil policy and its implications for socio-economic development.

Alexis Rwabizambuga is a Harvard Fellow at the Weatherhead Centre for International Affairs, Harvard University. His current research and publications centre on business and development, and environmental security and development. He has previously worked in insurance and finance, business consulting and development in Europe and Africa.
Email: arwabizambuga@wcfia.harvard.edu

This chapter first undertakes an examination of the goals, objectives and interests of both oil-producing states and multinational oil companies in the context of international investment, exploration and production licensing in the oil industry. Second, it examines the significance of oil revenues to the Nigerian economy, the development of the country's oil policies and the socio-political context in which oil exploitation agreements were negotiated. Third, this chapter highlights how socio-political instability, which often coincided with the fall in oil prices, gave rise to and perpetuated Nigerian dependency on oil revenues. Fourth, it argues that the state's relative negotiating power and its national oil exploitation policy were submerged under the struggles among community elites to control oil revenues, while the power of commercial stakeholders grew proportionally.

Goals and objectives of oil producers and commercial stakeholders

The oil-producing states

The overarching goal of an oil-producing state is in most circumstances the maximisation of a number of pre-selected socio-economic benefits. These include the control of oil production operations to ensure that the industry develops in an orderly way as well as the state's full participation in oil production activities, enabling indigenous industrial development to emerge (Fee 1988). The level of its participation in oil operational activities is essentially determined by the reality of the exploration and production situation existing in each country. This generally consists of the size of the reserves and state capacity, in terms of its access to finance and technology, as well as whether the state has participated financially in the business venture (Fee 1988).

The key strategic factors that govern the state's strategic decisions over its petroleum exploitation strategy are the levels of the oil reserves, and the government's access to capital and its level of technological advancement (Khan 1994). For instance, an important feature of state–company relations is the government's need to strengthen its control over the oil companies' operations, thus ensuring that the exploration and development programmes entered into by these companies are carried out according to the initial terms agreed. To maximise these interests and attain its overall objectives, the state must establish the fiscal and legal arrangements that define its relationship with the companies involved in the oil exploitation process. These arrangements consist of the type of exploitation agreement, the type of licensing policy and the levels of loyalty and taxation policy negotiated (Fee 1988). While oil-producing states may generally pursue similar objectives, they differ in terms of implementation, institutional, technological, and financial capabilities, and will experience different outcomes accordingly.

It is said that what is distinctive about oil producers in developing countries is that they are often reliant on commercial stakeholders, including multinational oil companies and multinational financial agencies in order to produce oil. Often, this has had far-reaching implications in terms of the agreements made between the governments and the oil companies to establish the framework for oil operations in the country. While the processes for oil exploitation consist of complex bargaining processes between commercial stakeholders and oil-producing countries, it is often claimed that the former have an upper hand during these negotiations due to their financial and technological superiority (Fee 1988).

This chapter objects to these arguments and argues instead that the state power is resilient and may use the competitive dynamics in the oil markets to gain negotiating power. Before we get to this discussion, the next section explores the goals, objectives and interests of the commercial stakeholders.

The multinational oil companies

The oil industry has its own set of strategic goals. From the strategic management vantage point, all patterns of decisions and actions related to oil exploitation are aimed at improving or maintaining the firm's profitability and growth (Prakash 2000). In the business of oil exploitation, each company often ranks exploitation ventures according to their profitability potential, and possesses various methods for assessing the portability of all exploration ventures. In general, the factors influencing commercial stakeholders' decisions to invest include a relatively good probability of locating sufficient reserves to warrant production, and a firmly based legal framework by which the search for oil is regulated, to ensure stability and predictability. The decisions to invest are often both governed and justified following specific capital budgeting criteria, such as the criteria for profit maximisation on which each individual project is assessed according to whether it meets or exceeds the company or industry target rate of return (Lax 1983). The rate of return of the investment depends on the size of the reserves, the cost of the project based on technology, market forces, and the total taxation package to be applied to the project.

Commercial stakeholders often worry less about oil prices or development costs since these are determined predictably by international market conditions. However, the taxation package, which can constitutes a major factor in reducing the profit of the project, is politically determined by the government policy on the official rate of petroleum extraction. Where political risk is high, companies either stop investing in such countries, or raise the capital required for investing in a them, requiring a higher discount rate or a higher return on investment. Hence, the assignment of risk premium is arbitrary, since it is negotiated amidst political and market uncertainty. In the international oil industry environment, commercial stakeholders are mostly worried about risks associated with ownership of resources, risks to oil company personnel and installations (Lax 1983). The fear of expropriation or fiscal risk, which is often high in developing countries, is offset by the dependency of these countries on resource extraction projects so they cannot afford to make commercial stakeholders uncomfortable by changing policy. In all, the factors influencing the maximisation of oil company profits are both geological and political (Lax 1983).

Having explored the goals and objectives of oil producers and commercial stakeholders and the factors determining their respective success, the next section explores the emergence of Nigerian oil industry and the state's relationship with oil companies, with the aim to examine whether corporate financial, technological and market powers have obfuscated the state's ability to determine oil policy and to pursue socio-economic development goals through the use of oil revenues.

Nigerian oil industry and the state's relationship with commercial stakeholders

The introduction of modern drilling techniques at the eve of the twentieth century led to an unprecedented expansion of oil exploration and production activities, enabling a growing number of oil-producing countries to emerge. Besides the new drilling techniques, another factor underlying the rapid international expansion of the oil industry in the late nineteenth and early twentieth centuries was the favourable concessions that were offered to commercial stakeholders. In the early years of the oil industry concessions were enormous and the early relations between the state and the companies were based on the colonial experience of the previous century (Biersteker 1987).

A joint venture between BP and Shell was granted the licence to explore for oil across the entire territory of Nigeria in the 1920s and framework conditions of the old concession system prevailed until the end of 1960s (Soremekun 1995), with little state participation in the oil industry. The companies benefited from a sympathetic system of oil licensing and a business-conducive legal framework. They were in a position to decide production levels and thereby influence the revenues the state could expect by way of taxes. The imbalance of power in favour of the oil companies meant that the basis of the relationship was the state permitting the company total freedom of action with regard to petroleum operations in the concession area (Soremekun 1995, p. 8). Nigeria was still a colony, or emerging from colonialism. Even after Nigeria gained its sovereignty and hurried to assume the control of its petroleum resources the country was still too weak to mount any policy control.

State, society and the economy

In 1954 Nigeria became a federal state with three ethno-linguistic regions. The federal government was responsible for foreign relations, defence and internal security, finance and trade while the regions mainly retained control of the remaining areas of policy, such as agriculture, education, public health and local government. The federal structure reflected the wide cultural and political differences between the country's largest ethno-linguistic groups that constituted the majority in each region, and the ethnic majority tended to exercise political dominance over minority ethnic groups (Forrest 1995).

Colonial policies of indirect rule favoured the complex regional system of separate administrations and the use of the local authority structure. In the process, the local systems of authority were often upheld and kept intact to form the basis of local government. They were seen as forming a valid basis for political and administrative action. As a result existing forms of leadership and authority were strengthened and centralised. However, these policies emphasised cultural and linguistic differences and to some extent encouraged the economic disparities and communal sentiments that went along with these differences (Forrest 1995). The emerging fragmented political structures and the overall political scene of the nascent state of Nigeria was characterised by patronage, and inter-regional competition for the control of the national government.

The political parties were regional in character and were built around the majority ethnic groups. They each generally controlled regional power, which they used as a basis to bid for the control of the federal government. Underlying this competition were a struggle for economic advancement by individuals and communities and the fear for economic and political domination (Forrest 1995). In this context, given the focus of political actors at the time, public policies and the general direction of development were not sharply defined and contested. Ideas about welfare, public ownership and the redistribution of income and wealth did not find a strong ideological or political expression. As the regional and individual struggle for power and wealth intensified, the basis for federal government and national policies was weakened. The steady expansion of state patronage in which political considerations rather than economic criteria were paramount adversely affected the allocation of resources.

This intensified after independence and the internal competition for power soon led to the secession of the eastern region dominated by the Igbos, with direct repercussions for the Nigerian economy through the loss of oil output, and the loss of exports revenues from other produces. The central government was re-enforced after the war of secession (1967–1970) and a new alliance between federal civil servants and the military was formed as regional autonomy weakened. The period also saw the rise of minorities, most of which were pro-federalist. They saw the federal structure as the only model that could guarantee them recognition and protection since regional states were dominated by the majority groups.

Oil policy development in the 1970–1990s

It is argued that Nigeria's oil policy has never been entirely coherent due to its social and political instability, leading to factors such as the frequent change of petroleum officials and differences in the ruling elite (Frynas 2000). The country's policy development is marked by four distinctive phases. The first extended from the colonial period up until the end of the 1960s in which there was very little state participation in the oil industry. The role of the state was reduced to collecting tax, rent or loyalty from the oil companies, while the old concession system prevailed. The revenues were shared equally after the companies deducted their operating costs. As a result of this formula, the state's real revenues were less than 50 per cent of the total revenue (Forrest 1995). During this period there were measured fiscal changes that saw the state increase its share of revenues without any direct participation in the oil venture.

After the military coup of 1966 the Petroleum Profit Tax Bill was amended in 1967. Nigeria was still at its earliest stages of nation-building and was torn between rival tribes. However, the war brought sections of the country's civil servants to realise the strategic importance of oil.

The second phase marked policy changes towards indigenisation as a response to the social and political changes during the civil war. The changed perceptions among the Nigerian elite of the strategic importance of oil, and the country's increasing dependence on oil revenues for economic development led to a move to increase control of its oil sector through increased participation in it (Pearson 1970). The Petroleum Profit Tax Bill gave Nigeria the legal basis for modifying the existing fiscal regime to increase its rent-taking, and its 1971 adhesion to OPEC marks a third phase in the country's policy shift towards oil.

According to Soremekun (1995) the state started to be involved in the oil industry in the 1970s, moving from the simple collection of oil rents to a direct intervention in running the oil industry. Joining OPEC marked Nigeria's own indigenisation policy, encouraged by OPEC (Frynas 2000) and which was also characterised by an acceleration in the increase of government's profit tax and profit intake. In the post-colonial period, the Petroleum Profit Tax increased from 50 to 55 per cent of total oil revenues in 1973. It subsequently rose to 67.75 per cent in 1974, reaching 84 per cent of total oil revenues in 1975. Royalties increased from 12.5 to 16.6 per cent in 1974 and to 20 per cent in 1975 (Khan 1994; Turner 1977). This policy of indigenisation of the oil industry was accelerated in the 1970s and by 1979 the state had acquired a 60 per cent ownership in all major foreign oil companies operating in Nigeria (Khan 1994; Turner 1977). The indigenisation also permitted a policy of the gradual employment of indigenous labour force at all levels.

During the indigenisation phase Nigeria embarked on developing the state's institutional capacity and indigenisation policies were accompanied by a restructuring of the state oil administration through the creation of the Nigerian National Oil Company (NNOC) in 1971, which joined foreign companies in the exploration, prospecting and production of oil directly or through its subcontractors or subsidiaries. The NNOC merged with the Ministry of Petroleum Resources in 1977 to become the Nigerian National Petroleum Corporation (NNPC). The NNPC also combined the functions of an oil company with the extended regulatory powers of a ministry (Frynas 2000). This peculiar role enabled NNPC to issue licences to its so-called competitors. Its ambitious goal was to eventually control the entire oil industry in Nigeria, including oil exploration and production (NNPC 1986b). Despite the creation of NNPC, which strengthened the government's negotiating

power, the multinational oil companies retained the operation of the joint ventures on behalf of the government and control over the joint venture operations (Biersteker 1987; Turner 1977). Despite the government's apparent political leverage, the balance of power had not shifted greatly, as 98 per cent of the country's export earnings depended on oil revenues, and the government depended on the presence of the oil companies.

The fourth phase marks the Nigerian oil policy in the 1980s, the 1990s and beyond. The energy conservation policies of the 1980s, coupled with low energy prices, saw a considerable decrease in exploration by foreign companies. As shown in Fig. 1, rises in poverty levels and the near bankruptcy of the state forced the government into greater accommodation with the oil companies to the extent that, between 1983 and 1997, the fiscal incentives for foreign oil companies improved several times (Barrows 1988).

It has been argued that this change in policy was a more eloquent manifestation of the growing dependence of the state on oil revenues and therefore of the imbalance of power in favour of the multinational oil companies, which seized the opportunity to negotiate beneficial fiscal terms for themselves. Faced with the immediate problems of falling oil revenue and political crises during the 1980s the government further improved the fiscal terms of oil company operators in order to woo investors in on-shore and offshore deep-water areas, including low royalty rates and higher allowances for cost recovery (Barrows 1997) for new oil exploration and production ventures (Frynas 2000). During

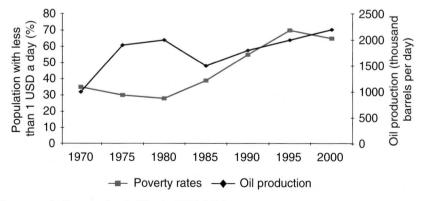

FIGURE 1. Poverty and oil production in Nigeria (1970–2000)
Source: BP Statistical Review of World Energy (2003); Sala-i-Martin and Subramia (2003)

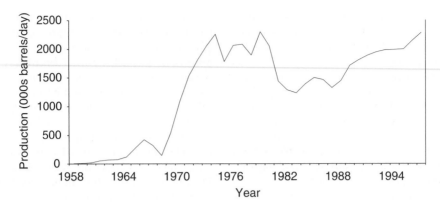

FIGURE 2. Nigeria's crude oil production (1958–1997)
Source: adapted from Human Development Index (2001)

the fourth phase of the Nigerian petroleum policy the government continued its policy of diversification and indigenisation strategies, granting a large number of licenses to indigenous oil companies through NNPC (Frynas 2000). The total area of the concession rose from 118,156 km^2 in 1966 to 225,444 km^2 in 1998 and it has expanded further since 1998. As shown in this section and in Fig. 2, Nigeria has depended heavily on oil revenues since the late 1960s, and, as such on the oil companies. But even since then the government's share of revenues has grown dramatically as production increased and the state gained more policy control and initiative. This shows that oil policy changes have often been sensitive to the level of investment in the sector, as the government was willing to offer beneficial terms to commercial stakeholders to maintain a high level of investment in exploration and production.

The fall in oil revenues due to global oil prices has had dramatic implications in the social and political stability of the country, as discussed in the section below.

Rising social and political instability

Oil production in Nigeria has depended largely on the oil companies' heavy investment in the sector. Oil exports exceeded other exports and hence the country's dependence on oil export revenues has grown ever since to its current levels. The decline in other exports brought Nigeria into relying exclusively on oil exports revenues, which account for more than 98 per cent of its export revenues. One of the main reasons for its increased dependence on oil revenues is the fall in production of other export commodities, which is blamed on the appreciation of the Nigerian Naira. This has exposed the Nigerian economy to the Dutch disease, and to the emergence of predatory social, political and economic institutions. It further resulted in slow long-term economic growth, turning the country into a quintessential example of resource curse (Sala-i-Martin and Subrahamanian 2003).

In terms of development, the country's performance since independence in 1960 has been dismal (Sala-i-Martin and Subrahamanian 2003). Nigeria's GDP has stagnated since the 1970s and it ranks among the 15 poorest countries in the world according to recent development indicators (African Development Bank 2007). Studies carried out on Nigeria's performance in terms of poverty reduction and income distribution show stunning under-performance in both areas. While the country's GDP of $1,084 million in 2000 is similar to its 1970 level, the poverty rate has increased from 36 per cent to close to 70 per cent, with 70 million people living on less than US$1 a day. The poverty rate increased despite cumulative earnings of about US$350 billion over the 35 years since oil was first produced in the country in 1957. During the same period, income distribution also deteriorated significantly. Whereas the top 2 per cent and the bottom 17 per cent earned the same income in 1970, by 2000 the top 2 per cent was earning the same income as the bottom

55 per cent. In addition, there is evidence that the oil revenues did not seem to improve the standard of living of the general population (African Development Bank 2007). While oil revenues per capita were about US$33 in 1965 and the per capita GDP was US$245, the latter remained more or less unchanged in 2000 even though oil revenues were US$325 per capita.

Repercussions on the economy and implications for social and political stability

As briefly described in this section, extensive research on the political economy of Nigeria has revealed how it is facing a damaging legacy of political corruption, repression, pollution, and destitution (Canagarajah and Saji 2001; Duruigbo 2003; Frynas 2000; Khan 1994; Sala-i-Martin and Subramahamian 2003; Soremekun 1995). Further research has revealed a significant relationship between a country's GDP per capital and its political stability as well as the effectiveness of its government. The same holds true for Nigeria, as described below.

The Nigerian oil sector is known for its volatility, violence and low levels of security. Oil conflicts, conflicts over territorial boundaries and control of resources, and political–military conflicts abound, especially in the oil-producing regions. This is demonstrated by the frequent disruptions of oil production activities and their repercussions on global oil prices and local political stability. The conflicts started off between local communities and the federal government over the lack of oil revenues flowing back from the federal government via the regional government to the local government. The latter has often responded to community protests heavy-handedly, rather than seeking dialogue and peaceful conflict resolution. The succession of dictatorial military regimes did little to appease these conflicts, but consolidated tactics for repressing dissent over the years.

While it is the responsibility of the government to guarantee operational security, the latter also used heavy-handed tactics to ensure its structural domination over communities. This has fostered a lasting climate of mistrust, not only between the government and communities but also between communities and multinational oil companies. As shown in Figs 3 and 4, the community protests made their ability to financially undermine company operations obvious through the blockade of oil facilities that affected delivery on time, an important constraint with serious financial implications. Hence most oil companies have approached community relations with a growing financial and institutional commitment.

Given the historically close collaboration that has existed between the Nigerian state and oil companies, the latter were increasingly perceived as an accomplice of the government. Thus, any attack on oil companies was regarded as an attack on the Nigerian government. They are accused of having supported the repressive tactics directed towards protesting communities. This response has fostered a lasting climate of mistrust not only between the government and communities but also among communities themselves.

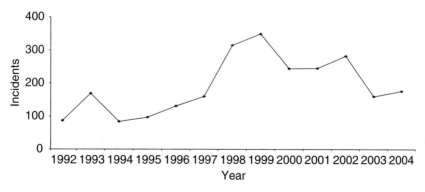

FIGURE 3. Trend of community incidents (1992–2004)
Source: Shell Petroleum Development Corporation (2005)

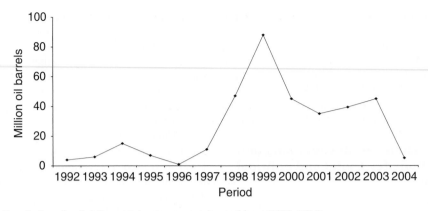

FIGURE 4. Trend of crude oil deferment due to community problems (1992–2004)

There has been a marked change of community dialogue strategy and tactics since the mid-1990s. The government now seems to prefer dialogue to its muscular tactics of past decades, while the oil industry has adopted a broad-based programme of community consultation. This perfect co-evolution between government's new approach to participation and social dialogue, and the oil companies' new conversion to the merits of stakeholder collaboration and consultation mark a new era in managing the complex relationships between companies, communities and the government. The return to democratic rule and the new discourse of corporate social responsibility in the extractive industries has compelled the main actors to employ new deliberative approaches in dealing with social protests against worsening socio-economic conditions.

As a consequence, the oil industry and the government have provided communities with financial support. As Table 1 reveals, for instance, Shell Nigeria has spent more than US$300 million in community development in Nigeria. As for the government, despite its implementation failures, it has created investment vehicles to channel 13 per cent of oil proceeds to the oil-producing regions as described in Box 1.

This new sensitivity recognises existing issues of environmental justice affecting oil-producing areas. The newly elected governments have also introduced major economic stabilisation reforms. Although there has been renewed hope for change in Nigeria since the 1999 democratically elected government has made tentative attempts to establish more responsible and accountable practices and standards for oil development, the burden of past abuses still heavily weighs on the present. Thus, a number of concessions made to the communities in an attempt to contain the increasing discontent have been little implemented, constrained by

TABLE 1. Shell Nigeria's community development spending profile (US$ million)

	1998	1999	2000	2001	2002	2003	Total
Roads and bridges	7.5	11.8	33.6	5.2	23.3	4.1	85.5
Education and schools	8	9.2	7.1	8.1	12.6	8	53
Electrification	0.4	0.5	1	7.2	6.7	4.8	20.6
Other infrastructure	7.2	11.1	0.5	13.3	5	2.9	40
Agriculture	2.8	1.7	1.9	3.8	4.8	2.3	17.3
Business development and micro-credit	-	2.7	0.5	2.9	4	1.9	12
Health care	5.7	5.8	5.9	4.9	3.9	2.6	28.8
Capacity, IEC and new ventures	6.8	1	1.2	2.2	3.8	2.5	17.5
Water schemes	4.2	8.2	8.5	4.4	2.8	1.7	29.8
Total	42.6	52	60.2	52	66.9	30.8	304.5

Source: Rwabizambuga (2007)
IEC, International Electrotechnical Commission standard.

Box 1. Government concessions to oil-producing communities and implementation failures (adapted from Duruigbo 2003)

Government concession	Year	Outcome	Issues
Justice Alfa Bagire Commission of Inquiry	1992	1.5 to 3% of government revenue. Creation of Oil Mineral Producing Area Development Commission	Low compensating rates, delays in payment
Revenue increase in 1999 Constitution	1994–1995	Proposed increase of allocations to 13% of total government oil revenues	Low compensating rates, delays in payment
Ministerial fact-finding team	1994	Recommendations to the government	Lack of supervision and absence of performance guidelines and controls
Creation of Delta State	1991	Better and direct control of oil proceeds	A concession to communities that wanted a larger share of the revenues
Concession of Bayelsa State,	1996	Better and direct control of oil proceeds	A concession to the communities that wanted a larger share of the revenues.
The Niger Delta Development Panel	1999	Framed new development policies for the oil producing states. Creation of NDDC increase of allocations to 13% of total government oil revenues	Lack of proper consultation and lack of discernible performance guidelines or control measures

poor governance, lack of accountability, transparency and corruption (Frynas 2000).

The cost of instability and the benefits of a good reputation

The increases in social investment described in the previous section were made during a period of intensified pressure from communities and non-governmental organisations, media and political scrutiny, as shown in Table 2. In an integrated supply chain the local practices of multinational company's business units do not go unnoticed. For instance, the intense media scrutiny shown in Fig. 5 shows that many international stakeholders were familiar with the problems being experienced by communities in the oil-producing regions of Nigeria.

TABLE 2. Media and political interest in Shell Nigeria operations (1997–2001)

Region	Number of diplomatic visits (1997–2001)	Visits from foreign journalists (199 –2001)	Destination of Nigerian exports (1997, % of total production)
North America	19	6	(USA only) 38
Europe	29	40	37.8
Africa	6	8	4
Asia	12	2	4.3
South America	3		4.3

In addition to the operational risks posed by local conflicts and community pressures, the Nigerian oil sector was receiving considerable political and diplomatic interest. As Table 2 shows, Nigerian oil-producing regions were receiving frequent visits from journalists and diplomats from Nigeria's major export markets. Between 1997 and 2001 there were 19 diplomatic visits and six media visits from the USA to Nigeria and 28 diplomatic visits and 40 media visits from EU. While these areas were the main destinations of Nigerian oil exports, they were also the major targets of environment and social rights activists who exposed the community grievances in Nigeria to the world. This generated pressure from home country consumers on Shell as many international stakeholders bercame familiar with the problems experienced by the communities in the oil-producing regions of Nigeria due to the media coverage in their respective countries.

Shell's operations were also being threatened at site level as a result of community protests, the sabotage of pipelines and the kidnapping of Shell personnel and other actions. Shell executives reported that these practices were becoming more widespread and the corporate social responsibility programmes were introduced in part to deal with them. The losses to Nigeria and to some multinational oil companies related to community sabotage and oil thefts are depicted in Fig. 4. The government of Nigeria and the oil industry faced a series of crises concerning their global and local reputation, increasingly negative responses

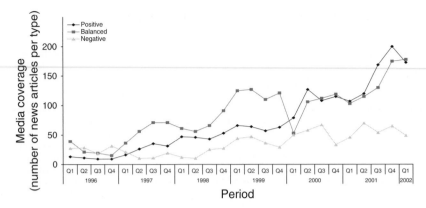

FIGURE 5. Media report analysis
Source: Shell Petroleum Development Corporation data (2005)

from global civil society and increasing media and public scrutiny, combined with the operational risks they were experiencing. They were compelled to respond to this situation through the launch of an ambitious social development programmes.

The constraints on Nigeria's oil policy control and socio-economic development

Nigeria did not gain control of its oil policy until the end of the 1960s. The evidence, however, reveals a growing awareness of the importance of oil after independence, which led Nigeria to gradually reclaim sovereignty over its national oil resources. It amended the taxation policy and increased state participation in the business. On numerous occasions the government was able to nationalise the assets of an oil company. There was at the same time great competition to gain access to Nigerian oil due to a favourable geological conditions and beneficial fiscal terms. Recent dynamics in the global oil industry have restored the influence of the state. The ever-increasing demand for oil has led to stiff competition for access to oil reserves, compelling investors and oil companies to court any potential oil producing country, however marginal. However, its ever-increasing dependence on oil revenues guaranteed the stability of the country's oil policy since the government could not afford to make major policy shifts that could unsettle the sector, with repercussions in terms of decreasing levels of investment and loss of revenues.

The lack of political stability limited government's leverage in negotiating extraction agreements, and may have spawned circumstances in which local institutions are too weak to make any effective use of oil proceeds to spur their social-economic development. Although Nigeria has earned over US$300 billion from its oil industry it has become more impoverished.

In terms of the development of the indigenous petroleum industry, the gradual increase in the assertiveness of the Nigerian state was followed by subsequent changes in the national policy for the country's oil resources. The country established key institutions such as the Department of Petroleum Resources and the NNPC in an effort to take control of the sector. However, these policies failed, not as a result of lack of access to funds and technology, but as a consequence of domestic social and political instability in general and failures in the country's oil policy, in particular. Caught in social and political struggles, successive governments focused more on maximising revenues from oil companies than on gradually building up a nationally sustainable oil industry. Their heavy dependence on oil revenues is an additional factor that has made the presence of multinational corporations in Nigeria and their constant investment in the sector a matter of vital importance to which other concerns have been subordinated.

The pursuit of socio-economic objectives through national oil policies did not succeed. The main factors underlying policy shifts are related to the country's dependence on oil revenues. This situation arose from the early socio-political instability which led to lack of attention to the need to diversify the country's exports and the protection of productive sectors. This left the country fatally exposed to fluctuations in the global oil prices. Another factor underlying the changes in the country's oil policy is closely related to the first. The level of investment in the oil sector has often forced the government to make lucrative concessions to the oil companies as an incentive to them to invest.

For instance, the fall in oil prices in the 1980s led to a disinvestment in the country's oil sector, which further led to a significant reduction in oil revenues. As a consequence, the country plunged directly into recession, suffering from deficits in the balance of payments, high unemployment and years of rationing. As expected, the situation led to high social unrests and political turmoil as regimes were frequently overthrown. Political competition saw in these upheavals an opportunity to seize power, and to loose it. This undermined the government's policy control, and made it more reliant on commercial stakeholders in the oil industry. The oil business is by nature capital intensive, and therefore is risk averse towards government policies that may affect the earning margins. There has never been any threat of that sort in Nigeria, as has been the case in states that produce oil, such as Norway and the UK. Nigeria is dependent on multinational corporations and its policies are submissive to the interests of the companies in order to safeguard their continued investment in the sector.

Conclusion

For historical reasons oil companies benefited from the colonial system and gained access to the vast oil reserves in Nigeria and the opportunity to set their roots deep in its oil sector as a basis for the long-term maximisation of value. Soon after the independence, however, the government increasingly took control of the industry. Nigeria has failed to convert this vast wealth into social and economic development due to domestic socio-political instability. The instability emanates from the socio-cultural and political context in which Nigeria emerged as a state. It also has to do with the weakness of newly established political institutions of the federal government of Nigeria in managing the challenges they inherited. While oil was at first a blessing, it soon became the main evil that has undermined the nation-building project in the country's post independence era.

On the other hand, the activities of the commercial stakeholders have always thrived in Nigeria. The main issue for an oil company is the operating agreement secured and negotiated with the host government. Such agreement covers all the economically vital aspects for the company. The threats that emerged later in the operating environment were brought about by the social communities among whom they worked and not the uncertainty of government policies.

The public oversight of oil projects in Azerbaijan, 2004–2007

Farda Asadov

The oil resources of Azerbaijan

Azerbaijan has played a special role in the history of the petroleum industry. This is defined not so much by its significance and relative weight in the global extraction industry and the development of oil extraction technology, as by the unique combination of the historical development of Azerbaijan's oil extraction industry with the factors of state construction, the national mentality and global political interests in the region.

Arabic sources dating from the Middle Ages and referring to the area of the town of Baku, tell of the extraction of "earth oil" in the tenth century. This is thought to be the earliest record of working oil deposits on land. It is generally believed that industrial petroleum extraction also began in Azerbaijan before anywhere else in the world, and the first oil well was drilled in the region of Bibi-Heybat in 1844, or 10 years earlier than the first oil wells to be drilled in Pennsylvania, USA. The peak of oil production in the pre-Soviet era was in 1901, when the oilfields of Baku yielded 11 million tonnes of oil. At this time world markets were dominated by Russian oil from Azerbaijan at 7.1 million tonnes, compared with the USA supply of 9.2 million tonnes. However, following this, oil extraction in Azerbaijan began to fall temporarily and the country's share of the world

oil supply fell in 1904 to 37.9 per cent, against 51.7 per cent from America. In 1905 this ratio shifted even more strongly in favour of the USA: 26.8:61 per cent (Sultanov 2000, pp. 12, 18).

For a long time Azerbaijan continued to extract more oil per head of population than anywhere else in the world, and conceded first place to Mexico only after the revolutionary shocks of 1917–1918. Using the index of volume extracted per square unit, Azerbaijan still continued to lead from the beginning of the twentieth century for five whole decades.

For 150 years the development of socio-economic relations and state institutions in Azerbaijan has depended closely on the conditions of development of oil production within the country and in the world. Baku, the modern capital of Azerbaijan, grew up first and foremost as the petroleum capital of the region, of Russia and later of the USSR. Even in the middle of the nineteenth century it was a small and unimportant town with a population of a few thousand people. The oil boom attracted workers and enterprise capital from the whole of Russia and neighbouring countries. The biggest companies in the world began to work and expand in the oilfields of Baku and the population of the town grew by 7.4 times in the last quarter of the nineteenth century alone. As the processes of urbanisation acelerated and the demographic and social make-up of the population

Farda Asadov defended his PhD thesis on Arab studies in Saint Petersburg in 1987 and has been awarded fellowships by the Oxford Centre for Islamic Studies in 1998 and UNESCO in 1999. He is the author of a monograph and a number of research articles. In 1998 he joined OSI-Azerbaijan and in 2001 was appointed as Executive Director of Open Society Institute–Assistance Foundation (Azerbaijan). OSI-Azerbaijan supports a number of programmes aimed at strengthening civil society in that country.
Email: fasadov@osi-az.org

changed, Baku became a Muslim town with a significant non-indigenous, non-Muslim population. The town took on the appearance of a multinational industrial town located in the Islamic East but becoming a place of intense cultural and economic exchange long before many other similar zones that are widely known today.

In the pre-war years of the Soviet period Azerbaijan was the absolute leader of the Soviet petroleum industry, both in terms of the volume of raw materials extracted and processed, and in developing and testing new technologies and educating and training the skilled workers needed in this industry. The contribution of Azerbaijan's oil workers was of special significance in the victory over fascism on the fronts of the Second World War. Approximately three-quarters of the oil extracted in the USSR during the war years was produced by Azerbaijani oil workers. During and immediately after the war the USSR repositioned its oil industry strategy towards developing alternative oilfields in the Urals and Siberia. The rapacious exploitation of the high yielding Azerbaijani oilfields was paradoxically combined with reduced capital investment the removal of equipment, companies and qualified staff to the eastern USSR. Azerbaijan's oil workers were now writing the history of the Ural–Siberian oil region, known as the "Second Baku", and later of western Siberia. However, irreparable damage was inflicted on the production of oil at home in Azerbaijan.

Nevertheless, in the history of the USSR Azerbaijan remained a country of oil workers. In the so-called "family of Soviet peoples", the group of figures symbolising the peoples of the different republics of the Union, contained the Azerbaijani oil worker, along with the Uzbek cotton-grower, the Ukrainian arable farmer and the Georgian wine maker.

As in other republics of the former USSR, as a result of non-commercial methods of management and its isolation from the world market and advanced technologies and production, the economy of Azerbaijan suffered losses that were very hard to make good. For an oil-producing country, along with a weakened economy, the ecology and productivity of the oilfield experienced a crushing blow. Neither the standard of living nor the social welfare for

the citizens compensated for the high price of Soviet administration. Azerbaijan was one of the worst provided-for republics of the USSR and was the worst off in terms of its income per head of population, and its access to quality education and health provision.

Thus, that at the moment when the USSR was dissolved and when each republic calculated what it had gained and lost during the 73 years of Soviet power, Azerbaijanis started to determine the role that developing of the oil industry could play in view of their need to build an independent state.

During the Soviet period reluctance to invest in expensive technology to work the deep-water oilfields in the Caspian Sea saved a limited part of the sea reserves from centralised extraction, and from the unfair redistribution of the revenue from these rich oil resources according to Soviet principles. Using these resources to strengthen the independent state as it entered the world market, and to help modernise public and state institutions, became the first priority. From the end of 1991 onwards, all national governments of Azerbaijan agreed upon the most important tasks for the national economy and foreign policy. These were to resolve the Karabakh conflict; to seek investment and advanced technology for exploiting hydrocarbon resources, and to resolve the problem of transporting crude oil to the world market.

Ultimately, it was the second of these problems that made a strategic alliance between Azerbaijan and the west necessary, as well as collaboration with western oil companies. However, it was not only the material and technical capabilities of western oil companies that pushed national government towards a logical and successful alliance with the west, but also the ecologically and socially destructive consequences of Soviet ownership of the Azerbaijani oilfields. The conclusion of the so-called "contract of the century" to work the richest of the Caspian oilfields, the Azeri-Chirag-Guneshli field, was a big political success for the government of President Heydar Aliyev. Intensive diplomatic efforts, as well as political consistency and flexibility, were required to resolve the question of oil transport. The solutions that were decided upon and implemented concerning pipelines for "early oil" and "principal oil" and finally securing a western transportation route were the result, not only of economic considerations, but also of great geopolitical foresight, requiring serious political weight and resolution to achieve them (Asadov 2000, pp. 210–211).

If, alongside political weight and foresight we also consider the broad responsibility for the choices made, then another important consideration was the task of neutralising the negative effects of Soviet ownership of the Caspian oilfields that, as noted above, must also have influenced the political will of the leadership of the republic. This meant taking responsibility for the rational use of the oil revenue and minimising the negative effects of oil extraction on the ecology, social relations and economy of the country.

Responsibility for the use of natural resources in the context of forms of power

The rational use of rich natural resources is one component of the general responsibility that a country's leadership shoulders in taking decisions and controlling their implementation. In the modern world these functions are performed either through a system of authoritarian rule or through democratic mechanisms. Each system uses various sources to form appropriate power structures on one hand, and on the other hand, to employ various mechanisms for using that power.

A digression into the Soviet past

The working principle of an authoritarian regime is the presence of a certain type of segregation, in which the privileged part of the population is the constant source of power. One legitimate mechanism for renewing power can be hereditary transfer, such as in a monarchy, in which the privileged group is a small number of family members or a ruling clan. Another mechanism for reproducing authoritarian rule is the use of the essentially democratic instrument of elections to legitimise an authoritarian regime. While illegitimate mechanisms of violent seizure also exist, for example, by establishing a military dictatorship or a dynastic or palace

revolution, those who have come to power sooner or later must face the problem of legitimising their rule.

The Soviet regime was a highly developed authoritarian system with a façade of nominally democratic institutions. In the Soviet state the source of power was a strictly centralised ruling communist party with a rigid hierarchy, each level of which enjoyed its own special privileges. The party practiced a clear-cut system of reproducing power in which its members were tested and promoted up to the most privileged levels of power. While a significant proportion of the population participated in the renewal of this socio-political institution, most received very little from their power, apart from their nominally privileged status. However, they had wider formal possibilities for career growth than those beneath them, and at the same time they shared the burden of ruling the country. This broad base of responsibility stimulated the development of a fixed standard of living and social conditions that had to be provided to ensure the viability of the whole system. This standard included a more or less even distribution of access to quality Soviet education and health care. Other social conditions, such as the provision of housing or full-value recreation, were not, however, guaranteed to the same level, so that some evidence of attempts to establish a fixed standard here can also be seen.

A country that marked the extraction of the billionth tonne of oil (8 billion barrels) in the 1970s, accompanied by good management of this wealth, hardly deserved its place at the bottom of the table of the USSR republics. However, the fixed Soviet standard of living created an illusion the society was fairly dealt with, and a powerful ideological machine supported a corresponding frame of mind amongst the people. After the breakdown of the USSR, when the Soviet practice and social institutions were destroyed and the ideology was debunked, questions arose about new conditions and living standards and the responsibility of the new leaders to provide them.

Alliance with the west or alliance with "western democracy"

Having achieved independence in 1991, the leaders of Azerbaijan were faced by the same problems as many other third-world countries that were rich in natural resources and had achieved independence in the last decade of the twentieth century: how could they secure an inflow of revenue from their natural resources and what the mechanisms of effective governance should be. We have shown above how successful the government of President Aliyev was in solving the first part of this problem.

The prospected reserves of Azerbaijani oil are conservatively estimated by experts at around 2–4 billion tonnes. However, some estimates are even higher, at between 8 and 20 billion tonnes (Guseynov 2002, p. 45). According to the calculations of the International Monetary Fund, with the price of oil at $US50 a barrel Azerbaijan's total income from selling profitable oil over 20 years will be more than $US150 billion (*Vergilyar* 2007) As the deep oil is owned by the state, this means a leap in budget credits, of which 60 per cent are already today met by revenue from oil. For comparison, relatively recently in 2002 the state budget of the country was around $US1 billion, in 2007 it reached the sum of $US7 billion, and in 2011 budget predictions indicate a budget of $US15 billion.

The experience of other independent oil-producing countries shows this money is not always managed successfully by the newly established state-political institutions to solve the problems of fighting poverty and raising living standards. A group of authoritative economists have conducted research into the effectiveness of using oil revenue by countries with authoritarian and democratic regimes, and have drawn paradoxical conclusions. By comparing data on the presence and functioning of democratic institutions and indicators of the country's economic development they found that if income from natural resources exceeded 8 per cent of the total national income, the advantage of democratic government institutions is lost. Statistical processing of the data led the researchers to conclude that a country in which revenue from natural resources makes up 20 per cent of the total national income sees a 3 per cent reduction in indicators of social growth when it transfers to a strongly competitive electoral system of political power.

The researchers explain these paradoxes by noting that democratically elected governments in newly independent countries do not properly develop their investment policy, prioritising instead the task of winning the next election and refraining from investing in projects that have no prospect of a positive effect before the next election campaign. Another negative practice is based on using excessive resources to finance election campaigns by directly bribing the electorate or smaller political parties, and consequently having to pay for this after a victory. As a result, the need to find money to pay these expenses can lead to corruption in managing the public finances and the government's investment projects (Collier 2007, pp. 43–44).

What is the fate of the democracies in oil-producing countries, and can an authoritarian regime guarantee an effective management of natural resources? The researchers believe that the most favourable conditions are created when democratic government is combined with a system of checks and balances, providing transparency and accountability of power. There are few such examples in the world. The often-cited experience of Norway is unhelpful, because democratic institutions and the necessary standards of accountability and transparency were in place before oil was discovered. Thus a more topical model recognises the need to develop in authoritarian regimes strong mechanisms and practices of accountability, transparency and civic involvement. The governments of many third-world countries are moving in the direction of this type of transformation with extreme reluctance.

There is an essential difference in the situation in Azerbaijan, which allows us to consider the experience of this country slightly differently from the well-known African examples. Inevitable transformations accompany the establishment of the country's sovereignty over its oil resources. The strategic energy alliance with the west and its geographic proximity to Europe predetermined the need for reforms that established the democratic mechanisms of checks and balances.

In fact, history left no other route for the transformation of society in Azerbaijan. The greater effectiveness of authoritarian management of natural resources mentioned above is seen in monarchical regimes of the Near East, in which patriarchal institutions and the particularities of national culture and religion play the roles of restraints and counterweights. The author of *The bottom billion* also diverges from the view of these economists, noting that a country with a small population extracting a fixed, high level of petroleum per capita can exist successfully as a rentier state, living exclusively on oil revenue and covering with interest the needs of the average family (Akhmedov 2006, p. 11). Nevertheless, it seems to me that without the pressure of traditional limitations or, in other words, without the foundations of patriarchal responsibility, there would be no mechanism to redistribute oil income that guaranteed citizens their share of the revenue.

In a post-Soviet country where the Soviet standards and controlling mechanisms have been lost, and the foundations of patriarchal responsibility had long since disappeared into oblivion, only the new requirements that arise upon entry into the European community zone and an alliance with western democracies are capable of standing in for the missing checks and balances.

These are the requirements for developing transparent and effective governance in which a significant role is assigned to civil society and for creating elements of community participation and surveillance, and also a culture of dialogue with the government. It is also worth bearing in mind that obstacles to absolute power include the most important institutions of democracies such as political pluralism, an independent judiciary and a free press. Azerbaijan took these obligations upon itself both within the framework of international agreements and in fulfilling its obligations as a member of the Council of Europe and as a country participating in the European Neighbourhood Policy proposed by the European Union.

Observing the principle of transparency as an element of national government policy

Azerbaijan's entry into the Council of Europe and its signing of the European Neighbourhood Policy Action Plan were voluntary acts, although they were also influenced by the dominant geopolitical tendencies in the region. Consequently, its observance of the require-

ments of transparency and accountability in administration were supposed to become elements of national policy in foreign relations and the internal affairs of the country. The Azerbaijani government did not fail to demonstrate these priorities in concrete foreign policy steps.

The Extractive Industries Transparency Initiative (EITI)

In 2002 the British government launched the EITI to enforce the declaration and certification of money received as revenue by national governments from natural resources extraction. This initiative was made possible partly as a result of the international movement, "Publish what you pay" founded by international civil society institutions and supported by a range of influential international organisations, including the Open Society Institute. Unlike a number of resource-rich states that showed, and in certain cases continue to show, reluctance to join the EITI (Collier 2007, p. 143), the Azerbaijani government announced it was joining the initiative at the first EITI summit in London in 2003. Henceforth, the actions of the government were also distinguished by being active and consistent. In the same year the State Committee for the EITI was established, beginning talks with oil companies about how to meet their obligations under this initiative.[1]

The dialogue that started up with civil society is particularly relevant here. The weakness of civil society institutions and their lack of previous experience of dialogue led to the government's initial reluctance to see that local non-governmental organisations (NGOs) must be involved in the EITI process. However, the international nature of the initiative, and the important role played by international NGOs in realising it, convinced government to meet Azerbaijani NGOs, which had by that time created a coalition to participate in this initiative. The Azerbaijani government, oil companies and the NGO coalition signed a memorandum on 24 November 2004 to collaborate in implementing this initiative in Azerbaijan.[2] Since then six half-yearly governmental reports have been published about the payments it has received, and the same number of aggregated audit reports based on a collection of individual reports from oil companies have been compared with the government accounts. As each of these was released the NGO coalition prepared an assessment, including, alongside the shortcomings noted, proposals to improve the process and the accounting regime.[3]

What does the EITI bring to help solve the problem of transparency in Azerbaijan?

For citizens this constitutes noticeable progress relative to Soviet practice, when apart from the triumphant reports about the tonnes of oil extracted, nobody in the country, and possibly even in the national government, had any idea how much revenue had been generated by the selfless labour of the oil workers. Reliable information about income has stimulated a sense of responsibility to spend it correctly. Moreover, as accountability became an important issue, some previously hidden problems in the transparent management of the country's oil industry started to appear. For example, it became evident that the state oil company, SOCAR, was involved in establishing accountability both as a representative of the government, giving data about the assignments of foreign companies, and as a commercial oil company, reporting on its own assignments. This drew attention to the need to reform SOCAR and increase its internal transparency.

It also drew attention to the fact that EITI reports are distributed only according to production sharing agreements (PSAs), whereas significant volumes extracted by SOCAR are not revealed (Coalition of Azerbijan NGOs 2005). One of the obscure aspects of accounting was the problem of associated natural gas. According to the PSA gas was transferred freely by SOCAR. The amounts of this gas were fully commensurable with its production and the level of internal consumption. However, in the first period of accounting evidence was produced only about the government receiving these amounts, and there were no data about the transfer of these amounts for comparison.

The regular presentation of EITI reports also led to greater committment to individual public reporting procedures by the extraction companies, strengthening their responsibility for payments and for giving details in the "miscellaneous payments" column in a form acceptable to the EITI.

The State Oil Fund of the Republic of Azerbaijan (SOFAZ)

The public are also concerned about several other questions that are not answered by the EITI. While it may be a reasonably effective instrument in defining the amount of income at the disposal of the government, the current agenda of the EITI does not open possibilities for providing transparency about how public money is spent. Nevertheless, the experience of Azerbaijan shows that it can serve as a good start for more detailed work limiting the uncontrolled expenditure of wealth from oil.

It is generally known that an effective means of preventing an influx of oil dollars that would harm the economy and entail the associated macroeconomic consequences known as "Dutch disease" is to collect a significant proportion of receipts outside general circulation, and more specifically, within specially created funds. The State Oil Fund of the Republic of Azerbaijan (SOFAZ) was created in Azerbaijan for this purpose, on the recommendation of international financial institutions (State Oil Fund of the Republic of Azerbaijan n.d.). A significant proportion of the receipts from oil companies, with the exception of direct tax payments, accumulate in SOFAZ, which represents the most transparent source of public finances. The assets of the Oil Fund today already exceed $US4 billion. According to some evaluations by IMF experts, with the price of a barrel of oil at $US45–50, it can be predicted that SOFAZ will receive up to $US45 billion before 2011.

Unlike in Norway, in Azerbaijan there would be little sense in saving this money for future generations. On the contrary, it constitutes the basis for developing a regular investment policy, again in the interests of the future of the country, as it stands on the threshold of necessary transformation. The government is already increasing the practice of making transfers from SOFAZ into the state budget, and also into special social programmes for refugees and investment in infrastructure (See SOFAZ, n.d.). These payments are already attracting public interest today, but the situation concerning the activities of SOFAZ opens up quite wide possibilities for public participation. Although it would be premature to assert that the government is ready to collaborate openly with the public through its policy of distributing SOFAZ money, there is nevertheless a basis for thinking that the wide SOFAZ investment programme and control over its effectiveness could not be managed without the representative participation of civil society.

Public control over natural resources–an important condition of institutional democracy

The importance of public information and participation in the management of natural resources does not consist only in achieving a necessary level of transparency and government accountability. Another condition necessary for transforming post-Soviet society is the creation of a working mechanism of public scrutiny over that management. Indeed, when the government sees that achieving a fixed international transparency standard in its management of oil income is a necessary element of its international reputation, mechanisms of public control can be created for this branch of industry that can serve as an example for institutional reforms in other areas of public policy. A full set of questions connected to the transparency of oil income can fit within the following three simple but fundamental problems.

How great is the oil revenue?

We have seen that the Azerbaijani government considers its obligations under this problem to be an important condition of its foreign policy and reputation. In this particular area Azerbaijan strives to maintain an advanced position in the world. The government is actively working in the international EITI institutions, and a government representative joined the International Advisory Group involved with the formation of these institutions. The government of Azerbaijan is at the time of writing joining the International Board of the EITI and actively supports strengthening the initiative, establish-

ing effective international instruments of control for meeting EITI obligations, and it even initiated a plan to raise the status of the EITI to the level of a UN convention.

A precedent was created in Azerbaijan within the framework of transparency of income for establishing a dialogue between the national government, international oil companies and a coalition of national NGOs. The government bodies participating in this process are the State Committee on the EITI and the State Oil Company. The State Oil Fund was also partly drawn into this process because the Director of the Fund is at the same time the Chair of the State Committee on the EITI and a large proportion of the payments reflected in the EITI reports sit within the Oil Fund. The regular reports from the Oil Fund are in turn good sources of information in determining the amount of oil revenue.

How transparently and effectively is oil revenue distributed?

Success in providing transparency in this area is not so impressive. It was noted above that a significant proportion of oil revenue has accumulated in the Oil Fund. The purpose and Regulations of the Oil Fund allow for the possibility of creating active mechanisms of transparency in distributing the Fund's resources. Despite regular information about payments from the Fund to different state programmes and government needs through budget transfers, public participation in decision-making is minimal, if not nonexistent. Part of the reason for this lies in lingering uncertainty over the purpose of the Fund. Currently, the distribution of money has the characteristics of a stabilisation fund, a fund for future generations, and a fund to support social programmes. There is no detailed public dialogue about the expenditure policy or distribution of money from the Fund. Decisions are taken in the habitual and unchanging style of managing state finances that has much in common with former Soviet practices. And although many payments from SOFAZ do not seem inappropriate in their purpose, neither the Fund itself, nor the other state organs that receive these payments, seem ready yet to let civil society participate in decision-making or in monitoring the effectiveness of the expenditure.

According to the estimates of IMF experts, oil revenue makes up around 60 per cent of the state budget income. Over recent years the budgetary process has undergone several positive changes. The current draft budget for next year represents quite a detailed document that is sufficiently informative to define concrete purposes for budgeted resources, although not all of its component parts are equally detailed. Experts from the International Budget Project regularly produce transparency ratings of budget processes for a whole series of Eastern European, Asian and African countries. According to the results of the report published at the end of 2005 Azerbaijan is not badly placed, occupying 11th place out of 36 countries, when ranked according to the transparency of the planning stage of the budget, ahead of such countries as Russia and Mexico or its neighbours Georgia and Kazakhstan.

However, when it is ranked according to indices of accountability and monitoring implementation, the country occupies a place at the very bottom of the table, 33rd out of 36. The rating for public participation in the budget process is also not high: the country has to be content with just 28th place (Open Budget Initiative 2006). Success in this area was most likely the result of collaboration between the government and international financial institutions, and as civil society had little noticeable involvement in the reforms it is not possible to speak about internal mechanisms of restraints and counterweights. It is likely that this is why the greatest progress is noticed at the stage of developing the draft budget, because it is here that the possibility of collaboration with and the influence of international institutions is greater. Where implementation and monitoring of the budgeted expenses are concerned, these international institutions are less able to have an effect and the main role has to be played by internal mechanisms of surveillance.

How much does it cost society to prioritise the development of the oil extraction industry?

At first glance this aspect of concern about transparency is not as significant as as the problem of accumulating and distributing income. It is clearly necessary to measure the inevitable ecological damage. The environmental costs of oil extraction could even be significant enough in certain cases for the feasibility of oil projects to be questioned. At the beginning of the oil discussions in Azerbaijan there were suggestions that the ecological damage to the Caspian could be so great that refusing to extract oil or exploit the bio-resources of the Caspian could turn out to be more rational than working the oilfield. It is known how difficult it was, for example, to decide about placing pipelines across the Georgian part of the Baku-Tbilisi-Ceyhan (BTC) project. Transit fees, even after the extremely favourable conditions proposed by Azerbaijan, will bring Georgia around $US60 million a year. For Georgians, comparing this income with the ecological costs of laying the pipeline could be a real reason for special concern.

Yet the ecological risks are not the only obstacle to oil projects. Again, comparison with the Soviet period inevitably arises. Those who have been to the Apsheron peninsular have seen with dismay the twisted remains of boring equipment and puddles of dirty and environmentally damaging water containing copious amounts of crude oil, which all create an impression of an ecological catastrophe.

However, the socio-economic cost was no less ruinous. The oil industry of the country developed under conditions of Soviet ownership and administrative command. The practice of public industrial relations served to inculcate these very principles and habits. Local enterprise and initiative, which had been present at the dawn of the Azerbaijani oil industry, were eradicated in Soviet times. The responsibility of citizens themselves for the efficiency of production and for reducing the associated social and environmental impact was exchanged for ideological beliefs of communist solidarity and Soviet patriotism. As a result, the country was completely unprepared for the inevitable market transformations and democratic reforms, and the people did not have the understanding and knowledge necessary to stimulate and implement these radical transformations. Such was the starting position after the breakup of the USSR.

New socio-political conditions brought about the emergence of new risks: dependence on oil dollars; indifference towards social reforms; increased risk of corruption and cynical practices and the same lack of civil responsibility as was manifested under the strict and authoritarian Soviet regime. It should be emphasised that this is not a question of using oil revenue to reform the economy and society. It means that as the practice of oil production influences social conditions and institutions, some habits, skills and behaviours are encouraged and some are rejected. It is this very aspect of being informed and responding that can have a serious transformative effect on societal structures in a country where most of the increase in gross domestic product is provided by oil projects.

Thus, informing the people about the effects of oil projects on the ecology, social environment and institutional development of the public sector can have transformational effects on social and political attitudes. To reason about this and to respond effectively to the possible negative consequences of oil exploitation depends on how well informed the people are. To inform the public effectively also requires the monitoring of large projects, with methodology and results that instill confidence in the person carrying out the project. To successfully monitor them requires access to information about the project, professional experience of working with project documents and conducting a full range of information, access to the project zone and readiness for dialogue about the results. Representatives of civil society in Azerbaijan encountered the absence of these very conditions when they expressed concern about the negative effects of one of the largest projects of the modern oil industry: the construction of the BTC oil pipeline.

The project of monitoring construction of the BTC oil pipeline

The BTC pipeline stretches for 1,768 km across three countries. The Azerbaijani section comprises 443 km, the Georgian part 249 km and the Turkish part 1,076 km to the port of Ceyhan on the Mediterranean Sea. It was proposed that the whole pipeline would be laid underground. The route crossed 1,500 rivers and rose to 2,800 m above sea level in the mountain sections. Digging the trenches, large-scale excavations and construction work would

- affect the ecology: condition of the soil, air and water, biodiversity
- create social problems: condition of the infrastructure and quality of social services, restoration of fertile soil
- affect economic conditions: influence the development of local business
- affect human rights: labour relations, rights of land ownership, whether affected by construction works or acquired for laying the pipeline
- cause cultural and material effects, including the conservation of archaeological finds and historical monuments along the pipeline.

The company British Petroleum (BP), the operator of the BTC project, had developed a policy for disclosing and managing these risks. There were several levels of monitoring and disclosing problems of construction. These were internal monitoring, existing within the project itself and external monitoring. The latter included the monitoring missions of the international financial institutions, the possibility of monitoring by national governments,[4] and international groups of experts nominated by the heads of companies to evaluate the impact of the project and tasked with consulting directly with the president of BP (reports from the Caspian Development Advisory Panel (n.d.) are held on their own Internet site). These efforts created the impression in the company that the resources for monitoring were sufficient and that it was therefore not necessary to create conditions for monitoring by local NGOs.

However, the problems listed above also worried local civil society activists. An initial set of construction problems led to a transparency requirement for the project. The first monitoring projects simply collected complaints from the inhabitants and evidence about how the leaders of BP were solving the problems. The following problems in carrying out monitoring were immediately revealed:

- There was a lack of information about project documents regulating the obligations of the operator and other participants in the project.
- Access to the sections under construction was limited.
- There was a lack of information about the conditions of other project monitors.
- The company's workers were unwilling to devote time to working with the monitoring team.
- No commitment had been given to respond to the shortcomings in the company's work noted by the group of monitors.

It became clear that in order to remove these obstacles a decision about monitoring by local NGOs should be taken at the highest leadership level of the company. Talks with the company were held by the Open Society Institute Assistance Foundation (OSI-AF), one of the largest funds supporting civil society in Azerbaijan, speaking on behalf of and in constant collaboration with local NGOs. Prolonged efforts led to the conclusion on 22 April 2004 of a bilateral memorandum about monitoring the BTC pipeline, which included a detailed description of the obligations of BP, OSI-AF and the monitoring groups. The Memorandum also set out the procedures for forming these groups, the development stages of the project, a chronological plan and forms of documentation for monitoring. One can read the text of the Memorandum on the OSI-AF site (2004) and also on the BP site.

The first phase of monitoring (2004–2005)

By the time monitoring began, practically 80 per cent of the work in laying pipelines was complete. Nevertheless the effects of the project on social problems of the people, the ecology and human rights were far from exhausted at the time. The obligations of each side according to the Memorandum are worth reproducing below, in so far as they quite clearly differentiate the functions of the three sides: the monitoring groups, the oil company (BP) and the donor (OSI).

Obligations of BP

- To render technical and organisational support (health and safety equipment, transportation and ecological training) to NGOs in the monitoring process.
- To discuss the results of monitoring with the working groups and answer questions about their content.
- To provide access to information about the methods used in production, current construction works and planned undertakings.
- In the case of their inability to present the monitoring groups with the required information, to provide a written explanation of the reasons why this was so.
- To co-finance the training required to broaden knowledge about pipeline construction and develop skills in managing monitoring projects.

Obligations of OSI-AF

- To facilitate the formation of monitoring groups using the criteria and selection mechanisms that had been developed.
- To coordinate the work of the monitoring groups.
- To stimulate the collective work of the members of the groups.
- To give technical support to the monitoring groups during the monitoring and reporting phases of the programme.
- To finance the implementation of the action plan for the monitoring project (such as travel expenses and honoraria for the experts).

Obligations of the monitoring groups

- To work as a team, develop and agree on a collective plan of action.
- To choose a coordinator and evaluator for each monitoring group.
- To conduct objective and unprejudiced monitoring of the construction project.
- To present a high quality and reasoned report according to the agreed standard.

- To evaluate their own work independently and highlight any learning points.

As seen by the division of responsibilities, the participants in the process were set the following tasks:

- To develop and test the monitoring skills of the representatives of the NGOs.
- To develop in the representatives of the NGOs an experience of collaborating in the framework of a single project.
- To establish first experience and a culture of dialogue with the oil company.
- To facilitate as far as possible the solution of problems caused by the social and environmental effects of construction.
- To provide maximum objectivity and independence of monitoring, with responsibilities and finances strictly differentiated between the donor and the company and between the donor and the NGOs.

Accomplishing these tasks could mean creating the first experience of complex problem-solving concerning the social and environmental effects of industry, and could set an example of successful interaction through the development of professional skills and the ability to reach compromises. Professionalisation, a culture of dialogue and the ability to reach a compromise are all necessary conditions for transforming a post-Soviet society and promoting reforms. Thus, the project could be used as an example for similar interactions in other spheres of public policy.

If we ask whether all these tasks were achieved successfully in the first phase of the project, then the answer would not be entirely positive. A definite amount of progress was made and project management skills were developed, full observation was conducted over the fulfilment of construction standards, and measurements and descriptions of physical effects on the infrastructure were produced. At the same time, during the discussions with the company about the results of the monitoring it turned out that a significant proportion of the remarks were not accepted as sufficiently reasoned. The comments and recommendations should have had stronger reasoning, based on good knowledge of the documented obligations of the company.

Second phase of monitoring (2005–2006)

This phase was characterised by more detailed work with the project documents, describing the obligations of the company during the realisation of the construction. This allowed the project to be defined as a citizen's audit of the construction, and this time not only of the BTC oil pipeline, but also the South Caspian Baku-Tbilisi-Erzurum gas pipeline. Along with the same five-themed monitoring groups as in the first phase, a group was also formed to monitor the fulfilment of the company's obligations to resolve the shortcomings noted earlier. A special characteristic of the organisational structure of the project was the creation of a group of mentor-consultants charged with forming new monitoring groups, collaborating on the revision of the action plan and advising and supporting the activities of the groups.

Third phase of monitoring (2007)

By the time the third phase began the construction of the pipeline was completed and the projects were entering the operating phase. The operator company lost its former motivation to support the continued efforts of civil society to survey the project. At the same time the task of reducing the operational risks and impact of the projects required the participation of civil society institutions.

In our opinion, it was not only the quantitative reduction of the amount of construction work that caused the company's interest in direct collaboration with NGOs to diminish. The operational phase is characterised by risks of the possible environmental effects of exploitation, ongoing labour relations, limited movement along the route of the pipeline and partially retained restrictions on land use. It is necessary now to create permanent mechanisms for public control and reaction by the inhabitants of the territories along the pipeline, rather than by the experts and NGO agents based in the capital who were the driving force of the previous phases of monitoring. These local inhabitants had been passive beneficiaries of the monitoring.

The next special characteristic of the operational phase was that the construction companies–the subcontractors, whose professional responsibility rested with the operator company (BP)–left the scene. At the same time, central government structures and local organs of power now moved to the leading edge of contacts with the local population. In other words, responsibility for the functioning of control mechanisms and interaction with the people was relocated with local authorities. In particular, responsibility for ensuring the security of the pipelines lay completely with the State Security Service in the Office of the President of the Republic of Azerbaijan. The entities that were created or renewed in the social investment programme such as social services or infrastructure (such as for water supply, health care, education and electricity supply) came under the management or control of the local authorities.

This created a qualitatively different situation, in so far as in Azerbaijan the sensitivity of local authorities towards the activities of NGOs remained quite high. Moreover, a phase now began of compensating for the investments made and receiving direct profits from the extracted oil and operation of the pipeline. Under such conditions direct collaboration with NGOs from the capital could seem to entail more political risks, as well as a less effective way of interacting with the local population and local authorities.

The NGOs, having gained significant experience of conducting monitoring and audits, also could not help but see the need to transform their efforts into local initiatives. Thus, former partners naturally turned out to be formally divorced in their later activities. NGOs reacting to this situation defined their aims in the following way:

- to develop a methodology and training plans for the public monitoring of extraction industry projects
- to carry out pilot projects for preparing and conducting monitoring by the local population
- to create mechanisms for permanently observing and responding to the risks during operation of oil projects
- to facilitate the creation and distribution of public response networks in the country.

OSI-AF enabled maximum development of the programme and the interaction of public sector

experts. Pilot projects were supported by the Foundation. The final results of the project are expected to be written reports on monitoring and the creation of public response mechanisms.

The fate of the partnership with the oil company

The partnership with the oil company in conducting the public scrutiny, although it did not formally continue after the pipeline had been constructed, did, however, bear fruit. The company created the Azerbaijan Social Review Council including four Azerbaijani experts in its international team, all of whom had been participants in the pipeline construction monitoring projects. One of the obligations of the Council is to produce biannual reports and recommendations for the company's social programmes. Contacts between NGOs and BP continue. Action plans are exchanged. Questions about the presentation of information from one side and the other are satisfactorily answered. The formal obligations of the preceding phases of monitoring continue to have an effect, and the previous links provide a certain level of trust and responsibility towards one another.

Regional significance of the pipeline monitoring projects in Azerbaijan

The efforts of the Azerbaijani NGOs in monitoring projects were catalysts for the activity of civil society in Georgia. The partners in the Azerbaijan project, BP and OSI, facilitated the exchange of experience and collaboration between Georgian and Azerbaijani NGOs. In September 2007 Georgian and Azerbaijani colleagues organised a conference in Baku on the experience of public monitoring of extraction industry projects. Taking part in the conference were representatives of the civil society sector from Turkey, Russia, Romania, Mongolia and the USA. The accumulated experience enabled a productive exchange on the problems of collaboration between civil society, national governments and foreign oil companies, and also on questions of transparency and the particular responsibility of national oil companies. During the working sessions specialists had the opportunity to discuss concrete questions about the methodology of monitoring the ecological, social and economic impact of extraction industry projects.

During the course of the conference it became clear that in each country, despite differences in the level of organisation of civil society and the level of interest of the government and company, there was unique and useful experience of civil activity. It was demonstrated that the link between national processes and regional initiatives is reciprocal. Progress on a national level brings investment in the regional process, and regional initiatives speed up the national process.

Moreover, regional exchanges ensure the effective participation of civil society in international initiatives. The session to discuss the agenda for a meeting of the International Board of the Extractive Industries Transparency Initiative in Oslo on 26 September 2007 was particularly useful from this point of view. With one member of the Board representing civil society from Central Asia, the Caucasus and Eastern Europe, NGOs at the conference benefitted from the opportunity to agree the key points of its position and the most important proposals for discussion in Oslo.

Conclusion

The Caspian region has entered the responsible phase of its development. Hydrocarbon wealth, the flow of which can appear quite short-lived, is capable of creating the conditions necessary for modernising society and improving the health and technological equipment of a nation's economy. However, it can also lead states to regenerate autocratic institutions, to limit the healthy creative potential of their citizens and to become disillusioned by the time natural resources are exhausted. In Azerbaijan there are signs that the government and citizens are quite well-informed about the acuteness of the problem. At the same time there are as yet in the country no mechanisms of joint response to the challenges of growing global needs for raw hydrocarbon resources in the interests of the country's citizens. Nevertheless, being well informed about the problem, integrated pro-

cesses and international obligations have created fixed mechanisms for stimulating reforms and the development of a system of checks and balances.

A successful application of the EITI in Azerbaijan can be regarded as a genuine achievement against the background of the as yet catastrophic lack of control of extraction and income in some developing countries of Asia and Africa. However, it is necessary to bear in mind the particular characteristics of Azerbaijan as a post-Soviet country, in which the national government never had full control over the extraction of natural resources, but at the same time managed the share which was given to it by the central Soviet government. On one hand, this led to risks of internal corruption and the ineffective management of money, especially in the area of state expenditure rather than in accounting for the wealth that had been extracted. It is not by chance that the national government, which works in collaboration with civil society on accounting for income, was not willing to extend this experience to the area of spending public finances. Dialogue with civil society is limited and remains sensitive towards broadening contact with NGOs and public accountability.

The partnership with BP within the framework of monitoring construction of the BTC oil pipeline and South Caucasus gas pipeline holds a special significance in formalising and developing a culture of dialogue with civil society. However, it is also significant that in limiting the participation of the company in relations with civil society to the operational phase, a more cautious approach to collaboration with NGOs by the company prevails. One can nevertheless hope that the positive experience of collaboration has created conditions for more active and professional work of NGOs whose mission is to spread a culture of responsibility and dialogue in the field of relations with local powers. The successful development of these initiatives in Azerbaijan can serve as an example both for countries within the region and also for others with economies based on extraction and processing natural resources.

Translated from Russian

Notes

1. See the decree of the President of the Azerbaijan Republic on the SOFAR website: http://www.oilfund.az/en/content/2

2. For the fulfilment procedures and text of the memorandum see http://www.oilfund.az/en/content/2

3. The site of the NGO coalition introduces the reports and opinions of coalition experts partly in English: http://www.eiti-az.org/ts_gen/eng/feal/eng_f10.htm, and in full in Azeri: http://www.eiti-az.org/ts_gen/azl/feal/index_f10.php

4. The Azerbaijani government did not conduct its own monitoring. The Georgian government conducted an audit mainly of ecological problems, however, no significant breaches of the accepted obligations were revealed. State Oil Fund of the Republic of Azerbijan (n.d.)

Energy relations in Russia: administration, politics and security

Andrey Makarychev

Introduction and theoretical notes

This chapter analyses energy relations through a prism of three interlinked concepts: administration, politics and security. It proceeds from the viewpoint that this triad describes the basic approaches to questions about energy: the technical, the politicised and the securitised (based on the primacy of the concept of security). These three concepts are logically linked to each another and represent an elementary matrix through which we can analyse different segments of the energy discourse.

The proposed scheme can be of research interest for several reasons. First, it allows us to see that communication problems between participants in energy relations arise when these three approaches are confused, whether consciously or unconsciously. For example, if one side explains its actions with reference to legal, economic or financial motives, but the other sees a political purpose behind the actions, then a communication breakdown occurs. This situation can be illustrated using the example of the energy dialogue between Russia and Europe.

Dr Andrey S. Makarychev is Professor of International Relations and Political Science, Nizhny Novgorod Linguistic University. His teaching courses include theories of international relations, international integration, international organisation and regionalism in world politics. His was formerly employed by the Centre for Security Studies and Conflict Research, Eidgenössische Technische Hochschule, Zurich (2000–2001) and the Danish Institute for International Studies, Copenhagen (2003–2004). He was Visiting Fellow at Jagiellonian University, Cracow; Copenhagen Peace Research Institute; Baltic and East European Graduate School, Sodertorn Hogskola (Sweden); Kennan Institute for Advanced Russian Studies (Washington, DC); The Netherlands Institute for Advanced Studies in Humanities, Wassenaar; George Mason University, Fairfax, VA and the Free University of Berlin. He is a member of the Programme on New Approaches to Russian Security and the Network of Institutes of Public Administration in Central and Eastern Europe, "Professionals for Cooperation" Alumni Association.
Email: amakarych@mail.ru

Second, in practice one country can have several different modes of communication in its arsenal. For example, western countries discuss energy amongst themselves in administrative terms but use a different, more politicised language when talking to Russia. Russia also tries to speak simultaneously in two different, albeit weakly connected languages. The first was heard when oil transport through Belarus was temporarily interrupted and Moscow first decided to start using depoliticised language when conversing with its closest ally. We heard the second language in Vladimir Putin's speech in Munich in 2007. He outlined the basic problem for Russia as being in security, and to be more precise, in the expansion of NATO military structures towards Russia's western borders, in the light of which any discussions about moving to world prices for energy appeared less convincing. If, during the "gas crisis" with Belarus, Russia acted within the framework of technological thinking, which did not leave space for friends or enemies, then the Russia that faced the world in Munich had switched to another, deliberately politicised language that was based not on economic arguments, but rather on the logic of inevitable conflict.

If the first logic can be called conditionally "gas industry speak", then the second is "geopolitical speak". It is surprising that the Kremlin showed a readiness to speak out in both languages, thus demonstrating either that it misunderstands the fundamental differences between them, or it wishes to experiment with different "voices". It turns out that Russia is trying to use both arguments simultaneously, creating an extremely confused situation, both for Europe and, more importantly, for itself.

Third, we can see the interconnectedness of two concepts important for understanding energy relations that are at first glance opposing: transparency and security. In fact, it is becoming ever more difficult to speak of security outside the context of transparency, just as it is to discuss transparency without resorting to the conceptual apparatus of security. This semantic pairing appears completely paradoxical: if the discourse on security places a strong emphasis on the exclusive, exceptional and specific nature of a situation, then conversely, the discourse on transparency is routine in character and is aimed at building an institutional base defining what the norm is.

The "security–transparency" link, from this point of view, shows the coexistence of two opposing processes. On one hand, a process of securitisation is happening, through which many social or economic problems are formulated and understood as problems of security. On the other hand, de-securitisation is also underway, whereby security problems are translated into the format of normal politics and subjected to its principles and mechanisms. In recognising the political subjectivity of the sources of security threats a political reaction is required, proposing possible solutions beyond the scope of the existing institutional order. For this very reason, it seems that the second of these two processes currently predominates, which leads to the formation of a depoliticised model of resistance to different threats as a consequence of linking the grammar of security with a whole series of administrative concepts, one of which is undoubtedly transparency. In this chapter the author repeatedly turns to the multifaceted concept of depoliticisation as it is applied to various spheres of energy relations.

Administrative technologies of transparency

The administrative strategy of developing energy relations is based on technical economic thinking, which presupposes a model of the state as an enterprise, an apparatus or machine for effective management. Carl Schmitt defined this model as an "absolute technicism" that is based on indifference towards a political goal, just as engineers can have no interest in how their invention will be used. This is a system of supposedly unerring objectivity in which "there should remain only organisational–technical and economic–sociological challenges, but there should be no more political problems. ... The modern state, it seems, has in fact already become what Max Weber regarded as a large enterprise" (Schmitt 2000, p. 96).

It is possible to use these apparently theoretical arguments to construct a logic for the development of energy relations, in that the contemporary management culture (both in Russia and in the west) bears a technologised character and is based on the concept of universally applying a series of standard practices. Using them presupposes that energy problems can be fully solved through the instrumental application of a certain set of methods, standards, rules and procedures. In practice this means that the modern state needs a new administrative technology. In the opinion of many authoritative specialists it is the state apparatus itself and not private corporations that can react most flexibly to the changing conjuncture of energy markets. Correspondingly, the state is more easily influenced by professional associations, civil society organisations and the mass media, which are all concerned with ideas of good governance. For example, several years ago the British government, under the former Prime Minister Tony Blair, set up the Extractive Industries Transparency Initiative (EITI) under the influence of international non-commercial organisations.

Moreover, this problem can be theorised within at least two different frameworks. First, these new technologies of state administration can be discussed in categories that touch on Michel Foucault's concept of "governmentality". It portrays flexible, fast-changing forms of power that do not belong to anyone and that take the form of networks with huge numbers of members. The key problem in this type of model is that it neglects the relationship between different languages of public communication. For example, there is a mass of economic research on energy problems, but this is not automatically translated into the language used by people in power or in civil society organisations. The ideal model of the organisation of such power could be represented by the citizen-expert: the individual who is capable of competently understanding where the budget has been spent.

Second, an institutional perspective is possible, which assumes that in order to remove socially defective institutions, which are taken to include corrupt practices, it is necessary to raise the cost of maintaining them. The key problem here is that it is quite possible for corrupt deals to be socially effective (although not irreproachable from a moral point of view), in so far as they satisfy the needs of certain groups. Moreover, as Joseph Stiglitz demonstrated in a recent publication, in so far as the strategic goal of business is to maximise profit, possibilities for corruption lie within the enterprise model itself (Stiglitz 2007, p. 21).

Transparency as an administrative concept

Administrative technology is most clearly expressed by the concept of transparency, which, along with accountability, is at the foundation of what is known as "good governance". Transparency is an interactive concept that is actualised when there is a contact between actors representing different spheres of professional activity (especially administrative structures, big business and the non-governmental sector). A strong system of external communication – including economic, political, social and professional communication – is believed to lead to greater transparency. In this way, transparency is in a social construct closely linked to information, expertise, public policy and symbolic capital. At the same time, transparency represents a particular characteristic of socio-economic relations, significantly changing the functioning of institutions connected with the efficiency of business and the legitimacy of its role in society with methods for the regulation and distribution of resources, and with the existence of certain models of corporate governance.

The EITI process is a good illustration of the transformation of transparency from an idea into a norm and then into an institution. The first stage of this process is connected to the understanding of transparency as an idea. Here it is appropriate to refer to one of the most influential representatives of the English school, Hedley Bull, for whom any rules are fundamentally intellectual constructs (Bull 2002).

Transparency as an idea is discussed in a great number of conferences and publications on this theme, both in academic circles and in the mass media. It is here that the basic arguments for and against it are voiced, the concepts are clarified and finally a vocabulary of public communication in this area is formulated. During this discourse transparency holds a strong ideological component: it is known that the voices that are most critical of the concept itself are traditionally heard from the left flank: thus, many neo-marxists and antiglobalists attribute transparency to the liberal political vocabulary and, correspondingly, blame it for neoliberal economic policy. However, since the mechanism of the EITI has begun to work, the situation looks somewhat different: global neoliberalism, as embodied by the structures supported by George Soros, began, in essence, to bring about a political agenda of the "new left" (including the fight against poverty in developing countries and the control of transnational corporations and international financial organisations) with the help of the instruments of transparency.

The second stage of the process that interests us is connected to the transformation of the idea into a norm, which takes on a definite shape and is interpreted, incorporated in different contexts and approved within a network. Let us suppose that this transformation happens when documents, such as the New Energy Policy of the European Bank for Reconstruction and Development, or the European Union Green Paper on energy security, are formulated on the basis of the concepts that have been developed. Concepts such as "responsible financing" (a term used as an ethical standard for evaluating the policy of giving credits to countries that are rich in natural resources) or the "project-oriented lobbyist coalition" (one of the organisational forms of groups who speak out in favour of transparency measures) come into play in this stage. It could be said that a kind of culture of transparency is being laid out, which is based to a large extent on persuasion and incentives, rather than on sanctions.

The essence of the second stage is that in order for the defined model of economic behaviour to be called the norm, it is delimited and contrasted with another model that is defined as a deviation. The norm goes beyond the limits of the minimum disclosure of information that is legally fixed (and required by law). The principles of the EITI deliberately encourage new countries to join voluntarily the efforts undertaken for disclosure of socially significant information (for example, in relation to financing social programmes from petroleum or gas money). In this way the norm promotes greater symmetry: all participants in the "transparency space" know who makes payments, how much, to whom and for what, which sharply reduces the probability of exclusive (privileged) transactions. On the other hand, opacity (including in the sense of confidentiality) always favours asymmetry based on political preferences.

In this sense the EITI represents a depoliticised move on a global scale, which is even more remarkable knowing the list of countries which are implementing the initiative. These include both states with stable political regimes and those that have recently experienced revolutionary changes. However, in both types of state the introduction of transparency norms flows in roughly the same pattern and follows a similar scenario, which underlines the depoliticised nature of the initiative itself.

Finally, in the third stage, the norm grows smoothly into an institution, based on a defined organisational foundation. For example, such a transition was observed within the framework of the EITI, in collaboration with Publish What You Pay (PWYP), when a dialogue was initiated with the international banks, requiring stricter standards of financial transparency from them. At the limit, institutionalisation leads to legalisation: that is, to subjects accepting legally precise obligations and in some instances delegating the rights of control in fulfilling these obligations.

Each participant in this system of institutional interrelation has its own role: the political elite provides general support for transparency measures at the state level; grant-making foundations (in particular the Open Society Institute) distribute the means to promote the idea, to

which transnational network coalitions (including PWYP) are attached. The problems of transparency are also built into different international formats, including the G8, the World Trade Organization and the four Common Spaces in relations between Russian Federation and the European Commission.

However, this process is long and complicated, in so far as the typical situation is one in which the key players – including the International Monetary Fund, the International Accounting Standards Board (IASB) and several others – cannot force countries to accept advanced methods of transparency as they do not have the formal authority to do so. Therefore, any agreements can be achieved only through a process of lengthy discussions, such as, for example, the many attempts of the PWYP to persuade the IASB to modify accounting standards towards a greater openness of information.

The institutional potential of transparency arises from its symbolic capital, its material resources and the contractual obligations that are adopted by the countries that subscribe to it. For example, a trust fund has been set up within the framework of the EITI that covers the expenses of maintaining the administrative apparatus of the Initiative, and that PWYP has created a fund for the legal defence of its workers, who risk prosecution in countries opposed to the introduction of standards of transparency in relation to the extractive industries.

The three-stage model described above has an internal dynamic, in so far as all three of its elements are conditional on each other. Thus, for example, the institutionalisation of transparency clearly leads to a change in the discourse. Moreover, within this scheme some so-called transitional situations stand out: the transition from transparency-as-discourse to transparency-as-norm requires an effort from public policy centres, combining civil activity with expert analytical capabilities. The transition from norm to institution then requires organisational and material obligations on the part of the state, which, in combination, create a solid basis for "petroleum governance".

As a result one can talk about the appearance of a "technology of transparency" within the framework of the international community, the essence of which consists in the smooth but strategically adjusted shift of emphasis from a fight against law infringement to a fight for the formulation of the key norms on a global scale. The transparency discourse is thus transformed into the most significant alternative to the repressive model of the fight against illegal activity. In other words, in place of exclusively legal qualifications of corrupt practices, a more complicated social technology forming the general communication space arises, constructed not on the opposing terms of "legal" and "illegal", but around the semantic pair of "norm" and "deviation".

Russian perspectives

Russia does not yet take part in the EITI process. There are neither statements from officials in this respect, nor a national coalition of non-commercial organisations ready to participate in realising this initiative. As one of the largest countries that extracts and processes natural resources, Russia falls outside (both organisationally and intellectually) the "transparency space" which has been actively created by its southern neighbours with the no less active support of international organisations.

It is known that within the founding mechanism of the EITI there is a strong interaction between three actors: the state, business and civil society. If, however, one of these actors refuses to participate, then the whole construction falls apart. What stimuli to join the Initiative exist in each of these three segments?

We will begin with the state, which, first, assumed definite obligations within the framework of the G8 agreement about the support of transparency in its various forms. Second, any government that adheres to the principle of transparency of financial information secures for itself the additional resource of public support, which clearly would not harm the Kremlin.

Third, the governmental apparatus needs transparency to control the petroleum and gas industry in order to meet the budget. Take, however, the EITI's strategy in relation to commercial banks, which proposes the repatriation of assets obtained illegally, the development of a "white list" of banks that adhere to the principles of information openness, the adoption of more effective legislation to prevent money laundering and the revision of the principles of confidentiality of banking information.

Finally, high levels of transparency could at the same time prevent some conflicts, such as those that have recently surrounded the Sakhalin-2 project. In this case the Production Sharing Agreement (PSA) was not made public when it was signed. If the PSA had been publicly disclosed and discussed it is possible that civil society and responsible government officials could have prevented certain articles from appearing in it, which 10 years later have been recognised as running counter to Russia's interests.

There are also potential stimuli for business. First, experience shows that transparency brings additional investment, which Russia needs, including in its extraction industry. Second, transparency requirements can be proposed by Russian business in cases when it takes on the role of investor itself and, as very often happens, it meets with a closed (in the sense of both information and politics) environment, fraught with discrimination towards domestic firms. This type of obstacle periodically occurs in the Baltic States and eastern Europe. Third, the Russian extraction business working in countries neighbouring the Russian Federation may be interested in the regular disclosure of information about the sums it pays each year into the budgets of these states. It is very likely that such evidence would reflect Russia's role in a fairer and more positive light in these close neighbouring countries. Finally, business can turn to transparency standards when competing in international markets (including within the Commonwealth of Independent States) with the biggest foreign companies, which abide by many obligations about divulging information (this concerns especially BP, Exxon Mobil, Statoil, Hydro and other companies).

Many spheres of business simply could not exist without transparency requirements as an integral element of carrying out any business. An audit or insurance of risks (including ecological risks), for example, is possible only when the most important operators in the market seek to create an economic environment that is transparent from the point of view of the rules of business behaviour. Transparency is necessary even in legal security, requiring the dynamic development of the consultancy field.

Many segments of the advertising business are oriented towards transparency. It is known, for example, that many petroleum companies spend significant resources on advertising, albeit with various aims. Some can be justified by the formulation of their own corporate image, which should be considered as promoting their brand through strengthening characteristics such as confidence, predictability and reliability. Advertisements for petroleum companies, as a rule, play up social motives such as those connected with job creation and the allocation of assets for ecological purposes.

Thus, transparency has become a proven method of advertising and marketing that gives a market advantage to those who practice it. This is replicated in the sphere of energy relations: for example, it is impossible to promote the new generation (Euro 4 level) of diesel oil products to the market without a clear, open demonstration of their technological characteristics and ecological purposes.

Second, transparency raises the level of trust towards those institutions that adhere to it. Examples from the administrative and governmental spheres are appropriate here, such as the live television broadcasts of parliamentary sessions or publication of materials from legislative hearings (for example, the US Congress). These are all aimed at demonstrating to voters how political questions are really discussed and how decisions that are important for society are made.

Third, realising one or another model of transparency is possible only in the form of a kind of convention, or an agreement between two or more players. This reveals its interactivity: transparency can only be reciprocal (bilateral or multilateral). This important quality relates directly to the EITI: for example a petroleum company working in one region or another and adhering to the principles of transparency has a right to expect similar transparency from the organs of power with which it comes into contact, and with which it may even sign agreements about interaction. A kind of transparency chain is formed: openness, as practiced in the petroleum business structures, demands gestures from their partners in return.

Finally, we come to civil society which, in the light of the political manoeuvres that have taken place in Russia over recent years, finds itself at a crossroads and needs a new definition of its social mission. The EITI would be unthinkable if non-governmental organisations

had not moved to the forefront, and their significance is defined by their public resources of influence and their ability to affect society's expectations with relation to transparency (DID 2005). The essence of the Initiative is reduced to prompting civil society organisations in countries rich in resources, and with the support of the international community, to control revenue from the extraction, transport and processing of these resources. Ideally the plan was that the non-commercial sector would help to influence interrelations between the state and the extraction industry towards greater transparency and predictability. The search by non-commercial organisations for new spheres in which to apply their efforts in this regard is natural. In this connection the creation of network coalitions of Russian non-state organisations concerned with problems of providing transparency in the petroleum sector could become very attractive. Moreover, it is possible that the Russian state could find in a non-commercial organisation additional leverage against oligarchical structures which are distinguished by their lack of openness.

Thus, although Russia may be interested in the possibilities presented by the EITI, it is likely that it will be able to participate fully in this Initiative only after its partners in the G8 join it not just as sponsors (or patrons), but as countries which take upon themselves the same transparency obligations as developing countries have. It is known that countries such as the USA have problems with their own petroleum business. A series of international non-governmental organisations (in particular, Global Witness) have drawn attention to the presence of the German Deutsche Bank and businessmen from the UK, Hungary, The Netherlands, Denmark, Cyprus and Austria as shareholders of the infamous company Eural Trans Gas in an international chain of dubious gas deals between Ukraine and Turkmenistan (Global Witness 2006). At the same time, under the aegis of PWYP, a report recently published reveals several problems in the USA relating to obstacles preventing the Americans from achieving the standards of transparency which Washington requires of other countries (Bugala 2006). Consequently, the key structural problem facing the EITI today is erasing the existing boundaries between a small group of "donors" and the countries that take upon themselves obligations within the framework of this initiative.

Politicisation of energy relations

What facilitates the politicisation of discussions about energy problems? Why is it that a purely administrative approach turns out to be inadequate, and one or another participant moves on to political arguments? The answers will probably be found by looking in several directions.

Firstly, energy problems are easily incorporated into various geopolitical schemes in which national interests form the basic category, but where states perceive each other, at best, as potential competitors or rivals and, at worst, as enemies. In this way the energy policy of Russia appears on the one hand to fit into the existing outline of fundamentally political interrelations with countries that Moscow considers to be hostile (Poland, Lithuania, Latvia and Estonia). On the other hand, the politicisation of energy relations can change external relations. Russia does this with the help of the concepts of "energy sovereignty" and "energy superpower", and the EU does it by broadening the possibilities for normalising energy markets on the basis of the European economic model.

The North-European Gas Pipeline (NEGP) is a classic example of how becoming a political subject is possible only through interaction with other subjects. As Russia becomes a subject, a new picture of the political space of Europe will appear. The NEGP is the factor which fixed Russian priorities in Europe outside the institutional context proposed by the EC: an alternative to the imaginary Moscow–Brussels axis is the real Berlin–Moscow axis (which was dreamed about long ago by people such as Aleksandr Dugin). Here the divergence between the positions assumed by Germany and the former Eastern Europe can bring a number of potential pluses for Russia. However, the reverse is inevitably to make the whole suite of relations between Russian and its neighbours in the west extremely complicated.

It is interesting that discourse games take place between countries participating in energy relations; the essence of which leads to them accusing one other of artificially politicising these relations. Thus, Russian officials recognised that if the Baltic states prioritised economic reasoning rather than politics, then the NEGP would pass through their territory and not through the depths of the Baltic Sea (Spruds 2006, p. 20). Here the NEGP represents a technical response to a hyper-politicised approach to a whole suite of interrelations with the Russian Federation on the part of Poland and the three Baltic states. The Baltic leaders then evaluate the NEGP as a political project, which in turn provokes a reaction from Moscow (and sometimes from Berlin) in the form of an accusation that they are using political rhetoric. What happens is something like double politicisation: the very act of pointing out political motives behind the actions of the opposing side becomes a sufficient basis for describing the act of pointing it out as political itself.

Second, yet another factor of politicisation is the possibility of taking decisions that are based not so much on economic expediency as on political will. The NEGP as an example of a political solution signifies the possibility of Russia positioning itself in Europe in a way that breaks loose from the existing structural circumstances (be it the Energy Charter or the road map that has not been ratified by the Russian Federation). It is for this reason that in many countries in the west such semantic constructions as "energy as a weapon" or softer allusions such as the "contradictory position of Gazprom" have arisen, indicating that behind Russia's actions are motives that differ from the declared logic of economic rationality and effectiveness.

Third, another condition of politicisation is that in the energy sphere there are many uncertainties over the rules of the game. The greater the lack of clarity, the greater the measure in which professional discussions acquire political connotations. Discussions turn around how to fill in the blanks, polarising those who participate, and they inevitably begin to resort to a political categorisation to defend their positions and explain the motives behind the actions of other actors.

In this sense, the discussions around the Sakhalin 2 project after Gazprom arrived, and concerning the prospects for the Shtokman gas field, could be considered a politicising factor (Kupchinsky 2007). The list of uncertainties relating to the NEGP is probably the longest: specialists have remarked upon the lack of clarity in relation to the resource base of the project, the absence of a public announcement by Gazprom about the conditions for accessing the Russian gas fields, inadequate information about all the potential receivers of gas, and also uncertainties about its exact cost and precise route (Loskot 2006, p. 50).

Fourth, politicisation frequently enables an artificial broadening of the spectrum of questions that all too easily become attached to energy. In the international press questions linked to the strategy of Gazprom on the European markets are often discussed in a deliberately broad context, which includes the nature of the political regime in Russia and Vladimir Putin himself, the Litvinenko affair and the death of the journalist Anna Politkovskaya, and Russia's withdrawal from the Conventional Forces in Europe treaty, among others. An important observation follows from this: western countries appear to politicise the whole range of energy problems to no lesser extent than Russia.

Energy security

In recent years it has become accepted to speak about many problems connected with extractive industries primarily in a security context. What is behind the fashionable term "energy security", and why has it received such wide circulation in different spheres? How inevitable is it that these problems should be infused with meanings related to security? In general, what meaning is intended by the term "energy security"? Is it the regular, stable and long-term delivery of power to the domestic market? The safety of its transportation (including in an ecological sense)? The creation of strategic reserves of energy materials? The diversification of sources of energy to avoid dependence on one type of fuel, or on one supplier state?

The first of the most widespread approaches to energy security as a concept in the academic literature was voiced by the well-known American specialist Daniel Yergin. He interprets the very idea of energy security as the broadening of former representations of relations within the energy sphere by including in them new risks and threats, such as those linked to terrorism, political instability, the growth of nationalism and geopolitical rivalry between the leading powers (Yergin 2006). Energy security is

thus turned into a type of umbrella term: within its framework there is room for climate change, pricing policy, the reliability of the oil and gas infrastructure and for technological innovation (World Economic Forum and Cambridge Energy Research Associates 2006, p. 8). A broader interpretation of energy security also includes an ecological component, such as supplying gas in a way that is not harmful to the environment, or ensuring that the operation of oil pipelines is ecologically safe.

An example of the tendency to broaden the problematic field of energy security is considering this concept through the prism not only of the reliability and stability of supplies of hydrocarbon products, but also the remaining links of this technological chain, including the extraction and processing of energy resources. However, any attempt to attach a universal description to the concept of energy security has not yet yielded satisfactory results: extracting, transit and user countries start from different understandings of what should be considered risks and threats.

For many user countries, raising the level of energy security is connected with partial access to Russia's energy resources through working with Gazprom and other large companies (Loskot 2006, p. 52). European countries define energy security as providing acceptable (that is stable and sensible) prices for oil, gas and their future equivalents, derived from reliable and diversified sources. There are two main threats from this point of view: high prices for energy and instability of supply. In other words, energy security is a means of creating regulatory regimes that would lower the risks of unexpected price changes, and would provide at the same time an appropriate level of openness in the markets.

For transit countries the source of danger is dependence on the supplier of energy resources. On the other hand, security is associated with the possibility of controlling the process of transit itself and receiving rent for it. In the opinion of Lithuanian specialists, for their country "the transit of gas to Kaliningrad is a source of revenue and creates a sense of security. Losing the position of transit state will make Lithuania more vulnerable to Russian politics" (Janeliunas and Molis 2006, p. 30).

For exporter countries such as Russia the main source of danger is dependence on transit across the territory of countries where the political mood is hostile (Kazin 2006, p. 62). At the extreme, the very process of transit itself contains threats. In addition, moving to the forefront of the Russian understanding of energy security is maximising the capitalisation of petroleum resources and using them to promote Russian economic interests in the west.

A second approach to analysing the concept of energy security can be found in turning to the so-called Copenhagen school, which defines security in the category of survival, and therefore proposes something that is peculiar, exceptional and goes beyond the bounds of normal, standard procedures. Security signifies the suspension of normal rules, which directly links the concepts of security and sovereignty. In other words, the exclusivity of the event dictates the exclusivity of the reaction to it.

More often than not, when a security vocabulary is used it indicates that one or another problem has departed from normal politics and taken on an exceptional character, with possible actions being proposed that go beyond the framework of the existing institutional order. The security discourse places a strong emphasis on the specificity or singularity of a situation. The term "securitisation" describes situations in which economic problems are formulated as security problems (this is exactly how constructs such as ecological or information security arose).

The problem here is that the range of problems that can be publicly presented through the prism of security is, in truth, limitless, and this in itself brings about anxiety due to several circumstances.

First, each time that we speak about something as a problem of security it follows that we understand that presenting the question in such a way inevitably assumes that the sphere of state regulation and control is broadened. For this reason, in the words of Slavoj Žižek, power often "endeavours to sell us insecurity" (Žižek 2006, p. 237). This tendency is expressed by the appearance in the language of new terms such as "risk governance". Thus, broadening the circle of security problems means that state participation in different spheres of our lives is gradually strengthening, and correspondingly, that the apparatus of power and different control techniques are growing.

Second, a stronger articulation of the concept of energy security implicitly creates a paradox, as was recently noted by a group of influential European experts: "The more one tries to securitise social phenomena in order to ensure 'security', the more one creates (intentionally and non-intentionally) a feeling of insecurity. ... As a logical consequence, the politics of maximal security are also politics of maximal anxiety" (CASE Collective 2006, p. 461). The question arises: who uses this situation and how? One of the directions of thought in this field lies in the understanding that many in the business world quickly understood that there is money to be made by playing on the universal anxiety about security questions. For example, this touches on insurance of investment risks. Large transnational business has formed its own agenda around global discussions in this problematic sphere. The smartest transnational companies proceed from the viewpoint that any problem can be used to create new markets. This could refer to the prospects for investing heavily in the production of energy from renewable sources, in the creation of new routes for transporting energy products and in new technologies for processing and cleaning them in accordance with increasing ecological standards. It is not by chance that the general direction of discussion in the west consists of linking energy security problems with an extremely wide range of other questions, including global climate change, sustainable development and the condition of the environment.

Third, considering the whole spectrum of energy problems through a security framework indirectly presupposes that non-governmental organisations are marginalised. The logic of the state could be, for example, that if we are discussing security then there is no room for the public activity of non-governmental entities, and the professionals should be left to deal with it. It is quite difficult for an non-governmental organisation to find its place in the security relations that are formed.

Depoliticisation and desecuritisation

Movement in the opposite direction, however, is also possible: from "energy security" to "energy effectiveness". This vector can be described as depoliticised, in so far as it consists of an understanding of the effectiveness of administrative structures, which is based on their being functionally separated from politics as a sphere of power relations.

Russia is gradually moving to a depoliticised language, which is associated with an expert–technical approach to the solution of problems and which, it would seem, ought to be understood by our European colleagues. This is a technical language of economic calculations that leaves no space for ideological or political rhetoric. Thus, when speaking about potential Russian investments in the economies of EU countries, Vladimir Putin drew attention to the fact that our "companies are meeting market conditions, investing, supporting jobs, and enabling economic development" (Putin 2007a). In his view the NEGP is an economic project which "raises energy security in Europe". Elsewhere we heard similar logic: "When we realized that the Baltic states were engaging in honest economic relations with us and that they were ready to transfer to world pricing, then we met them halfway" (Putin 2007b). Practically the same declaration was also made by the ex-President concerning conflicts with transit countries about the price of energy resources: "Our actions are not politicised. These are not political actions" (Putin 2007c).

Watching fragments of the parliamentary session at the height of the Russian–Belorussian gas crisis (January 2007) on television reminded us more of a meeting of the board of directors of Gazprom: not a word about geopolitics, about friends or enemies: all the President's questions were about how matters such as how much of the Russian budget was lost due to Minsk's position, and whether Belarus was in worse conditions than similar countries. In essence, we were witnessing an extremely important change, not only of language, but of the whole practice of international positioning of Russia.

Depoliticisation is understood by Vladimir Putin in the context of the second most important component of the discourse that forms it: the concept of universality. He calls the Russian position in the energy arena "market-oriented in relation to all our partners irrespective of how our political relations are at the time" (2007a). Vladimir Putin is increasingly inclined to refer to universal rules, norms and

procedures to be applied to all participants in international economic relations without exception. In other words, market universality is opposed to the singularity and uniqueness of the political interventions it stirs up. For example, his argument in relation to the conflict around the Sakhalin 2 project is that Gazprom paid to join a market in the project. The same logic applies in relation to the attempts of Russian companies to penetrate European markets: they "arrive with investments that are badly needed by the economy" of these countries.

The crisis surrounding the interruption in the supply of Russian gas to European countries is an example of the kind of complications that can arise in such approaches. The user countries accused Russia, not so much because Moscow increased the price of gas for Belarus, but because of its reluctance to consult with European countries earlier about the unfolding situation. As a result a conflict between two norms arose: market price, on the one hand, against transparency, on the other. Russia's behaviour was interpreted by the user countries as a demonstration of its indifference to the way it would be perceived in the world. And this accusation was in many ways fair: if Russia constantly insists on adding the adjective "strategic" to describe a partnership with the European Union, then the conflict with Belarus could be seen as a model situation proving that Moscow is correct. Alas, the opposite occurred: Europe, not knowing what to do with Moscow's proposal for a strategic partnership, can now easily convince itself that nothing much stands behind it.

However, some signs that Moscow is ready to admit the presence of problems and to give back do exist. Igor Jurgens, for example, remarked that pretensions that Russia has towards the signed but not yet ratified Energy Charter, are not "obstacles which cannot be removed" (*Rossiyskaya Gezeta* 2007, p. 5). In his opinion, in the long term "such situations as those in Belarus or Ukraine, if, God forbid, they are repeated, will not be the subject of bilateral concern of Russia and the country which has broken a rule, but the concern of the international community" (*Rossiyskaya Gezeta* 2007, p. 5).

The situation is growing more complicated and underlines the frequently encountered thought that desecuritization can never really be complete, as the production of insecurity and the designation of issues and actors as enemies of the state and the community is always part of the production of social identity. States or communities can never be fully desecuritized, as such stasis ... would mean their disintegration. (Benhke 2007, p. 110)

It is in this context that we should evaluate how Russia and the EU use questions of energy security to reformulate their images and impressions of each other and, in the end, to formulate their own international identity.

Conclusion

This chapter has analysed three modalities of the discourse about energy relations, which prove to be closely interconnected, and which have practical significance for understanding the political and economic sides of the energy factor for countries such as Russia.

From the point of view of what is happening in Russia, it is not difficult to see that the Russian petroleum business is simultaneously both depoliticised and hyper-politicised. Depoliticisation in this context can be understood in two ways: on one hand as the non-participation of a petroleum business in political processes as a fight for power (companies either behave quietly and are unnoticed, or use technical expert arguments), and on the other hand as the Russian state acquiring managerial qualities and taking on the role of a big national corporation. The opposite of this situation is hyper-politicisation, presenting a tendency to use the petroleum business as a weapon or instrument of the power elite.

In terms of the international effects of this situation, the west more often refuses to see behind the actions of the Russian leadership economic calculations, an example of which is the move to world prices for energy. Europe and the USA still cannot resist the temptation to offer an oversimplified interpretation of Russia as an imperial state, despite the evidence of Russia's attachment to egotistical and extremely individualistic diplomacy, its adherence to unilateral action and its reluctance to meet the cost of friendly relations with its neighbours from its own budget. The concept of friendship was practically never actualised in the foreign policy of the Russian Federation, because the material cost is too high and Moscow is not prepared to pay. There is a mass of supporting evidence that the Kremlin is often motivated by economic considerations which, naturally, do not have to be at all democratic in essence.

On the basis of the above we can assume that in the near future the language games in the energy sphere between Russia and the west will essentially consist of each attempting to catch the other out in contradictions. Brussels and Washington will continue to try to see a hidden political logic behind the economic steps favoured by Moscow, and because of this will receive in response reproaches that are all the more excessively politicised.

Russia on the whole will not escape from the general tendency of extracting states to turn into something like corporations (Baker Institute 2007). In this respect the metaphor "Russia, Inc." appears completely appropriate. In theory, for the west to work with an administrative state should be easier than with a state which thinks exclusively in geopolitical categories. But this is only hypothetical, in so far as there is a basis for proposing that the depoliticisation we observed during Vladimir Putin's presidency is one of the means of strengthening Russia's power in the world.

Translated from Russian

Doing business with integrity: the experience of AngloGold Ashanti in the Democratic Republic of Congo*

Paul Kapelus, Ralph Hamann and Edward O'Keefe

Introduction

The Democratic Republic of Congo (DRC) has for many years been the epitome of what the Organization for Economic Cooperation and Development (OECD) calls "weak governance zones". A weak governance zone is defined as an investment environment in which governments are unable or unwilling to assume their responsibilities. These "government failures" lead to broader failures in political, economic and civic institutions that, in turn, create the conditions for endemic violence, crime and corruption and that block economic and social development. About 15 per cent of the world's people live in such areas, notably in sub-Saharan Africa (OECD 2006).

The DRC's human development index is among the lowest in the world and it has fallen throughout most of the period in which this index has been measured, from 1975 to 2003, with a slight rise in 2004 (OECD 2005; UNDP 2006). The conflict that engulfed much of the country from 1996 to 2001 (though conflict is still occurring in the north-eastern DRC) claimed almost 4 million lives and

Paul Kapelus has 15 years' experience in the field of corporate responsibility with a focus on mining, oil, infrastructure development, finance and telecommunications. He works in emerging markets with a significant focus in Africa. He is a director of Synergy Global Consulting and a founder of the African Institute of Corporate Citizenship.
Email: info@synergy-global.net
Ralph Hamann is senior researcher at the University of Cape Town Environmental Evaluation Unit.
Email: ralph.hamann@uct.ac.za
Edward O'Keefe is a Director of Synergy Global Consulting in the UK. He has worked for the UK Department for International Development and international non-governmental organisations, and has consulted with various organisations including Shell, IFC, Fauna & Flora International and Hewlett Packard to understand and integrate complex social issues into management systems.
Email: info@synergy-global.net

involved numerous other African countries. Parts of the country experienced the highest estimated conflict-related mortality rates in the world (Guha-Sapir and van Panhuis 2003). While the extractive sector historically accounted for about 25 per cent of gross domestic product (GDP), this had declined to about 7 per cent in 2001 (Extractive Industries Transparency Initiative [EITI] 2007).

Primarily due to this conflict, international investment in the DRC has been very limited. The only sectors that experienced some investment have been extractive industries and related service providers. Given the DRC's large deposits of gold, copper, cobal, and other metals and minerals, and given the increasing global demand and the concomitant decrease in accessible deposits in more stable countries, resources companies have been the most likely to discount the political and economic risks associated with doing business in the DRC. This is especially true for junior mining companies and small, unlisted companies (OECD 2005), which have a greater appetite for risk and which generally experience a smaller degree

*This chapter was first published in *The Business of Sustainable Development*, published by Unisa Press.

of international scrutiny by government and civil society organisations. In some cases this increased risk has been rewarded with significant returns. As noted by one mining company CEO: "It's the holy grail of the copper industry – companies are saying: to hell with the political risk, we just have to be here!" (Clive Newall, CEO, First Quantum, quoted in Global Witness 2006). The global economic downturn in 2008 has had a massive impact on copper mining, with many of the mines closing down due to low copper prices. This has had an impact on the livelihoods of communities, especially those working on the mines.

Over and above the direct risks to companies' employees or operations through physical violence, disruptions due to destroyed or faulty infrastructure and expropriations, companies operating in weak governance zones also face a number of indirect risks associated with the international corporate responsibility movement. These include risks to their reputation and stakeholder relations if they are seen to become complicit in human rights abuses. Companies have been accused of supplying the economic resources that provide the motives and means to perpetuate conflicts, especially if this has involved the payments of bribes or remittances to armed groups.

There have been numerous initiatives to clarify these risks and responsibilities of business with regard to human rights. The most prominent is the UN Global Compact, in which currently over 4,000 corporations have commited themselves to abiding by 10 principles derived from international agreements, including the Universal Declaration of Human Rights. Two of these principles are focused on human rights issues (UN Global Compact n.d.)

Principle 1: Business should support and respect the protection of internationally proclaimed human rights within their sphere of influence and

Principle 2: Business should make sure that they are not complicit in human rights abuses

The two key terms are "sphere of influence" and "complicity". Both are still open to some interpretation, though an important commentary has been provided, for instance, by the UN High Commissioner on Human Rights (2005):

A company is complicit in human rights abuses if it authorises, tolerates, or knowingly ignores human rights abuses committed by an entity associated with it, or if the company knowingly provides practical assistance or encouragement that has a substantial effect on the perpetration of human rights abuse. Four situations illustrate where an allegation of complicity might arise against a company. First, when the company actively assists, directly or indirectly, in human rights violations committed by others; second, when the company is in a partnership with a Government and could reasonably foresee, or subsequently obtains knowledge, that the Government is likely to commit abuses in carrying out the agreement; third, when the company benefits from human rights violations even if it does not positively assist or cause them; and fourth, when the company is silent or inactive in the face of violations.

With regard to sphere of influence, the commentary is vague, arguing that the larger the business entity "is, the larger the sphere of influence is likely to be" (UN High Commissioner on Human Rights 2005).

Various initiatives have focused more particularly on the role of business in conflict or weak governance zones. These include, for instance, the Voluntary Principles on Security and Human Rights (n.d.) and the OECD risk awareness tool for multinational enterprises in weak governance zones (OECD 2006). Other initiatives have focused on particular sectors or issues, whereby the EITI (n.d.) is a prominent effort to enhance the disclosure of information on payment of taxes and royalties by companies in the extractives industry. Another example is the Kimberley Process (n.d.) which brings together governments and companies to eradicate so-called "blood" or "conflict" diamonds.

The DRC has been a prominent test case for these international efforts to break the link between corporate activity and conflict and human rights abuses. For a start, a panel of experts mandated by the UN Security Council identified a number of corporations, including some that are well-known, which were part of, or contributed to, the proceeds of elite networks including rebel groups and Congo army officials, as well as armies from other African countries. These elite networks fought over and funded their hostilities with the proceeds of natural resources extraction (Global Witness 2006; UN Security Council 2002). Outcomes similar to those of the UN expert panel study were arrived at in a study conducted by a Congolese

Parliamentary Commission led by parliamentarian Christophe Lutundula.

The UN expert panel study contributed to various subsequent studies and investigations, including those by the Dutch and British national contact points established for the implementation of the OECD guidelines for multinational enterprises (OECD 2005), and the Lutundula Commission's findings have eventually – in early 2007 – led to a review of contracts entered into during the period prior to the 2006 election. Nevertheless, the implementation of the recommendations of either the UN expert panel or the Lutundula Commission remains limited and civil society organisations, in particular, have bemoaned the "impunity of individuals . . . involved in the pillage or the natural resources [and in] one-sided, illegal, and unethical contracts" (Publish What You Pay Coalition of the Democratic Republic of Congo 2007).

One of the most prominent cases illustrating the challenges and complexities faced by companies operating in weak governance zones, and in the DRC in particular, was that of AngloGold Ashanti (AGA). The company has a licence to explore a gold deposit in Ituri District in the north-east of the country (see Fig. 1). The exploration area is near the town of Mongbwalu and covers an area of approximately 10,000 km². Ituri District has been one of the most volatile in the country, even after the large-scale deployment of the UN peace-keeping force Mission des Nations Unies en République Démocratique du Congo (MONUC) in 1999 and the establishment of a transitional government in 2003. Clashes between the DRC military and the Front des Nationalistes Intégrationnistes (FNI), the main rebel group in the area, have taken place as recently as October 2006.

In January 2005 the staff of the AGA exploration team in Ituri District made a US$8,000 payment to the FNI, which was controlling much of the Ituri District during the civil war, and which has been accused of committing extensive human rights abuses (Human Rights Watch 2005). In addition, the AGA exploration project provided FNI with accommodation and access to transport, and paid levies on cargo flown into the local airport. The payment and assistance provided established a relationship between AGA and the FNI and provided the FNI with legitimacy.

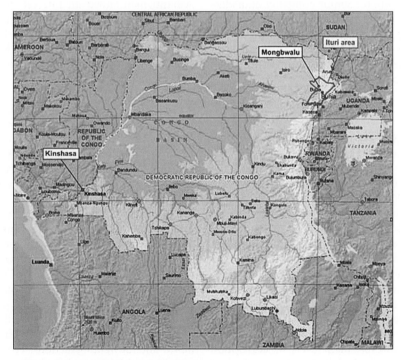

FIGURE 1. Map of Mongbwalu, Ituri area and the DRC
Copyright AngloGold Ashanti. Permission to reproduce granted.

In June 2005 Human Rights Watch (HRW) released a report, *The curse of gold*, which provided details of the financial and material assistance provided by AGA to the FNI and stated that AGA had obtained permission from the militia group to enter the area, despite being warned against this at the start of operations in Mongwalu by MONUC. For many observers this represented an example of reprehensible corporate irresponsibility in a weak governance zone, and it was used to argue that companies such as AGA should not be operating in such areas in the first place (HRW 2005). The company admitted that a mistake had been made, but it argued that the interests of local people and the DRC in general are better served by its remaining in the area (AGA 2005).

Based on document sources and interviews with senior company managers, the aim of this case study is to provide an analysis of AGA's management responses to working in a weak governance zone fraught with violent conflict. It considers whether and under what conditions it is possible for a company such as AGA to conduct business with integrity in such a context. Particular emphasis is placed on the lessons emerging for senior company managers in the wake of the payment made at the local level to the FNI. Broader issues, such as the implications of the UN Global Compact – to which AGA is a signatory – and the EITI are also considered.

History of the company's presence in the area

Gold was first discovered in north-eastern Congo in 1903. Exploitation started in 1905 as the Belgian colonial authorities exploited the gold through private companies. As with other mines under colonial rule, the mining companies took a paternalistic approach and provided social services to the local community. After independence in 1960 the President of the renamed Zaire, Mobuto Sese Seko, nationalised the mines and continued the high levels of social service provision through external agencies, such as the churches. However, high levels of corruption and patronage resulted in few long-term economic benefits flowing to local communities.

There was then a slow decline in the production of gold until the early 1990s when a joint venture agreement was established between the government company Kilo-Moto, Okimo, Mindev (a DRC company) and the International Finance Corporation. This created a company called KIMIN, which had the explicit support of the Zairean parliament as being in the best interests of the country. Later, a South African company called Gold Fields considered investing in KIMIN but did not do so. The International Finance Corporation also pulled out of KIMIN as the threat of violent conflict in the country increased. By 1996 debts continued to mount and in order to raise finances the Ghanaian mining company, Ashanti Goldfields Company Limited (Ashanti) was successfully invited to invest in KIMIN. Ashanti began more detailed exploration of the Mongbwalu concession in 1996.

Ashanti halted its activities around Mongbwalu in 1998, when it became clear that what was to become the second civil war in the country would make exploration activity in the region impossible. Over the next four years the war in the DRC escalated. Despite the conflict, Ashanti maintained an interest in the concession. In November 2000 Ashanti secured a majority stake in KIMIN, and the company was renamed Ashanti Goldfields Kilo (AGK). However, as a result of the continuing war, no mining and only limited exploration took place. The retrenchment of workers and a subsequent dispute over the payment of salaries led to tensions between the local mining company management and workers, most of whom are from the Mongbwalu area. These tensions have contributed to the difficult and complex relations and mistrust between the mining company and local communities in the area.

As the war in the DRC increased with involvement from Uganda, Rwanda and Zimbabwe, the UN published the above-mentioned report by a panel of experts that linked the war to mineral resources extraction (UN Security Council 2002). In July 2002 the Ashanti personnel left the exploration site. However, in the chaos of the conflict, some prospecting continued on the basis of personal contacts between mining operators on site and the fighting factions. Towards the end of 2003 MONUC established a base in Ituri and engaged in repeated clashes with FNI.

Also at the end of 2003 AGK returned to the site to set up a base. In March 2004 the self-styled president of the FNI, Floribert Njabu, returned from his base in Kinshasa to Mongbwalu and engaged with AGK. According to internal AGA documentation, he told AGK that they were welcome to return to the area, that the war was finished and that FNI wanted to become a political party. FNI set itself up as the authority in the area and gave its permission to AGK to continue exploration activities in the concession area. There are different positions about the extent to which AGK actively sought this permission, thereby providing political legitimacy to the militia group, or whether it was granted without the company soliciting it.

Over the next year and a half after AGK re-established a presence in the area, the FNI was provided with financial payments and other support, including accommodation, transport and levies for cargo flown into the area by AGK. The reasons for this support of FNI are disputed. Commenting on this period, AGA emphasises that AGK's support to the FNI was essential to ensure the safety of employees whose lives were threatened by the group, which had established itself as the authority in the area. HRW, on the other hand, emphasises that this support ensured that AGK had control of the concession area. In the HRW report, *The curse of gold*, a local observer is quoted as saying, "Njabu [President of the FNI] now has power due to the gold he controls and [the presence of] AngloGold Ashanti".

In April 2004 Ashanti and the South African mining company AngloGold Limited finalised their merger. The two major mining companies became the largest gold mining company in the world, AngloGold Ashanti (AGA). AGA is headquartered in Johannesburg and has its primary listing on the Johannesburg Securities Exchange. It is also listed on exchanges in Australia, New York, London, Ghana, Paris and Belgium.

It is apparent that, the usual diligence studies notwithstanding, the merger between Ashanti and AngloGold did not involve a process in which social and political risks, especially those associated to business activities in weak governance zones, were adequately considered. This raises the important, broader question of the extent and manner in which corporate responsibility principles are integrated in mergers and acquisitions. The AGA example suggests that they play, at best, a secondary role and that this can have significant implications for the new company's reputation.

After the merger the company developed a new set of business values and principles to guide their operations and exploration activities (see Table 1). These relate to ethics and governance, occupational safety and health, regional health threats, labour practices, the environment and the community. These values and principles set high standards for the company, which are in line with international standards and guidelines, such as the UN Global Compact (though note, in this context, Reich's [2005] concern that there is, in fact, little global convergence in such corporate codes of conduct). The question remains, however, as to what extent these new business principles were embedded in the new company's procedures and culture, bearing in mind that this is a complex process that takes significant time (e.g., Sinclair 1993). This complexity is increased significantly by the new company's international spread of operations, and – in some instances – their setting in weak governance zones.

The decision to re-enter the Ituri District

In November 2004 AGA consulted a range of external informants on the situation, assessed the risks and opportunities involved and made a strategic decision to continue exploration in Mongbwalu, despite continuing conflict in Ituri District. Steve Lenahan, AGA's corporate affairs executive, argues, "The judgment, on balance, at that time, based on the views of a wide range of stakeholders, was that there was an appreciable measure of risk associated with the venture, but that it was manageable" (Lenahan 2006).

One management response to the decision to re-establish activities in the conflict zone was to build relations with the UN peace-keeping force, MONUC. MONUC was operating in the Ituri District at the time and there are differing views on the relationship between AGA and MONUC. In particular,

TABLE 1. AngloGold Ashanti business values and principles

Business values

Anglo Gold Ashanti consistently strives to generate competitive shareholder returns. We do this by replacing profitable gold reserves and by continuously improving the performance of our key resources – our people, our assets and our product. We conduct ourselves with honesty and integrity.

We provide our employees with opportunities to develop their skills while sharing risks and rewards in workplaces that promote innovation, teamwork and freedom with accountability. We embrace cultural diversity.

Every manager and employee takes responsibility for health and safety; and together we strive to create workplaces which are free of occupational injury and illness.

We strive to form partnerships with host communities, sharing their environments, traditions and values. We want the communities to be better off for Anglo Gold Ashanti's having been there. We are committed to working in an environmentally responsible way.

Principles

We will comply with all laws, regulations, standards and international conventions which apply to our businesses and to our relationships with our stakeholders. Specifically, Anglo Gold Ashanti supports the Universal Declaration of Human Rights, the Fundamental Rights Conventions of the International Labour Organization (ILO) and those principles and values referred to in the United Nations Global Compact.

Should laws and regulations be non-existent or inadequate, we will maintain the highest reasonable regional standard for that location.

We will fully, accurately and in a timely and verifiable manner, consistently disclose material information about the company and its performance. This will be done in readily understandable language to appropriate regulators, our stakeholders and the public.

We will not offer, pay or accept bribes, nor will we condone anti-competitive market practices and we will not tolerate any such activity by our employees.

We prohibit our employees from trading shares when they have unpublished, material information concerning the company or its operations.

We require our employees to comply with all money handling requirements under applicable law, and we further prohibit them from conducting any illegal money transfers or any form of "money laundering" in the conduct of the company's business

We will require our employees to perform their duties conscientiously, honestly and in ways which avoid conflicts between their personal financial or commercial interests and their responsibilities to the company.

We will take all reasonable steps to identify and monitor significant risks to the company and its stakeholders. We will endeavour to safeguard our assets and to detect and prevent fraud. We will do this in a manner consistent with the international human rights agreements and conventions to which we subscribe.

We will promote the application of our principles by those with whom we do business. Their willingness to accept these principles will be an important factor in our decision to enter into and remain in such relationships.

We are committed to seeking out mutually beneficial, ethical long-term relations with those with whom we do business.

We encourage employees to take personal responsibility for ensuring that our conduct complies with our principles. No employee will suffer for raising with management violations of these principles or any other legal or ethical concern.

Although employees are encouraged to discuss concerns with their direct managers, they must, in any event, inform the group internal audit manager of these concerns. Mechanisms are in place to anonymously report breaches of this statement of principles.

The company will take the necessary steps to ensure that all employees and other stakeholders are informed of these principles. If an employee acts in contravention of these principles, the company will take the appropriate disciplinary action concerning such contravention. This action may, in cases of severe breaches, include termination of employment. In addition, certain contraventions may also result in the commencement of civil proceedings against the employee and the referral of the matter to the appropriate enforcement bodies if criminal proceedings appear warranted.

Source: AngloGold Ashanti n.d.

there is lack of clarity about whether or not MONUC advised AGA that it was feasible to re-enter the area and the level of support which AGA understood would be provided by MONUC to avoid negative relationships with rebel groups. The absence of a clear commitment in writing from MONUC to this effect means that the company could not rely on this crucial support and that MONUC was not accountable for providing it.

In early 2005 the leadership of FNI was detained in Kinshasa in connection with the killing of UN peace-keepers. Further UN peace-keepers were then deployed in Mongbwalu to manage the conflict. At this stage the AGA exploration staff returned and the corporate affairs and community development team from AGA head office visited the site. This visit illustrates the realisation among head office managers that, with the exploration team commencing its activities on site, the operations in the area might have posed significant risks to the company and that existing management systems to manage this risk may not be adequate.

The decision of AGA management to commence exploration activities, despite ongoing fighting in the area and the support being provided by company personnel to a rebel group, is at the heart of the difficulties subsequently experienced by the company. Company respondents argue that the decision was made following a careful risk assessment, including some level of stakeholder engagement. However, with hindsight, it is apparent that this risk assessment was not adequate. As noted in the introduction, the information that local AGA staff made payments and gave support to FNI in early 2005 became a global reputation liability for the company. As noted by Steve Lenahan:

Events proved that we had got our timing wrong and that, consequently and with the benefit of retrospect, our assessment of the manageability of the risk had been (again on balance) flawed. In January 2005, our colleagues in Mongbwalu were forced to pay to the FNI a sum of $8,000. We knew, at that time and now that this was quite obviously inconsistent with both our own business principles and commonly accepted conventions for the protection of human rights. (Lenahan 2006)

This raises many important questions: how can the risks of commencing activities in an area with weak governance be adequately assessed in a way which is consistent with a company's business principles? How much risk is manageable, especially in such unpredictable conditions? If a decision is made to enter an area with weak governance, how does a company ensure heightened managerial care? In hindsight, it is apparent that there was insufficient communication and oversight between the local and corporate management. It may also be argued that the skills and experiences of the local management team were not adequately considered. A formal stakeholder engagement strategy, which would formally document interactions with, for instance, MONUC, was also not in place.

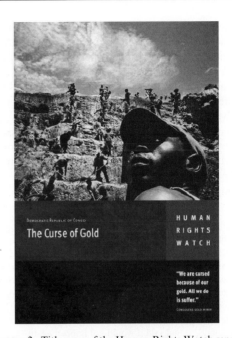

FIGURE 2. Title page of the Human Rights Watch report *The curse of gold*
Copyright AngloGold Ashanti. Permission to reproduce granted.

The HRW report and the company's response

The publication of the HRW report *The curse of gold* (see Fig. 2) in June 2005 contained detailed information about the payment of bribes to the FNI and made serious allegations of irresponsibility against AGA.

As a company with public commitments to corporate social responsibility, AngloGold Ashanti should have ensured their operations complied with those commitments and did not adversely affect human rights. They do not appear to have done so. Business considerations came above respect for human rights. In its gold exploration activities in Mongwbalu, AngloGold Ashanti failed to uphold its own business principles on human rights considerations and failed to follow international business norms governing the behaviour of companies internationally. Human Rights Watch has been unable to identify effective steps taken by the company to ensure their activities did not negatively impact on human rights. (HRW 2005, p. 2)

HRW's fundamental concern was that AGA put business interests above human rights and compromised the company's own policy commitments to ethical and responsible business. Anneke van Woudenberg, the report's author, argued that AGA should never have entered the area until peace had been secured, and that any involvement in the area which was under the control of the FNI would give the FNI more power and political legitimacy and ultimately the ability to commit more crimes against civilians.

The report and the associated international media attention prompted an unprecedented response by AGA. In a press release, the company argued:

Firstly, yielding to any form of extortion by an armed militia or anyone else is contrary to the company's principles and values. It is not condoned by AngloGold Ashanti, under any circumstances. That there was a breach of this principle in this instance, in that company employees yielded to the militia group FNI's act of extortion is regretted. In mitigation, it should be noted that as soon as it came to our attention we publicly acknowledged it, condemned it and said it would not happen again.

Secondly, in contemplating whether to operate in a conflict zone, we believe we have a moral right to do so only if, after due consideration, we can honestly conclude that, on balance, our presence will enhance the pursuit of peace and democracy. ... We believe that, if our exploration programme does yield a mine, it will be of significant benefit to the DRC government and local communities, by providing revenue, employment and access to social development opportunities – and, of course, returns to our shareholders. (AngloGold Ashanti 2005)

AGA thus argued that the payment to the militia group was an isolated, once-off aberration. It also insisted that it would not happen again. Steve Lenahan (2006) argues, "If it becomes clear to us that local conditions have changed to the extent that it is not possible to act within the boundaries of our own business principles, we will go".

The company also insisted that it had been "given the repeated assurance of the DRC Government, at various levels, that it was confident that, with the continuing collaboration of the UN force MONUC, the peace and political processes would yield positive results in the Ituri region and beyond" (AngloGold Ashanti, 2005). However, there was no documentary evidence to back up this claim, with the result that counter-claims by HRW could not be allayed.

The HRW report and AGA's response rapidly resulted in wider discussion at an international level about the events in DRC. Debates were held in the media, on television, at conferences and at the UN Global Compact meeting in Shanghai. Journalists, non-governmental organisations (NGOs), including the NGO that the lead author of this chapter is part of), and AGA themselves wrote articles about the issue. AGA's public engagement on the issue included a press conference the day after the report was publicised; press releases and articles written for the media; text on the AGA website and in its 2005 *Report to society* (including a mention in the CEO statement and a dedicated case study discussion); various live and recorded electronic media interviews; detailed interviews and site visits with the *Financial Times,* numerous interactions with shareholders (mostly by e-mail); and a presentation by the AGA President, Sir Sam Jonah, to the UN General Assembly. At one of the press conferences, CEO Godsell publicly admitted that the company "had messed up" in the DRC (*Mail & Guardian* 2005).

This comprehensive engagement on the issue is in contrast with a "ignore and deny" strategy that some other companies have followed in similar circumstances. AGA's engagement has contributed to international debates on the role of big companies in weak governance zones, and anecdotal evidence suggests that a broad range of stakeholders views positively the company's open approach to the accusations by HRW. The significant debate and controversy surrounding what some commentators anecdotally characterised as a minor sideshow in the context of the DRC's broader challenges also attests to the significant global interest in multinational enterprises and international corporate responsibility principles. The smaller companies deserve similar scrutiny but remain under the radar to a significant degree.

It may also be noted that the company did not raise an argument in its defence that has commonly been raised in the context of similar situations, such as the case of Talisman Energy in Sudan. That is, companies such as AGA, which have at least committed themselves formally to human rights principles and agreements, such as the UN Global Compact, and which furthermore have prominent exposure to international shareholders, including large socially responsible investment funds, and an international network of advocacy NGOs, may be a better bet for the human rights of local communities than companies that are smaller or have different jurisdictions, and that may not enjoy such scrutiny. From a moral point of view, this argument is given some support by French (2005).

At a local level, AGA consulted with a variety of stakeholders about their presence in the area. As noted by Steve Lenahan (2006):

In the period immediately after January 2005, management asked every organisation or leader to whom we spoke in Ituri whether, in their candid view, we should cease our activities there and go and, if not, what should we do better. The view was unanimous. We should stay, but we should ensure that we were more visible in the community and we should establish structures which ensure that our development initiatives enjoyed a reasonable degree of consensus in the surrounding communities.

The results of this stakeholder engagement have been cited by AGA as the reason why the company remained in operation in Mongwalu. Sir Sam Jonah, the AGA chairman at the time, published an article in a South African newspaper which explained why AGA took the management decision to remain in the DRC despite the issues surrounding the conflict and the risks they might pose to the company (Jonah 2006).

AngloGold Ashanti certainly found itself with dirty hands when in January its employees at its exploration camp were forced to hand over US$8,000 (R55,000) to members of the National Integrationist Front militia. Our mandate to operate derives from the transitional authority whose legitimacy is extensive. And that authority and the one that succeeds it after the elections need economic progress to sustain them. That said we still need to ensure that our presence does more good than harm.

How do we think we can do that? First, our policy must firmly state that no financial or logistical assistance can be given to rebel groups. Where a situation threatens that it may be unavoidable we need to withdraw. Second, we will not initiate any contact with such groups. Where such contact takes place unavoidably at their behest its nature needs to be recorded and limited to ensure it meets the above basic constraints. Third, continued dialogue must be maintained with legitimate authorities over these matters. We will also maintain communication with relevant non governmental organisations.

And finally as we continue our local economic development activities in the region we will redouble our efforts to ensure that it is done on a non partisan basis. We believe that continuing our activities on this kind of basis will do more for the peace process than those who would prefer to keep their hands clean by advocating an economic scorched earth approach. They might find should they succeed that they end up with far dirtier hands than ours'.

The responses outlined in the article by Jonah have begun to be put in place at a local level. AGA now states that in their current practice in Mongbwalu every time there is some form of interaction of any kind with any third party, from the mayor to the local commander of the MONUC force stationed in the town, a record is made and a summary of these interactions is regularly shared with executive management, local politicians, the UN and its joint venture partners, OKIMO. One of the key benefits of this, according to AGA, is that it makes project management reflect on their proposed actions before committing to a process:

Before he agrees to meet a local business owner or a political party leader, the manager asks himself, "Will I be happy for my corporate office, the UN Group of Experts on the DRC and HRW to know about this meeting?" If the answer is positive, there's a good chance that it passes the test of consistency with our business values. (Lenahan 2006)

AGA has also focused more attention on its approaches to local stakeholder engagement. Prior to the HRW report AGA had set up a community forum to act as a body to engage with the company. A total of 23 different community groups, from women's groups to indigenous pygmy groups, is represented. Representatives are elected by the constituent groups. The community forum initiates community development projects with the support of the company and it oversees their implementation and management. Most of these projects are in the fields of health care, education and infrastructure development. The community forum is also intended to be the vehicle through which the disbursement of foreign donor aid in the community is directed.

The establishment of a community forum is critical in ensuring a greater degree of communication and accountability between parties. It provides the community with more responsibility for communication and ensures that the mining company has a legitimate group to engage with. However, HRW has highlighted potential challenges to the community forum in acting as an effective mechanism for stakeholder engagement (Van Woudenberg, pers. comm.). For a start, the forum has to deal with historically complex relations with workers, traditional authorities, the community and artisanal miners. The process of electing people to the forum contributed to ethnic tensions and the mayor had to stop the elections at one point. Added political complexities were based on previous militia personnel being linked to participation in the forum. Furthermore, the forum has the potential of undermining the traditional rights of the local chief Nyali, the chief of the Kilo (the original inhabitants of the land, who were promoted as farmers under Belgian rule). The country's new mining code, which was established in 2003, provides traditional authorities with rights over the process and proceeds of mining and the chief may feel his authority is undermined by having to go through the forum in order to engage with the mining company.

Furthermore, HRW argues that the dual roles of the forum for stakeholder engagement, on the one hand, and the disbursement of development funds, on the other, may create tensions. However, HRW's suggestion that two separate bodies be established to carry out these different roles may be impractical, considering the dominant role of the mining company in the area and the need to reduce the duplication of community representation structures. Despite, or perhaps because of, the complexities and tensions at the local level surrounding the mine and exploration site, the company's attempts to develop a representative forum are well considered, though much depends on the skills and facilitation abilities of company staff that support and engage with the forum.

The future of mining in Ituri District

The mineral resource at Mongbwalu appears to look promising and AGA is willing to develop the project further. A second drill rig has recently arrived on site to speed up the feasibility studies. AGA now faces the challenge of rapidly developing the project while simultaneously building trust with local stakeholders and ensuring the project delivers sustainable benefits to the region and supports the strengthening of governance structures.

At a local level AGA faces challenges in how it makes social investments in community development projects. The key issue is that there are massive expectations of AGA to deliver development and these have to be managed. The community remembers the social benefits afforded to them by previous mining companies in the area, which have included schools, hospitals and libraries. The key management issues that AGA will need to address will be those faced in other mining areas with a similar history of paternalism, in which local communities expect development backlogs that were caused by previous joint ventures' failure to keep their promises to be fulfilled. Initial social investments during the exploration, development and construction phases will necessarily be small as revenues are not being generated. A fund of \$50,000 has been established, and there is an agreement that 1 per cent of pre-tax profits will be contributed to local sustainable development.

More generally, the limits of the company's responsibilities are unclear. In particular, in post-conflict areas with weak governance, there will be expectations that companies need to assume responsibilities that coincide with those of local governments and civil society. Collaborative approaches will be central to successfully negotiating these shared responsibilities (Hamann *et al.* 2005).

An additional local development challenge for AGA is that of artisanal mining. Artisanal mining has been on the increase in the Ituri area. There are approximately 100,000 miners operating in the area of the gold reserve. Many of these are former militia and are likely to be reluctant to leave the area and cease mining. The new mineral legislation recognises the status of artisanal miners but leaves their access to ore bodies up to negotiations between the artisanal miners and the company that holds the mineral rights. The presence of these miners increases the volatility of the situation because they have strong political allegiances and are firmly entrenched in the political dynamics of the area.

The social complexities in the area are significant. Political factions, the legacy of the war, high levels of poverty in communities, relations with the workforce, and artisanal miners are all connected. Establishing a successful mine in the context of a severely degraded social environment requires a focus on human rights and the role of the mine can play in both their protection and advancement. The mine and associated exploration activities and their complex interrelationships with the various stakeholders in the area, are firmly entrenched in communities' perceptions of their long-standing suffering.

At a wider level, AGA also needs to address its role in supporting good governance in the area. The DRC's new Constitution places heavy emphasis on local autonomy and, more significantly from the perspective of mining companies, cedes significant control over mining regulation and revenues to provincial governments. In addition, extensive autonomy has been granted to local governments. As with other countries where decentralisation has taken effect, mining companies in DRC shoulder increased burdens to assist with the delivery of public services and infrastructure on behalf of the local authority. Local authorities are often unable to meet the increased demand for public services and infrastructure resulting from the development of mining projects, particularly before they benefit from the increased revenue streams associated with the projects. As experience has also shown in other resource-rich states with weak governance, increased revenues and opportunities for rent-seeking can result in high levels of corruption.

The EITI, in which AGA is an active participant, is a global multi-stakeholder initiative focusing on the management of revenues and more transparent governance in resource-rich countries. Its key stipulation is that companies and host governments report on and account for all payments made by companies to host governments. The actual implementation of this objective may vary from country to country, but there generally needs to be an aggregating body that receives the information from the companies and the government. In other words, companies are not actually required to report

such information publicly. In contrast, the NGO coalition, Publish What You Pay, asks companies to make all its payments public.

The DRC government committed itself to the EITI in 2005 and a national EITI committee was set up with financial support from the government. Nevertheless, EITI requirements have yet to be implemented as at the time of writing. Instead, companies such as AGA have been constrained from publicly reporting on its payments to the government by a law that requires any such information to be vetted by parliament. Hence, AGA currently provides figures for payments to all relevant host governments except that of the DRC on its company website (see AngloGold Ashanti, n.d.). There is thus increasing pressure on the DRC government to implement its EITI commitment more rigorously (see, for instance, Publish What You Pay Coalition in the Democratic Republic of Congo, 2007) and there are recent signs that there is some renewed momentum with the establishment of a new multi-stakeholder EITI Committee in September 2007.

Conclusions

Investing in and re-entering the DRC during the period of conflict was clearly an incorrect decision to make by AGA. Though there is likely to be little legal certainty on the extent to which the company became complicit in human rights abuses or whether the actions of the FNI are within the company's sphere of influence, the company suffered significant reputation damage as a result of the publicity surrounding the payment. The risk of complicity in human rights violations could probably not be assessed well enough in such difficult and chaotic circumstances and there ought to be a precautionary principle guiding such decisions. Such a precautionary approach would generally emphasise a more risk-averse approach, taking into consideration the possibility of unforeseen events or circumstances. In this example, the company relied on a particular role by the UN in the area, and this reliance may have been part of the reason why the company was exposed to extortion by the rebel group. It also seems that these risks were not sufficiently considered during the merger between AngloGold and Ashanti, bearing in mind the complex history of interactions between the latter and the local communities. This experience therefore illustrated the broader importance of including human rights and other corporate responsibility considerations more carefully in mergers and acquisitions.

The company's decision to remain in the area subsequent to the payment is also difficult to assess, because so much depends on how the local and national governance system develops. There is little doubt that a mining operation such as AGA's proposed Ituri mine can provide crucial employment and income opportunities to the local population, the region and the country as a whole, as long as legitimate decision-making processes are established and supported at various levels of government. The present trajectory may be more benign than when AGA made its initial decision to re-enter the region in late 2004, and the company has also shown that it can make a contribution to improved governance at various levels. At the local level, this includes, for instance, the establishment of a local decision-making forum to guide the development of the mine and the company's social investment programme. At the national level, there is much hope that the EITI can become a catalyst for greater transparency in the payment and allocation of mining-related revenues, and the recent establishment of a new, multi-stakeholder EITI Commission with representatives from government, extractive industry companies and civil society is an encouraging development.

To conclude, AGA's experiences in the DRC and the company's engaged response to the HRW report arguably made an important contribution to the international debate on the role of big extractive companies in weak governance zones. The case highlights how difficult it is to assess and manage the risk of complicity in human rights abuses in such areas, and weighing these risks against the socio-economic development that large-scale investments promise is even more fraught. Another, broader question is whether – in the context of increasing pressure on companies to invest in such resource-rich areas – these risks to complicity in human rights abuses are being adequately considered, particularly among smaller companies that are less in the spotlight than companies like AGA.

The International Petroleum Industry Environmental Conservation Association social responsibility working group and human rights

Jenny Owens and Richard Sykes

Introduction: the oil and gas industry working together

The oil and gas industry operates in some of the most challenging places in the world and faces complex human rights-related issues in many of those locations. Ensuring good human rights policy and practice, both internally and externally, has become an important issue, not only for the communities in which the industry operates, but also for the worldwide reputations of the companies in the industry and for their ability to pursue future business opportunities.

Sharing information and experiences on human rights among companies is one valuable way in which the oil and gas industry seeks to improve its effectiveness in promoting human rights. The International Petroleum Industry Environmental Conservation Association (IPIECA) provides a forum for the open discussion of good practices on a variety of issues, including human rights. Since 1974 IPIECA has brought together oil and gas companies and associations to address existing and emerging social and environmental issues that arise from oil and gas operations.

Jenny Owens is social responsibility project manager and Richard Sykes is the executive secretary at the International Petroleum Industry Environmental Conservation Association (IPIECA), which was founded as a non-profit organisation in 1974. It is the single international association representing both the upstream and downstream oil and gas industry on key global environmental and social issues. IPIECA fosters dialogue between the industry and many international bodies, including the UN, and draws on the skills and experiences of its international membership through a number of working groups supported by a small secretariat.
Email: jenny.owens@ipieca.org
Richard Sykes attended Shell as a geologist in 1975 and took up the position of Group Environmental Manager in 1998. He has been active in climate change, biodiversity and public assurance and reporting and was chair of the IPIECA Climate Change Working Group from 2001–2005. In 2007 he joined IPIECA as executive secretary.
Email: Richard.sykes@ipieca.org

Currently it has over 30 member companies and 12 association members.

IPIECA draws on the expertise and experience of its members' representatives who come together in specialised work groups, such as climate change, biodiversity, oil spill preparedness and response, human health and social responsibility. In this way IPIECA also helps members to identify emerging global issues and assesses the potential impact those issues may have on the oil and gas industry.

Human rights fall under the jurisdiction of the Social Responsibility Working Group (SRWG), which was formed in 2002 to find ways to address key social responsibility issues such as human rights, capacity building and community development. This group provides a forum for IPIECA members to share information and enhance their understanding of social responsibility issues, challenges, and implications for the oil and gas industry; to engage with stakeholders and to co-ordinate on joint actions, such as participation in external initiatives and the development of good practices guidance on key subjects. The group aims to develop a consistent and credible industry voice on social responsibility issues and, in particular, to develop and share sound business practices to promote human rights.

How individual companies define the scope and nature of their responsibility when assessing and addressing human rights issues is being addressed by the industry and through the SRWG. There is no single answer to this question, especially as social and political environments vary greatly among the regions where companies operate. Additionally, there can be differing expectations among stakeholders on what role business should play in influencing human rights issues – sometimes to the point that certain organisations expect companies to fill the role that only governments have the legitimacy and responsibility to play. Companies therefore need to assess where and when they can be effective in improving social and environmental conditions, and make clear what roles they can play on local, regional, national and international levels. The next section explores the role the oil and gas industry can play in meeting human rights challenges in varying capacities.

Responsibility and influence

Under the Universal Declaration of Human Rights (UDHR), governments bear primary responsibility for protecting and promoting respect for human rights. However, the scope, scale and impact of the oil and gas industry in many countries can make oil and gas companies influential organs of society. Many reasonably expect that the companies will use what influence they have to promote respect for human rights.

In the oil and gas industry human rights issues are raised in differing circumstances with a wide variety of stakeholders. Depending on the stakeholder group, a company's ability to influence behaviour varies. In some stakeholder groups companies have a direct influence. In others, the company's role may be to influence behaviour indirectly. A useful framework, developed at a stakeholder workshop by IPIECA, seeks to divide responsibility and influence for promoting human rights in the oil and gas industry into three categories: direct responsibility, shared responsibility and indirect influence.

Direct responsibility

This refers to responsibilities that relate directly to company operations and to situations in which the company can exert direct influence. Human rights issues of concern to the oil and gas industry in this category include employee behaviour and rights (including health and safety and freedom of association) and, in some circumstances, the behaviour and rights of contractors working at company facilities, including security contractors.

Shared responsibility

This refers to responsibilities that are directly related to company operations, but which require joint action by several stakeholders. Examples of shared responsibilities in other social impact management areas may include working with impacted communities to improve their skills development, capacity building and education, and the long-term economic development of the community.

Another common shared responsibility that oil and gas companies may face is the possibility of influencing the behaviour of security forces assigned by the national government to protect their facilities. This may include insisting that training on human rights and acceptable security practices be provided to those security forces and urging that appropriate authorities investigate alleged human rights violations when the company has reason to believe those security forces may contribute to such violations. In attempting to influence the behaviour of security forces, oil and gas companies share responsibility with host national governments, human rights groups, community leaders, international organisations and other interested parties.

Indirect influence

This refers to issues indirectly related to company operations with respect to which a company may have an opportunity to support desired outcomes. The area of indirect influence of an oil and gas company may include its potential influence at a national or international level to encourage the general improvement of the human rights environment in a country. The oil and gas industry acknowledges that all parts of society, including business, are participants in that society who should proactively encourage the promotion and support the protection of such rights.

These three categorisations of influence for the oil and gas industry are explored in more depth here through a discussion of company and IPIECA activities, with specific case studies to illustrate a real life application of human rights activities.

Direct responsibility

The influence and accountability of a company for human rights starts in its immediate operations and extends at lesser levels to impacted communities and to regional and national stakeholders. Many believe that promoting human rights where companies have the greatest influence often produces the greatest demonstrable results. Communicating human rights policies and opening dialogue within the company and then progressively engaging local, regional and national actors can have an impact on the human rights environment surrounding a project and beyond.

Most companies operating in the oil and gas sector recognise the importance of putting in place effective human rights policies and practices – not only for their employees, but also for external stakeholders, such as their suppliers, local partners, local communities, security forces and governments. Accordingly, oil and gas companies throughout the world are now involved in promoting ethical business practices and human rights in a number of ways.

Social impact assessments (SIAs)

SIAs can assist oil and gas companies to understand the legal framework (including human rights) in a country, conducting social baseline studies, and engaging with the local community to develop a greater understanding of local values and customs. Knowledge gained from such efforts help companies develop programmes for community engagement, social investment, local content and economic development, monitoring and reporting frameworks, fair compensation for land acquisition and other measures that lead to broader human rights awareness and cultural sensitivity.

Through companies' internal departments and through IPIECA, the oil and gas industry continues to review and improve practices for understanding and managing potential social impacts of oil and gas activities. IPIECA has published a *Guide to social impact assessment* (IPIECA 2004) to promote the understanding and use of SIAs within the industry. The *Guide* provides managers of existing or new projects with an understanding of how to best use SIAs.

Human rights impact assessments (HRIAs)

In areas with high risks of human rights issues arising some companies are also implementing specific impact assessments for human rights. HRIAs help companies to ensure that the company's operations, local employees and private security personnel make the promotion and respect of human rights part of their core activities. This identification, assessment and planning for human rights issues is increasingly done before entering a country to help identify the degree of risk a potential investment faces in general. HRIAs also specifically help the company to anticipate and mitigate the risk of human rights abuses occurring from its activities or from external actors, such as public security forces assigned to protect the company's operations. Participants in the International Business Leaders Forum (IBLF), International Finance Corporation (IFC) and UN Global Compact (GC) have recently collaborated to produce a comprehensive guide to human rights impact assessment and management for business which will be road-tested with companies, including in the oil and gas industry over two years, culminating in a final revised publication in 2010).

Human rights and ethics training programmes

Many companies implement human rights and ethics training programmes for audiences ranging from lower level employees to management. Sometimes companies provide programmes for various community groups in their areas of operation as well.

In 2005 the member companies of IPIECA identified a need for general guidance for training managers and staff about human rights. In response IPIECA member companies shared human rights expertise, practices and policies and, working with human rights experts, developed an industry-wide template. The result was the publication in 2006 of the *Human rights training toolkit* – a training template that companies can customise to fit their existing human rights policies and applicable laws and regulations (IPIECA 2006).

The *Toolkit* consists of a presentation, a workbook, a trainer's manual and a resource guide. Core issues covered include labour rights, indigenous rights, security and law enforcement arrangements, dealing with corruption and transparency, and stakeholder issues.

The *Toolkit* also includes an overview of core international human rights treaties and instruments, a discussion of the role of business in general and the petroleum industry in particular on human rights, and an overview of the stakeholder concept.

One of the main strengths of the *Toolkit* is its versatility; companies can customise it to reflect their own human rights policies and to include regional or operation-specific materials. The *Toolkit* is being used by many companies to complement their existing human rights training sessions. The global audiences range from security personnel, corporate social responsibility (CSR) and human resources staff, and employees in high-risk countries. The *Toolkit* is currently translated into French and Spanish, with further translations possible in the future.

Building on the success of the *Toolkit*, the SRWG decided to hold several regional workshops to raise awareness of human rights issues among stakeholders and promote the use of the *Toolkit* for the oil and gas industry. The workshop concept was piloted in London in February 2006 to test the *Toolkit* with key stakeholders. A second workshop was held in Kuala Lumpur in November 2006. The objectives of this second workshop were to use the *Toolkit* to provide a high-level introduction to the topic of business and human rights to IPIECA members in the Asia–Pacific region and then to examine in more depth Asian perspectives on human rights and company experiences in the region. This workshop brought together experts from academia, business, and government, and international non-governmental organisations (NGOs).

Several key points were concluded from the workshop, some specifically addressing issues in

Asia and others applicable worldwide. Among the key conclusions were the importance of recognising indigenous rights as a distinct issue in human rights and of understanding companies' role in addressing indigenous rights issues. A third workshop held in Calgary in June 2007 concentrated specifically on indigenous peoples and the extractive industry, highlighting the experience of indigenous communities and resource development in North America – primarily Canada and Alaska. The fourth workshop was held in Buenos Aires in 2008, and IPIECA partnered with ARPEL, the Latin American regional association, to reach out to a wide membership. IPIECA plans to hold similar events in two further events in Cape Town in 2009 and the Middle East in 2010, and then to produce a document of good practices from the workshops for the industry.

Both the *Guide to social impact assessment* and the *Human rights training toolkit* provide companies with important baseline knowledge for raising awareness and improving practices on impact assessment and human rights. These publications are available for public use to encourage awareness of key industry issues, foster good practices, and promote dialogue with stakeholders. The *Guide* and the *Toolkit* are available to download free of charge on the IPIECA website at www.ipieca.org. IPIECA encourages not only its member companies, but also others in the industry and from different sectors to review, utilise and provide feedback on all publications.

Stakeholder engagement

Companies' relationships with external stakeholders, which may include governments, NGOs, local communities and security forces, are an important part of managing human right issues. Consultations and sharing information for constructive purposes between stakeholders help to maintain good relationships, which in turn facilitate dialogue on human rights between communities, countries and industry. For example, SIAs and HRIAs are not just tools for industry; they can also be used as a means of informing stakeholders, listening to their concerns and building their trust. Although SIAs and HRIAs may be carried out by the government, an external contractor, an NGO, or an internal team within the oil and gas company, they should include input from community members to build confidence that the impact assessment is objective.

The case study below describes one IPIECA member company's approach to assessing the potential social and human rights risk associated with its operations. Occidental Petroleum Corporation (Oxy) is a global oil and natural gas exploration and production company and a major North American chemical manufacturer.

Oxy: a constructive collaboration with International Alert and Fundacion Ideas Para la Paz (FIP) in Colombia

In 2005 Occidental de Colombia (Oxy) agreed with Ecopetrol (Colombia's national oil company) to jointly operate an enhanced oil recovery project at the La Cira oil field in the Middle Magdalena Valley, a region that has been impacted upon by violence and diminishing economic opportunities for the local population. Much of the project's future success depends on proactively addressing security, human rights, and social issues. In 2006 Oxy and Ecopetrol partnered with two NGOs to conduct an innovative social risk assessment of the project and the region. The purpose of the assessment was to identify issues that needed remediation, to find opportunities that could be developed and to comply with a key requirement of Oxy's human rights policy.

International Alert, a London-based conflict resolution and peace-building NGO that has been actively engaged in global multistakeholder initiatives to address development issues, was selected to conduct an independent assessment. International Alert used its proprietary tool, *Conflict sensitive business practices* (CSPB 2005), which allows companies to apply a two-way risk and impact analysis with a specific, but not exclusive, focus on issues of security and human rights. International Alert teamed with its local Colombian partner, FIP, on the pilot application of a human rights and social risk programme in La Cira to test the CSBP approach it had developed based on field research and consultation with various stakeholders.

The staff of Oxy and Ecopetrol, from managers to fieldworkers, participated in this collaborative effort through workshops, training, interviews and an extensive review of the project documents and socio-economic information on the region. After a three-month pilot a full risk assessment, including fieldwork, was conducted, providing valuable analysis and recommendations for addressing the social, security and economic impacts of the project. FIP and International Alert provided guidance in conducting the field analyses, as well as training for the La Cira project teams. To ensure the independence and autonomy of all parties involved, a formal memorandum of understanding (MoU) was drafted. This MoU set forth the specific roles of the NGOs and the companies in the effort.

The utilisation of the CSBP and the coaching from the NGOs provided guidance for current and future stakeholder consultation on issues including

- identifying specific actions for furthering engagement with private and public security forces in the region
- providing valuable feedback on key aspects of the La Cira project, including managing land issues with neighbours
- promoting safe utility use by local residents who had installed unsafe connections to the oil field pipes.

The most important long-term effect of the NGO collaboration has been the introduction of risk analysis and stakeholder engagement as a continuous practice.

Shared responsibility

Particularly in developing countries, oil and gas company activities can have socio-economic impacts on the surrounding communities. While these impacts are related to the oil and gas company's activities, they are influenced by a number of stakeholders. Common ways in which the industry is addressing some of its shared responsibilities are listed below.

Working with indigenous communities

The industry acknowledges indigenous communities' assertions of their customary rights to land and the communities' desire to maintain traditional ways of life, and it recognises that these issues must be resolved fairly. In addition to promoting indigenous rights' awareness, the industry plays a role in building capacity in indigenous communities and helping to strengthen communication between governments and communities for improved relationships.

The human rights concerns of indigenous people that may be implicated by company activities include respect for indigenous cultures and traditional land rights. Common issues include their rights to exist as distinct peoples, their continued practise of traditions and customs, and their continued use of traditional land. It is crucial in these cases that companies work with qualified partners to engage in meaningful consultations, especially as many indigenous communities live in political environments in which various groups have differing views on their rights to land and resources.

Indigenous communities are particularly vulnerable because they often have the least access to government channels of decision-making. Oil and gas companies are therefore working with communities or organisations that represent communities to ensure that decisions regarding land and resource usage and the implications of these are made with the understanding and support of communities.

Developing partnerships

The past decade has seen a substantial increase in the number of multi-stakeholder partnering initiatives in the oil and gas industry. These initiatives derive value from the different perspectives and skills of the various partners. The industry has utilised different combinations of NGOs, governments, international governmental organisations, international finance institutions and community groups to advance research, develop policy and implement programmes.

Experience in the industry has shown that multi-stakeholder partnerships make greater progress toward human rights goals than one company can achieve acting alone. In July 2006 IPIECA published a document called *Partnerships in the oil and gas industry* (IPIECA 2006). This document shares the successes, challenges and lessons learned by IPIECA members and their partners working together to address a number of

issues including human rights. And in 2008 IPIECA hosted a two-day dialogue with nearly 50 stakeholders drawn from member companies and external stakeholder groups such as academia, civil society and government to validate that IPIECA is addressing the right issues as the basis for the direction and content of its work plan.

Partnerships enable oil and gas companies to contribute to human rights initiatives with a reduced risk of being solely responsible for deliverables outside their expertise, while at the same time offering their competencies to assist partners in project development and implementation. Partnerships thus enable the sharing of costs, benefits, risks and responsibilities for an initiative, and they can provide some legitimacy to oil and gas companies' commitment to address human rights issues. Additionally, multi-stakeholder partnerships can enhance the quality of initiatives. Involving a number of parties – particularly if they come from different sectors and have not worked together before – can leverage additional resources, bring new knowledge and build a platform for innovation and creativity.

Successful partnering initiatives are those that include actors such as governments that are capable of long-term commitments and that can build institutional capacity. While having a national government as a partner presents both risks and opportunities, its presence increases the chance of influencing behaviour in a broad societal context, and it offers a long time-frame to develop the kinds of relationships that are needed to effect substantive change. Creating effective partnerships with governments, NGOs and communities through the implementation of social investment projects help to ensure their sustainability. Past experience has shown that projects based solely on financial support from companies do not, most of the time, outlast the company's presence in the region.

A partnership approach has also been effective when significant social tensions, such as human rights issues, exist between local communities and oil companies. Where a company and an NGO have a long-standing, strategic partnership, the NGO is often able to act as a conduit for the company to engage with local communities. These relationships can prevent conflicts by creating open channels of communication and by building a fund of trust that companies and communities can draw on when they need to discuss local grievances.

Partnerships are essentially about joint action. The act of jointly establishing a partnering relationship, jointly designing and managing an initiative, and jointly sharing risks, costs and benefits is an intensive undertaking that requires – and can generate – a close working relationship. In addition, partnerships work only if they deliver benefits for all partners. They require an appreciation and leveraging of complementary competencies and they can take time to deliver outcomes, but some outcomes cannot be attained except through partnership, and partnerships often achieve more widely accepted and lasting results.

Supporting and participating in external initiatives

A significant number of oil and gas companies are supporting the development of international voluntary initiatives on human rights and ethics, including the UN Global Compact, the Voluntary Principles on security and human rights (Voluntary Principles) and the Extractive Industries Transparency Initiative. Many companies have joined these initiatives or have adopted parts of them for their corporate policies and practices and some have incorporated aspects of the initiatives into contracts with suppliers.

IPIECA monitors and participates in a number of these external initiatives. It regularly updates member companies on these initiatives in an effort to foster understanding, raise awareness, encourage involvement and identify the potential implications of these initiatives for its members.

The Voluntary Principles are an attempt to address a specific issue of human rights and security with respect to extractive industries' operations. In early 2000 the USA and the UK governments, a number of mining and oil and gas companies, several international human rights NGOs and a trade union initiated a year-long, multi-stakeholder effort to address security and human rights concerns. The participants drafted guidelines to address security issues. The principles were designed to provide practical guidance on implementing the guidelines. Officially announced in December 2000, the Voluntary Principles cover three key areas: conducting risk assessments in the context of security and human rights issues; engaging with public security forces (military and police); and engaging with private security forces.

The Voluntary Principles illustrate the opportunities and challenges of a multi-stakeholder approach. Their success will depend on the strengths and legitimacy that each partner brings to the process. Companies offer the experience of working on the ground and of implementing programmes at an operational level. Home governments are able to convene diverse stakeholders around mutual goals and provide diplomatic channels to engage host governments. NGOs bring expertise in human rights issues, including knowledge of local civil society in the regions in which companies operate. IPIECA is an official observer to the Voluntary Principles process together with the International Committee of the Red Cross and the International Council on Mining and Metals. Many of IPIECA's member companies are among those involved in the process. In addition, numerous other companies that are actively implementing the Voluntary Principles already have shown interest in joining the initiative and, conversely, the participants of the Voluntary Principles are continually reaching out to companies, governments and NGOs who fit the participation criteria to join as members.

The Voluntary Principles have gained support from the private, public and civil sectors globally since their launch eight years ago. In addition to the current 29 official participants a number of other companies have adopted and implemented the Voluntary Principles or portions of them. Moreover, multilateral institutions, such as the International Finance Corporation and the Organization for Economic Cooperation and Development, are now referencing the Voluntary Principles in their guidelines and standards.

Due to their unique systems and policies, each of the company members of the Voluntary Principles has implemented the principles in a different way, and their progress has varied. However, companies on the whole have achieved significant milestones in the initiative's first eight years. Specifically, several companies have procedures for anonymously reporting human rights abuses and offer whistleblower protection. Many companies believe the Voluntary Principles have increased awareness of human rights and security issues among their staff and a number of companies have conducted related training for public and private security personnel and company staff. All participating companies report on their implementation of the Voluntary Principles in their corporate responsibility reports. Other IPIECA member companies, which are not yet full participants in the Voluntary Principles, apply the principles in their security operations.

The three pillars of the Voluntary Principles (governments, companies and NGOs) represent diverse stakeholders with varying objectives and approaches. These stakeholders have identified common interests and have worked together constructively to reach consensus on a set of principles, but translating this consensus on the principles into agreement on practical action has proved challenging. An important milestone was achieved in Washington in May 2007 with agreement on participation criteria aimed at enhancing the credibility of the initiative. Further work on governance and reporting criteria is continuing. The participants welcome the forum provided by the Voluntary Principles to share best practices and discuss common challenges related to security in difficult environments.

The Voluntary Principles for security and human rights have continued to develop since their launch in 2000, gathering momentum and winning acceptance by a number of major companies in the industry. While continued effort will be necessary to promote the adoption of the Voluntary Principles throughout the industry, this initiative demonstrates that a multi-stakeholder partnership can begin to address human rights issues that would be impossible for any single actor to resolve alone. (For more information see Voluntary Principles on Security and Human Rights n.d.). BP, a global energy company, has been an active participant in the Voluntary Principles initiative. In the case study that follows, BP provides an example of how it has utilised these principles in one particular area of its operations.

BP: embedding human rights and the Voluntary Principles in the Tangguh Project, Indonesia

The Tangguh liquefied natural gas project is located about 3,200 km from Jakarta on the south shore of Berau–Bintuni Bay in the new Regency of Teluk Bintuni. The communities around the bay consist of small, isolated villages with between 30 to 100 families.

BP supports the UDHR and the Voluntary Principles on security and human rights. It has embedded human rights within the whole Tangguh project, including in its approach to communities, the workforce and security. Dialogue is an important channel for BP when trying to promote a wider understanding of human rights with stakeholders and when trying to foster greater understanding and the use of best practices.

BP's approach to providing security is an integrated community-based security programme with the view that community support is the best security for the project. The programme draws on human rights principles and partnerships. BP has developed field guidelines, agreed to by Papua police and endorsed by related government agencies, which clarify roles and responsibilities in security provision. The Voluntary Principles and independent assessment are incorporated into these guidelines. They include procedures on investigation and reporting of alleged human rights violations.

One important aspect of the Tangguh operations is that the security forces, who are Papuan, are required to be unarmed. In 2005 and early 2006 the training of security personnel was carried out in collaboration with leading Papuan-based human rights organisations. There are a number of initiatives to promote good relationships and partnership between the company, the community and the police. These initiatives include community policing, the establishment of 24 village forums, and training and facilitation support.

Indirect influence

The area of indirect influence is one of the most complex for oil and gas companies. Different actors in society with an interest in an oil and gas project may have differing views of the potential impact of a company's indirect influence on human rights issues in the area around the company's operations or within an entire country. Defining and agreeing upon the boundaries of companies' roles and responsibilities with regard to human rights is often difficult. Improving engagement with all stakeholders is critical to achieving a consensus on those issues.

Opinions also differ on whether and how a company's indirect influence might be exercised and whether it is more productive to have detailed rules to determine behaviour or general statements of values that a company can use to guide operational decisions. Although the scope of a company's indirect influence will depend on the local conditions, companies can sometimes play a role in positively influencing government human rights practices.

The case study that follows from a Norwegian oil and gas company, StatoilHydro, illustrates how a successful partnership with a national NGO has been utilised to promote international human rights law in Nigeria, outside the company's direct project operations.

StatoilHydro: human rights training of Sharia judges in Nigeria

StatoilHydro has been exploring oil and gas in Nigeria since 1992 and has supported CSR projects in the county since 1996. StatoilHydro CSR projects entail partnerships with either NGOs or UN organisations. The company does not have its own field staff for these projects, choosing instead to focus on its area of expertise – exploring for oil and gas – while its partners implement the selected CSR projects.

After years of undemocratic leadership and neglect and numerous breaches of human rights, Nigeria turned its attention to addressing human rights issues. In 2001 StatoilHydro decided to support organisations working on human rights issues in the country. This support was in addition to its award-winning Akassa community development project and less extensive support of other NGO projects.

StatoilHydro spent significant time and effort screening potential cooperation partners and meeting the 10 organisations on its shortlist. The company asked for proposals for projects that could be implemented within one year. It also stated its intention to establish a long-term partnership after the first year if both parties saw value in doing so. From the proposals submitted, StatoilHydro selected those from three organisations: the Civil Liberties Organisation,

the Prisoners Welfare and Rehabilitation Action, and the Legal Defence and Assistance Project (LEDAP), which is described here.

Established in 1996, LEDAP is an NGO with headquarters in Lagos and branch offices in five Nigerian states. LEDAP's members are lawyers or others with professional legal training. The organisation disseminates legal knowledge and insight about human rights and good governance in Nigeria.

The LEDAP proposal that StatoilHydro agreed to fund was to teach and train Sharia judges from a number of northern states that have implemented Sharia, or Islamic law. Sharia judges at local level often have limited formal legal training. Some might be illiterate. They are mainly religious leaders and make their judgements by drawing on Islamic teachings and guidelines from the Koran. Many of the judges are unaware of Nigeria's position regarding the UN UDHR and other human rights resolutions.

LEDAP developed and delivered two-day training seminars for the Sharia judges on human rights principles, women's rights, just interrogation principles and their integration into the administration of Islamic law, and legal procedures and administration. Three years of training have given 450 Sharia judges from seven northern states (approximately 20 per cent of the Sharia judges in the country), some insight into human rights issues. Both StatoilHydro and LEDAP report that their experiences have been positive and that their initial concerns have proved unfounded. Specifically, StatoilHydro has had no accusations from government officials or observers of interference in the country's political processes. Moreover, administrators in some states have established links to LEDAP and from time to time use its staff as legal consultants and advisers.

Most importantly, the training has been popular and well received by the Sharia judges. For instance, in the evaluations of two seminars in 2004, all participants stated that the training had given them knowledge that was directly applicable to their daily work as Sharia judges. The relationship between StatoilHydro and LEDAP has gradually developed from one in which StatoilHydro provided support to an NGO "working on a good cause" into a partnership that involves consultations on questions of strategic significance.

From the StatoilHydro–LEDAP partnership to date we have learned the following:

- Be bold when picking partners and projects. According to some observers, selecting human rights, partnering with LEDAP and training Sharia judges were bold actions.
- Spend time evaluating potential partners and selecting partners.
- Build relations with people, not only with organisations.
- Spend time on mutual understanding of project tasks and expectations.
- Set up a simple but clear partnership contract. Be sure to build in start and ending dates.
- Establish a tight dialoguing and monitoring system.
- Release funds based on milestones and reporting.
- Ensure that the funder has a way to exit the partnership so that the ending of the funding will not harm the project.

Statoil initially considered that its reputational risk in setting up an NGO human rights partnership in Nigeria was high and the chances of gaining the desired reward were limited. Now, this type of human rights partnership is at the core of the company's CSR strategy and is the reason the company has undertaken similar initiatives elsewhere.

Going forward

Although much has been achieved in the last few years, there is a recognition that the private sector can continue to build expertise and knowledge in this area to support human rights. In addition, although many companies in the oil and gas industry are implementing sound policies and striving to achieve long-term benefits, a gap remains between what society (especially NGOs) expect of companies (as opposed to governments) and what is within these companies' expertise and capacity to achieve.

Recognising this fact and responding to continued discussion on the issue of human rights and transnational corporations and other business enterprises, in July 2005 the then UN Secretary General Kofi Annan appointed Harvard Professor John Ruggie as a Special Representative on business and human rights. Professor Ruggie's mandate was to identify and clarify standards of corporate responsibility and accountability with regard to human rights. In March 2007 Professor Ruggie presented his second report on business and human rights. The report represents a staging post towards completing his mandate. Central to the report is the recognition that international law firmly establishes that governments have a duty to protect human rights and that laws enacted or recognised by states set the standards with which all social actors, including businesses, must comply. The industry believes that governments' duty to protect and promote human rights should not be diminished and that ensuring governments discharge their human rights obligations effectively remains an essential requirement to progress in this area.

The special representative's findings uphold the view that international human rights instruments do not impose direct responsibilities on corporations. In addition, the second report confirms the emergence of Coluntary initiatives involving governments, business and civil society, and points to the key role that these mechanisms will play in charting the future course of human rights efforts and filling gaps in the international legal framework. Initiatives such as the Voluntary Principles attest to the growing attention paid by oil and gas companies to human rights. The success of these voluntary initiatives will, in large part, depend on each pillar's willingness to engage constructively with prospective applicants that are seeking assistance with improving human rights awareness and implementation. The Special Representative's final report was presented in 2008. It summarised Professor Ruggie's strategic assessment of the legal and policy measures that states and other social actors could take, including views and recommendations about which options or combinations might work best to create effective remedies on the ground. The report sets out a three-pronged framework: the state's duty to protect human rights; corporate duty to respect human rights; and the need for greater access to remedy for human rights grievances. Professor Ruggie's mandate was extended a further three years to 2011, during which time he and his team will work to provide practical recommendations on how to implement this framework.

To date there has been significant research into understanding, anticipating and assessing the impact of steps to deal with human rights dilemmas that the industry may face. IPIECA's SIA guidance and the *Human rights training toolkit* are products of this research. Further research is continually being conducted into other critical human rights issues where companies have direct or shared responsibility, such as working in conflict zones, or perhaps where there is an opportunity to indirectly improve communities' access to human rights through developing sustainable social investment projects.

The world's increasing demand for energy is pushing the oil and gas industry into ever more difficult areas of the world, including areas suffering from conflict or the threat of conflict. Conflict zones raise human rights challenges for oil and gas companies trying to operate in them and one area for industry to explore is constructive engagement. A *Guide to operating in areas of conflict for the oil and gas industry* has now been published was produced by IPIECA in 2008 to provide company managers with an accessible tool to assess and manage risk when operating in an environment of potential or already existing conflict, paying special attention to the importance of human rights and, where possible, encouraging their promotion.

Another issue that IPIECA members have explored is how to is implement sustainable social investment projects. Many companies have implemented social and community investment programmes in the areas where they operate with the aim of promoting socio-economic development. However, companies often find it difficult to quantify and measure the long-term impacts of their social investment performance and what influence it may have on their access to human rights. With a defined or limited life-span of any operation in a specific region, it is important for companies to build sustainability into their social investment programmes to ensure the benefits survive its presence in a community. An IPIECA *Guide to creating successful, sustainable social investment for the oil and gas industry,* published in 2008, summarises best practices and lessons learned, and provides a framework model for success, including indicators or methods to measure social investment impacts.

IPIECA and its member companies are working to understand these issues better, and the recent publications are now available for companies to use for training employees or to incorporate into their operational planning. However, discussion continues on how the private sector can become more proactive in promoting the principles set out in the UDHR. One suggestion has been for companies to report regularly on steps taken and results achieved with respect to human rights. The *Oil and gas industry guidance on voluntary sustainability reporting* (IPIECA 2005) includes a human rights indicator. However this performance indicator, like many used in other sectors, only measures effort. The difficult challenge of measuring impact is yet to be met in both the public and private sector. Measuring performance on human rights could encourage all companies in the industry to join voluntary initiatives and to implement human rights policies and practices.

Preventing human rights abuses will continue to be a matter of growing importance for the foreseeable future. Dialogue must continue in the industry and between the industry and governments, multilateral organisations and NGOs to understand and define the roles and responsibilities of the different sectors, public, private and non-government; to develop and implement actions and partnerships to promote human rights; and to measure performance in this area. Perhaps the most noteworthy conclusions of the Special Representative's second report are that "no single silver bullet can resolve the business and human rights challenge" and that "a broad array of measures is required, by all relevant actors" based on the notion of shared responsibility (Ruggie 2007). In particular, governments must meet their responsibility to address human rights and revenue management issues.

References

ACEMOGLU, D. AND ROBINSON, J. A. 2000. "Political losers as a barrier to economic development (political economy, governance and development)", *AEA Papers and Proceedings*, 90 (2), 126–130.

ACEMOGLU, D. AND ROBINSON, J. A. 2006. "Economic backwardness in political perspective", *American Political Science Review*, 100 (1), 115–131.

ACEMOGLU, D., JOHNSON, S. AND ROBINSON, J. 2001. "The colonial origins of comparative development: an empirical investigation", *American Economic Review*, 91 (5), 1369–1401.

ACEMOGLU, D., JOHNSON, S. AND ROBINSON, J. A. 2003. "An African success story: Botswana", *In:* Rodrik, D., ed. *In search of prosperity: analytic narratives on economic growth*. Princeton NJ: Princeton University Press, 80–119.

ACHEN, C. 2000. *Why lagged dependent variables can suppress the explanatory power of other independent variables*. Paper read at the Annual Meeting of the Political Methodology Section of the American Political Science Association, UCLA 20–22 July.

AFRICAN DEVELOPMENT BANK 2007. *Selected statistics on African countries*. Vol. 26. Economic and Social Statistics Division. Tunis: 1–300.

AHEAD ENERGY CORPORATION. 2007. *Professional resources to optimize sustainable solutions*. Rochester, NY: AHEAD.

AKHMEDOV, I. 2006. *Neftyanoy blesk economiki*. Baku: CBS-PP.

AMNESTY INTERNATIONAL 2005. "Nigeria: New evidence of human rights violations in oil-rich Niger Delta" AFR 44/025/20053 November. Available online at http://www.amnesty.org/en/library/info/AFR44/025/2005 Accessed 30 October 2008.

AMUDSEN, I. AND ABREU, C. 2006. *Civil society in Angola: inroads, space and accountability*. CMI Report No. R2006:14. Bergen: Chr Michelsen Institute.

ANGLOGOLD ASHANTI n.d. Home page. Available online at http://www.anglogoldashanti.com. Accessed 11 September 2007.

ANGLOGOLD ASHANTI 2005. "Human Rights Watch report on AngloGold Ashanti's activities in the DRC". News release 1 June 2005. Available online at http://test.anglogold.co.za/Press/Press + Releases.htm Accessed 4 November 2008.

ANON 1994. "Viet Nam finds success in program aimed at building oil and gas capacity", *The Oil and Gas Journal*, 92 (48). Available online at http://www.ogj.com/display_article/13692/7/ARCHI/none/none/1/VIET-NAM-FINDS-SUCCESS-IN-PROGRAM–AIMED-AT-BUILDING-OIL-AND-GAS-CAPACITY/ Accessed 4 November 2008.

ASADOV., F. 2000. "Oil caravans of XXI century on the Great Silk Road: what the future has in store for Azerbaijan and Kazakhstan", Online. Central Asia and the Caucasus (Sweden), No 6.

AUTY, R. M. 1990. *Resource-based industrialization: sowing the oil in eight developing countries*. Oxford: Clarendon Press.

AUTY, R. M. 2000. "How natural resources affect economic development", *Development Policy Review*, 18 (4), 347–364.

AUTY, R. M., ed. 2001. *Resource abundance and economic development*. Oxford: Oxford University Press.

AUTY, R. M. 2007. "Patterns of rent-extraction and deployment in developing countries: implications for governance, economic policy and performance", *In:* Mavrotas, G.

and Shorrocks, A., eds *Advancing development: core themes in global development*. London: Palgrave, 555–577.

AUTY, R. M. AND MIKESELL, R. F. 1998. *Sustaining development in mineral economies*. Oxford: Oxford University Press.

BACH, T. S. 2001. "Civil society and NGOs in Vietnam: some initial thoughts on development and obstacles". Paper presented at the Meeting with the Delegation of the Swedish Parliamentary Commission on Swedish Policy for Global Development to Vietnam 26/2–3/3/2002 available online at http://www.ngocentre.org.vn/files/docs/CSandNGOs%20in%20Vietnam.rtf Accessed 18 January 2009.

BAKER INSTITUTE 2007. "The changing role of national oil companies in international energy market". Policy report No. 35. April. Houston, TX: James A. Baker III Institute for Public Policy.

BANK OF BOTSWANA (2006). *Annual report 2006*. Gaberone: Bank of Botswana.

BARROWS, G. 1988. "A survey of incentives in recent petroleum contracts", *In:* Beredjick, N. and Wälde, T., eds *Petroleum investment policies in developing countries*. London: Graham & Trotman.

BARROWS, G. 1997. *World fiscal systems for oil*. New York: Barrows Company.

BASEDAU, M. AND LACHER, W. 2006. "A paradox of plenty? Rent distribution and political stability in oil states", GIGA WP 21/2006. GIGA research program: dynamics of violence and security cooperation. Hamburg: German Institute for Global and Area Studies.

BEBLAWI, H. 1990. "The rentier state in the Arab world", *In:* Luciani, G., ed. *The Arab state*. Berkeley, CA: University of California Press.

BECK, N. AND KATZ, J. N. 1995. "What to do (and not to do) with time-series cross-section data", *American Political Science Review*, 89 (3), 634–647.

BECK, N., KATZ, J. N. AND TUCKER, R. 1998. "Taking time seriously: time-series-cross-section analysis with a binary dependent variable", *American Journal of Political Science*, 42 (4), 1260–1288.

BEHNKE, A. 2007. "Presence and creation: a few (meta-)critical comments on the c.a.s.e. manifesto", *Security Dialogue*, 38 (1) March 105–111.

BELLIN, E. 2004. "The political-economic conundrum: the affinity of economic and political reform in the Middle East and North Africa", The Middle East series No. 53. Washington, DC: Carnegie Endowment for International Peace.

BEVAN, D. L., COLLIER, P. AND GUNNING, J. W. 1999. *Nigeria and Indonesia: the political economy of poverty, equity and growth*. New York: Oxford University Press.

BIERSTEKER, T. J. 1987. *Multinationals, the state, and control of the Nigerian economy*. Princeton, NJ: Princeton University Press.

BLACK, T. AND MARTINEZ, A. 2008. *Pemex missteps pare oil revenues, pave way for Petrobras entry*, Bloomberg, 31 March. Available online at http://www.bloomberg. com/apps/news?pid = 20601086& refer = latin_america&sid = a7pcyPC6LgXk Accessed 4 November 2008.

BOLT, K., MATETE, M. AND CLEMENS, M. 2002. "Manual for calculating adjusted net savings", Environment Department. Washington, DC: World Bank.

BOURGUINON, F. 1988. "Venezuela: absorption without growth", *In:* Gelb, A. H., *Oil windfalls: blessing or curse?* NewYork: Oxford University Press, 289–325.

BRAMBOR, T., ROBERTS CLARK, W. AND GOLDER, M. 2006. "Understanding interaction models: improving empirical analyses", *Political Analysis*, 14 (1), 63–82.

BRAUMOELLER, B. F. 2004. "Hypothesis testing and multiplicative interaction terms", *International Organization*, 58 (4), 807–820.

BP 2007. *BP statistical review of world energy 2007*. London: BP.

BUENO DE MESQUITA, B., DOWNS, G. W., SMITH, A. AND CHERIF, F. M. 2005. "Thinking inside the box: a closer look at democracy and human rights", *International Studies Quarterly*, 49 (2), 439–457.

BUGALA, P. 2006. *Transparency begins at home. An assessment of United States revenue transparency and EITI requirements*. Oxham America and Publish What You Pay, June.

BULL, H. 2002. *The anarchical society. a study of order in world politics*. New York: Columbia University Press.

BULTE, E. H., DAMANIA, R. AND DEACON, R. T. 2005. "Resource intensity, institutions and development", *World Development*, 33 (7), 1029–1044.

CANAGARAJAH, S. AND SAJI, T. 2001. "Poverty in a wealth economy: the case of Nigeria", *Journal of African Economies*, 10 (2), 143–173.

CAREY, S. AND POE, S. C., eds 2004. *Understanding human rights violations: new systematic studies*. Aldershot: Ashgate.

CASPIAN DEVELOPMENT ADVISORY PANEL (n.d.) Home page. Available online at http://www.caspsea.com Accessed 30 October 2008.

CENTRAL INTELLIGENCE AGENCY 2007. *The world factbook*. Available online at https://www.cia.gov/ library/publications/the-world-factbook/index.html Accessed 4 November 2008.

CHANG, H. 2007. *State-owned enterprise reform*. United Nations Department for Economic and Social Affairs. Available online at http://esa.un.org/techcoop/ documents/PN_SOEReformNote. pdf Accessed 4 November 2008.

CHAUDHRY, K. A. 1997. *The price of wealth: economies and institutions in the Middle East*. Ithaca, NY: Cornell University Press.

CINGRANELLI, D. L. AND RICHARDS, D. L. 1999. "Measuring the level, pattern and sequence of government respect for physical integrity rights", *International Studies Quarterly*, 43 (2), 407–417.

CIRI HUMAN RIGHTS DATA PROJECT (n.d.) Home page. Available online at http://ciri.binghamton.edu/ index.asp Accessed 30 October 2008.

COALITION OF AZERBIJAN NGOS (2005) "For improving transparency in extractive industries". Press release 31 March. Available online at http://www. eiti-az.org/ts_gen/eng/feal/eng_ f11_PR_2005_03_31.htm Accessed 30 October 2008.

CASE COLLECTIVE 2006. "Critical approaches to security in Europe: a networked manifesto", *Security Dialogue*, 37 (4), 443–487.

COLLIER, P. 2007. *The bottom billion. Why the poorest countries are failing and what can be done about it*. New York: Oxford University Press.

COLLIER, P. AND GODERIS, B. 2007. *Commodity prices, growth and the natural resource curse: reconciling a conundrum*. Centre for the Study of African Economies. Working paper series 2007–15. Oxford: University of Oxford.

COLLIER, P. AND HOEFFLER, A. 1998. "On economic causes of civil war", *Oxford Economic Papers*, 50, 563–573.

COLLIER, P. AND HOEFFLER, A. 2004. "Greed and grievance in civil war", *Oxford Economic Papers*, 56 (4), 563–595.

COLLIER, P. AND HOEFFLER, A. 2005. "Resource rents, governance and conflict", *Journal of Conflict Resolution*, 49 (4), 625–633.

COLLIER, P. AND HOEFFLER, A. 2006. "Testing the neo-con agenda:

democracy in resource-rich societies". Working paper, Oxford: Department of Economics.

COLLIER, P., ELLIOT, L., HEGRE, H., HOEFFLER, A., EYNAL-QUEROL, M. AND SAMBANIS, N. 2003. *Breaking the conflict trap: civil war and development policy*. Oxford: Oxford University Press.

COLLIER, P., HOEFFLER, A. AND SODERBOM, M. 2003. "On the duration of civil war". Available online at http://users.ox.ac.uk/~econ0109/jpr04.pdf Accessed 1 December 2007.

DAUNDERSTÄDT, M. AND SCHILDBERG, A. 2006. *Dead ends of transition: rentier economies and protectorates*. Frankfurt: Campus.

DAVENPORT, C. AND ARMSTRONG, D. A. II. 2004. "Democracy and the violation of human rights: a statistical analysis from 1976 to 1996", *American Journal of Political Science*, 48 (3), 538–554.

DE RENZIO, P. AND KRAFCHIK, W. 2007. *Lessons from the field: the impact of civil society budget analysis and advocacy in six countries*. Washington, DC: International Budget Project.

DE SOYSA, I. 2002. "Paradise is a bazaar? Greed, creed and governance in civil war, 1989–1999", *Journal of Peace Research*, 39 (4), 395–416.

DE SOYSA, I. 2006. "The empirical evidence for the resource curse", *In:* Daunderstädt, M. and Schildberg, A., eds *Dead ends of transition: rentier economies and protectorates*. Frankfurt: Campus.

DE SOYSA, I. AND NORDÅS, R. 2007. "Islam's bloody innards? Religion and political terror, 1981–2000", *International Studies Quarterly* 51927–943.

DELL, M. 2004. "The devil's excrement: the negative effects of natural resources on development", *Harvard International Review*, 26 (3), 1–5.

DEMING, D. 2003. "Are we running out of oil?" *Policy Backgrounder*, 159 29 January.

DEPARTMENT FOR INTERNATIONAL DEVELOPMENT 2005. *Extractive industries transparency initiative*. Source Book.

DIETSCHE, E. 2007. *The quality of institutions: a cure for the "resource curse"?* Oxford: Oxford Policy Institute.

DIETZ, S., NEUMAYER, E. AND DE SOYSA, I. 2006. "Corruption, the resource curse and genuine saving", *Environment and Development Economics*, 12 (1), 33–53.

DREHER, A. AND RUPPRECHT, S. M. 2007. "IMF programs and reforms: inhibition or encouragement?", *Economic Letters*, 95 (3), 320–326.

DURUIGBO, E. 2003. *Multinational corporations and international law: accountability and compliance issues in the petroleum industry*. Ardsley, NY: Transnational Publishers.

EASTERLY, W. AND LEVINE, R. 1997. "Africa's growth tragedy: policies and ethnic divisions", *Quarterly Journal of Economics*, 112 (4), 1203–1250.

EBENHACK, B. W. 2005. "Clarifying the limits of petroleum production", Paper read at the 2005 Annual Meeting of the American Institute of Chemical Engineers (AIChE) in Cincinnati, Ohio.

ECKSTEIN, H. 1966. *Division and cohesion in democracy, a study of Norway*. Princeton, NJ: Princeton University Press.

ECONOMIST INTELLIGENCE UNIT 2007. *Angola: country profile 2007*. London: EIU.

ENERGY INFORMATION ADMINISTRATION (EIA 2006). *Country analysis briefs*. Available online at http://www.eia.doe.gov/emeu/cabs/ Accessed 4 November 2008.

EIFERT, B., GELB, A. AND TALLROTH, N. B. 2003. "Managing oil wealth", *Finance and Development*, 40(1). Available online at http://www.imf.org/external/pubs/ft/fandd/2003/

03/eife.htm Accessed 4 November 2008.

ELIAS, V. J. 1978. "Sources of economic growth in Latin American countries", *Review of Economics and Statistics*, 60 (3), 362–370.

ENVIRONMENTAL RIGHTS ACTION AND FRIENDS OF THE EARTH NIGERIA 2005. *Flaring gas in Nigeria: a human rights, environmental and economic monstrosity*. Environmental Rights Action and the Climate Justice Programme, Amsterdam, June 2005. Available online at http://www.foei.org/en/publications/pdfs/gasnigeria.pdf Accessed 4 November 2008.

EXTRACTIVE INDUSTRIES TRANSPARENCY INITIATIVE n.d. Home page. Available online at http://www.eitransparency.org Accessed 3 November 2008.

EXTRACTIVE INDUSTRIES TRANSPARENCY INITIATIVE (EITI) 2005. *Extractive industries transparency initiative source book*. Available online at http://eitransparency.org/document/sourcebook Accessed 1 December 2007.

EXTRACTIVE INDUSTRIES TRANSPARENCY INITIATIVE (EITI) 2007. "Democratic Republic of Congo (country profile)". Available online at http://www.eitransparency.org Accessed 4 September 2007.

FEARON, J. D. 2005. "Primary commodities exports and civil war", *Journal of Conflict Resolution*, 49 (4), 483–507.

FEARON, J. D. AND LAITIN, D. D. 2003. "Ethnicity, insurgency, and civil war", *American Political Science Review*, 97 (1), 1–16.

FEE, D. 1988. *Petroleum exploitation strategy*. London: Belhaven Press.

FEDERAL EMERGENCY MANAGEMENT AGENCY (FEMA) 2007. *Energy security and sustainability in Africa*. Nairobi: FEMA.

FERGUSON, J. 2006. *Global shadows: Africa in the neoliberal world order.* Durham, NC: Duke University Press.

FORERO, J. 2003. "Texaco goes on trial in Ecuador pollution case", *The New York Times,* October 23. Available online at http://query. nytimes.com/gst/fullpage.html? res=980CE1D81731F930A15753 C1A9659C8B63

FORREST, T. 1995. *Politics and economic development in Nigeria.* Boulder, CO: Westview Press.

FRASER INSTITUTE (n.d.) Home page. "Free the world". The Fraser Institute. Available online at http:// www.freetheworld.com/ Accessed 30 October 2008.

FREEDOM HOUSE 2008. *Freedom in the world: the annual survey of political rights and civil liberties.* New York: Rowman and Littlefield.

FREIDMAN, T. 2006. "The first law of petropolitics", *Foreign Policy,* May-June 28–36.

FRENCH, P. A. 2005. "Inference gaps in moral assessment: capitalism, corporations and individuals", *International Social Science Journal,* 185, 573–584.

FRIEDMANN, J. 1966. *Regional development policy: a case study of Venezuela.* Cambridge MA: MIT Press.

FRYNAS, J. 2000. *Oil in Nigeria: conflict and litigation between oil companies and village communities.* Munster, Hamberg, Berlin, Vienna, London and Zurich: Lit Verlag.

GELB, A. H. 1988. *Oil windfalls: blessing or curse?* New York: Oxford University Press.

GLAESER, E. L., LA PORTA, R., LOPES-DE-SILANES, F. AND SHLEIFER, A. 2004. "Do institutions cause growth?" NBR working paper 10568, Cambridge MA: National Bureau of Economic Research.

GLEDITSCH, N. P., WALLENSTEEN, P., ERIKSSON, M., SOLLENBERG, M. AND STRAND, H. 2002. "Armed conflict 1946–2001: a new dataset", *Journal of Peace Research,* 39 (5), 615–637.

GLOBAL WITNESS 2006. *Digging in corruption: fraud, abuse and corruption in Katanga's copper and cobalt mines.* London: Global Witness.

GLOBAL WITNESS 2006. *Funny business in the Turkmen–Ukrainian gas trade.* A report by Global Witness, April.

GUHA-SAPIR, D. AND VAN PANHUIS, W. G. 2003. "The importance of conflict-related mortality in civilian populations", *The Lancet,* 36, 2126–2128.

GURR, T. R., JAGGERS, K. AND MOORE, W. 1990. "The transformation of the western state: the growth of democracy, autocracy, and state power since 1800", *Studies in Comparative International Development,* 25 (1). pp. 73–108.

GUSEYNOV, V. A. 2002. *Caspian oil.* Moscow: Olma Press.

GWARTNEY, J. AND LAWSON, R. 2005. *Economic freedom in the world 2003: the annual report.* Vancouver: Fraser Institute.

GYLFASON, T. 2000. *Natural resources, education, and economic development.* London: Center for Economic Policy Research.

GYLFASON, T. 2001. "Natural resources, education, and economic development", *European Economic Review,* 45 (4–6), 847–859.

HAFNER-BURTON, E. M. 2005. "Right or robust? The sensitive nature of repression to globalization", *Journal of Peace Research,* 42 (6), 679–698.

HAMANN, R., SONNENBERG, D., MACKENZIE, A., KAPELUS, P. AND HOLLESEN, P. 2005. "Local governance as complex system: lessons from mining in South Africa, Mali and Zambia", *Journal of Corporate Citizenship,* 18, 61–73.

HAMEED, F. 2006. *Fiscal transparency and economic outcomes.* IMF working paper WP 05/225. Washington, DC: International Monetary Fund.

HAMILTON, K. AND CLEMENS, M. 1999. "Genuine savings rates in developing countries", *World Bank Economic Review,* 13 (2), 333–356.

HAMILTON, L. C. 1992. *Regression with graphics: a second course in applied statistics.* Belmont, CA: Duxbury.

HARVEY, C. AND JEFFERIS, K. 1995. "Botswana's exchange controls: abolition or liberalization?" IDS discussion paper 348,. Brighton: Institute of Development Studies.

HARVEY, C. AND LEWIS, S. 1990. *Policy choice and development performance in Botswana.* Houndmills: Macmillan.

HAUSMANN, R. 1999. "Dealing with negative oil shocks: Venezuela's experience in the 1980s", *In:* Collier, P. and Gunning, J. W., eds *Trade shocks in developing countries: volume 2, Asia and Latin America.* Oxford: Oxford University Press, 120–163.

HAUSMANN, R. 2003. "Venezuela's growth implosion: a neo-classical story?", *In:* Rodrik, D., ed. *In search of prosperity: analytic narratives of economic growth.* Princeton NJ: Princeton University Press, 244–270.

HEALD, D. 2003. "Fiscal transparency: concepts, measurement and UK practice", *Public Administration,* 81 (4), 723–759.

HENDERSON, C. 1991. "Conditions affecting the use of political repression", *Journal of Conflict Resolution,* 35 (1), 120–142.

HILL, C. B. AND KNIGHT, J. 1999. "The diamond boom, expectations and economic management in Botswana", *In:* Collier, P. and Gunning, J. W., eds *Trade shocks in developing countries: volume 1 Africa.* Oxford: Oxford University Press, 303–50.

HOMER-DIXON, T. F. 2000. *The ingenuity gap.* New York: Alfred A. Knopf.

HOYOS, C. 2007. "The new Seven Sisters: oil and gas giants dwarf western rivals", *Financial Times*, 11 March. Available online at http://www.ft.com/cms/s/2/471ae1 b8-d001–11db-94cb-000b5df10621. html

HUBBERT, M. K. 1949. "Energy from fossil fuels", *Science*, 109 (2823), 103–109.

HUMAN DEVELOPMENT INDEX (2001).

HUMAN RIGHTS WATCH 2004. *Some transparency, no accountability: the use of oil revenue in Angola and its impact on human rights*. New York: Human Rights Watch.

HUMAN RIGHTS WATCH 2005. *The curse of gold*. New York: Human Rights Watch.

HUMPHREYS, N. M. 2005. "Natural resources, conflict, and conflict resolution", *Journal of Conflict Resolution*, 49 (4), 508–537.

HUNTINGTON, S. P. 1997. *The clash of civilizations and the remaking of world order*. New York: Touchstone Books.

IBNEY, M. AND DALTON, M. 1996. "The political terror scale", *In:* Cingranelli, D. L., ed. *Human rights and developing countries*. Greenwich, CT: JAI Press.

IIMI, A. 2007. "Escaping from the source curse: evidence from Botswana and the rest of the world", IMF Staff papers, 54 (4), 663–699. Washington, DC: International Monetary Fund.

IPIECA 2005. *Oil and gas industry guidance on voluntary sustainability reporting*. London: IPIECA.

IPIECA 2006. *Human rights training toolkit*. London: IPIECA.

INTERNATIONAL BUDGET PROJECT 2006. *Open budget questionnaire*. Center on Budget and Policy Priorities. Washington, DC: International Budget Project.

INTERNATIONAL MONETARY FUND (IMF) 1999. *IMF staff country report 99/132: Botswana: selected issues*. Washington DC: International Monetary Fund.

INTERNATIONAL MONETARY FUND (IMF) 2004. *Peru: report on the observance of standards and codes: fiscal transparency module*. Country report No. 04/109. Washington DC: International Monetary Fund.

INTERNATIONAL MONETARY FUND (IMF) 2005. *IMF staff country report 05/212: Botswana: selected issues*. Washington DC: International Monetary Fund.

INTERNATIONAL MONETARY FUND (IMF) 2007. "Guide on resource revenue transparency". Available online at http://www.imf.org/ external/np/pp/2007/eng/051507g. pdf Accessed 4 November 2008.

INTERNATIONAL MONETARY FUND (IMF) 2007a. *Guide on resource revenue transparency*. Washington, DC: International Monetary Fund.

INTERNATIONAL MONETARY FUND (IMF) 2007b. *Vietnam: 2007 Article IV consultation*. IMF Country report No. 07/387. Washington, DC: International Monetary Fund. Available online at http://www.imf. org/external/pubs/ft/scr/2007/ cr07387.pdf Accessed 14 January 2008.

INTERNATIONAL OPEN BUDGET INITIATIVE 2006. Home page. Available online at http:// www.openbudgetindex.org Accessed 1 November 2008.

ISAKSEN, J., AMUNDSEN, I., WIIG, A. AND ABREU, C. 2007. *Budget, state and people: budget process, civil society and transparency in Angola*. CMI Report No. R2007(7). Bergen: Chancellor Michelsen Institute.

IVANHOE, L. 1997. "King Hubbert updated", *Hubbert Center Newsletter*, 97 (1), 1–1–1–4.

JANELIUNAS, T. AND MOLIS, A. 2006. "The NEGP ends Lithuania's hopes of becoming a transit country", *Baltic Mosaic*, 1 (5), 30.

JENSEN, N. AND WANTCHEKON, L. 2004. "Resource wealth and political regimes in Africa", *Comparative Political Studies*, 37 (7), 816–841.

JOHNSON, P. M. 2005. "A glossary of political economy terms". Available online at http://www.auburn.edu/ ~johnspm/gloss/agency_problem Accessed 30 October 2008.

JONAH, S. 2006. "Why AngloGold must not desert the DRC", *The Star*, 15 June: 15.

JONES LUONG, P. 2004. *The transformation of central Asia: state–societal relations from Soviet rule to independence*. Ithaca NY: Cornell University Press.

KAREN, M. 2007. "Fighting the resource curse: the Azerbaijan response", *Developing Alternatives*, 11 (1), 23–26.

KARL, T. L. 1997. *The paradox of plenty: oil booms and petro-states*. Berkeley, CA: University of California Press.

KARL, T. L. 1999. "The perils of the petro-state: reflections on the paradox of plenty", *Journal of International Affairs*, 53 (1), 31–48.

KAZIN, P. 2006. "The NEGP and the global strategy of Gazprom", *Baltic Mosaic*, 1 (5), 62.

KHAN, S. A. 1994. *Nigeria: the political economy of oil*. Oxford and New York: Oxford University Press.

KIMBERLEY PROCESS n.d. Home page. Available online at http:// www.kimberleyprocess.com Accessed 3 November 2008.

KITTEL, B. AND WINNER, H. 2005. "How reliable is pooled analysis in political economy? The globalization-welfare state nexus revisited", *European Journal of Political Research*, 44 (2), 269–293.

KRUEGER, A. O., SCHIFF, M. AND VALDES, A. 1992. *Political economy of agricultural pricing policies*. Baltimore MD: Johns Hopkins University Press.

KUPCHINSKY, R. 2007. "Russia: BP–TNK, Gazprom, and the Kovytka gas field", Radio Free Europe/ Radio Liberty, 13 June. Available online at http://www.rferl.org Accessed 4 November 2008.

LA PORTA, R., LOPEZ-DE-SILANES, F., SCHLEIFER, A. AND VISHNY, R. 1998. "The quality of government", NBER working paper 6727. Cambridge, MA: National Bureau of Economic Research.

LAL, D. AND MYNT, H. 1996. *The political economy of poverty, equity, and growth.* Oxford: Clarendon.

LANDES, D. S. 1999. *The wealth and poverty of nations: why some are so rich and some so poor.* New York and London: W.W. Norton & Company.

LANDMAN, T. 2005. *Protecting human rights: a comparative study.* Washington, DC: Georgetown University Press.

LANGE, G. AND WRIGHT, M. 2004. "Sustainable development in mineral economies: the example of Botswana", *Environment and Development Economics*, 9 (4), 485–506.

LAX, H. L. 1983. *Political risk in the international oil and gas industry.* Boston, MA: International Human Resources Development Corporation.

LEDERMAN, D. AND MALONEY, W. F. 2007. *Natural resources: neither curse nor destiny.* Stanford, CA: Stanford University Press.

LEE, C., LINDSTRÖM, R., MOORE, W. H. AND TURAN, K. 2004. "Ethnicity and repression: the ethnic composition of countries and human rights violations", *In:* Carey, S. and Poe, S. C., eds *Understanding human rights violations: new systematic studies.* Aldershot: Ashgate.

LEITE, C. AND WEIDMANN, J. 1999. "Does mother nature corrupt? Natural resources, corruption and economic growth". Working paper No. 99/85. Washington, DC: International Monetary Fund.

LENAHAN, S. 2006. "Humanitarian and security challenges". Presentation to the Fifth Annual Transatlantic Dialogue Symposium on the humanitarian crises in Darfur and the DRC, 5–6 October,

Chicago: Northwestern University School of Law.

LOSKOT, A. 2006. "The NEGP: strategic interests and a number of unknowns", *Baltic Mosaic*, 1 (5), 50.

MACINTYRE, A. 2000. "Funny money in Indonesia", *In:* Khan, M. H. and Jomo, K. S., eds *Rents, rent-seeking and economic development.* Cambridge: Cambridge University Press, 248–273.

MAI, P. H. 2003. "The economic impact of foreign direct investment flows on Vietnam: 1988–98", *Asian Studies Review*, 27 (1), 81–98.

MAIL & GUARDIAN 2005. "Anglo 'messed up' in the DRC". 2 June. Available online at http://www.mg.co.za/articlePage.aspx?articleid = 242206&area = /breaking_news/ breaking_news__business Accessed 4 November 2008.

MARCEL, V. 2006. *Oil titans.* London: Royal Institute of International Affairs.

MARQUEZ, G. 1995. "Venezuela: poverty and social policies in the 1980s", *In:* Lustig, N., ed. *Coping with austerity: poverty and inequality in Latin America.* Washington DC: Brookings Institution, 400–452.

MARSHALL, M. AND JAGGERS, K. 2000. "Polity IV project codebook". Centre for International Development and Conflict Management, College Park, MD: University of Maryland.

MARSHALL, M. G. AND JAGGERS, K. 2005. *Polity IV project: dataset users' manual.* Polity IV Project. Arlington, VA: George Mason University.

MOFFET, M. 2007. "Beyond 'petrosaurus': how a sleepy oil giant become a world player", *The Wall Street Journal*, 30 August, A1.

MOST, B. AND STARR, H. 1989. *Inquiry, logic, and international politics.* Columbia, SC: University of South Carolina Press.

NIELSEN, F., ALDERSON, A. AND BECKERFIELD, J. 2005. "Exactly how has income inequality changed? Patterns of distributional change in

core societies", Luxembourg Income Study Working paper series. Available online at http://www.lisproject.org/publications/LISwps/422.pdf Accessed 4 November 2008

NIGERIAN NATIONAL PETROLEUM CORPORATION (NNPC) 1986. *NNPC annual report 1986.* Lagos: NNPC.

NØRLUND, I. 2007. "Civil society in Vietnam. Social organizations and approaches to new concepts", *Asien*, 105, 68–90.

OPEN BUDGET INITIATIVE (2006) "More public information needed to hold governments to account". Available online at http://www.openbudgetindex.org/SummaryReport.pdf Accessed 30 October 2008.

ORGANIZATION FOR ECONOMIC COOPERATION AND DEVELOPMENT (OECD) 2001. *OECD Best practices for budget transparency.* Public Management Committee, Public Management Service. Paris: OECD.

ORGANIZATION FOR ECONOMIC COOPERATION AND DEVELOPMENT (OECD) 2003. "Regulatory reform in Norway". Paris: OECD.

ORGANIZATION FOR ECONOMIC COOPERATION AND DEVELOPMENT (OECD) 2005. "Conducting business with integrity in weak governance zones: issues for discussion". Background document for consultations that provided inputs to the OECD risk awareness tool for multinational enterprises in weak governance zones.

ORGANIZATION FOR ECONOMIC COOPERATION AND DEVELOPMENT (OECD) 2006. *OECD risk awareness tool for multinational enterprises in weak governance zones.* Paris: OECD. Available online at http://www.oecd.org/dataoecd/26/21/36885821.pdf Accessed 4 November 2008.

OXFAM AMERICA 2008. "Take action protect community: rights and resources", March. Available online at http://www.oxfamamerica.org/whatwedo/campaigns/extractive_industries/news_publications/RKRDFactSheet.pdf Accessed 4 November 2008.

PAPYRAKIS, E. AND GERLAGH, R. 2004. "The resource curse hypothesis and its transmission channels", *Journal of Comparative Economics*, 32 (1), 181–193.

PEARSON, S. 1970. *Petroleum and Nigerian economy*. Stanford, CA: Stanford University Press.

PETRIE, M. 2003. "Promoting fiscal transparency: the complementary roles of the IMF, financial markets, and civil society". IMF working paper WP/03/199. Fiscal Affairs Department. Washington, DC: International Monetary Fund.

PLÜMPER, T., TROEGER, V. AND MANOW, P. 2005. "Panel data analysis in comparative politics: Linking method to theory", *European Journal of Political Research*, 44 (2), 327–354.

POE, S. C. 2004. "The decision to repress: an integrative theoretical approach to the research on human rights and repression", *In:* Carey, S. and Poe, S. C., eds *Understanding human rights violations: new systematic studies*. Aldershot: Ashgate.

POE, S. C., TATE, C. N. AND KEITH, L. C. 1999. "Repression of the human right to personal integrity revisited: a global cross-national study covering the years 1976–1993", *International Studies Quarterly*, 43 (2), 291–313.

POE, STEVEN C., CAREY, SABINE C. AND VAZQUEZ, TANYA C. 2001. "How are these pictures different? a quantitative comparison of the US State Department and Amnesty International Human Rights reports, 1976–1995", *Human Rights Quarterly*, 23, 650–677.

PRAKASH, A. 2000. *Greening the firm: the politics of corporate environmentalism*. Cambridge: Cambridge University Press.

PRZEWORSKI, A. 1999. "Minimalist conception of democracy: a defense", *In:* Shapiro, I. and Hacker-Cordón., C., eds *Democracy's value*. Cambridge: Cambridge University Press.

PUBLISH WHAT YOU PAY COALITION OF THE DEMOCRATIC REPUBLIC OF CONGO 2007. "Final statement of the workshop to build awareness on the Extractive Industries Transparency sInitiative". Available online at http://eitidev.forumone.com/UserFiles/File/drc/drc_pwyp_statement_feb_08_07.pdf Accessed 4 November 2008.

PUTIN, V. 2007a. "Press conference and answers to questions at the end of talks with the President of Greece Karolos Papoulias", 31 May. Official site of the Russian President. Available online at http://www.kremlin.ru/text/appears/2007/05/132212.shtml

PUTIN, V. 2007b. "Interview with G8 member countries newspaper journalists", 4 June. Official site of the Russian President. Available online at http://www.kremlin.ru/text/appears/2007/06/132365.shtml English translation. Available online at http://www.information clearinghouse.info/article17855.htm Accessed 4 November 2008.

PUTIN, V. 2007c. "Press conference and answers to questions at the end of talks with the Portuguese Prime Minister Jose Socrates". Official site of the Russian President. Available online at http://www.kremlin.ru/text/appears/2007/05/131976.shtml

RABE-HESKETH, S. AND EVERITT, B. 2004. *A handbook of statistical analysis using STATA*. 3rd edn. London: Chapman and Hall and CRC.

RADON, J. 2007. "How to negotiate an oil agreement", *In:* Humphreys, M., Sachs, J. and Stiglitz, J., eds *Escaping the resource curse*. New York: Columbia University Press, 101.

RAMKUMAR, V. AND KRAFCHIK, W. 2007. *The role of civil society organizations in auditing and public finance management*. Washington, DC: International Budget Project.

REGAN, P. M. AND HENDERSON, E. A. 2002. "Democracy, threats and political repression in developing countries: are democracies

internally less violent?", *Third World Quartely*, 23 (1), 119–136.

REICH, S. 2005. "When firms behave 'responsibly', are the roots national or global?", *International Social Science Journal*, 185, 509–528.

RICHARDS, D. L., GELLENY, R. D. AND SACKO, D. H. 2001. "Money with a mean streak? Foreign economic penetration and government respect for human rights in developing countries", *International Studies Quarterly*, 45 (2), 219–239.

ROBINSON, M. 2006. *Budget analysis and policy advocacy: the role of non-governmental public action*. IDS Working Paper 279. Brighton: Institute of Development Studies.

RODRÍGUEZ, F. AND SACHS, J. D. 1999. "Why do resource-abundant economies grow more slowly?", *Journal of Economic Growth*, 4 (XX), 277–303.

ROSS, M. 1999. "The political economy of the resource curse", *World Politics*, 51 (2), 297–322.

ROSS, M. 2001. *Extractive sectors and the poor: an Oxfam America report*. October. Available online at http://www.sscnet.ucla.edu/polisci/faculty/ross/oxfam.pdf Accessed 4 November 2008.

ROSS, M. L. 2001. "Does oil hinder democracy?", *World Politics*, 53 (XX), 325–361.

ROSSER, A. 2006. "The political economy of the resource curse: a literature survey", IDS working paper 268. Brighton: Institute of Development Studies.

Rossiyskaya Gazeta 2007. 17 January: 5.Online.

RWABIZAMBUGA, A. 2007b. "Negotiating corporate social responsibility policies and practices in developing countries: an examination of the experiences from the Nigerian oil sector", *Business and Society Review*, 112 (3). pp. 407–430.

SACHS, J. D. 1989. "Social conflict and populist policies in Latin America". Working paper 2897.

Cambridge MA: National Bureau of Economic Research.

SACHS, J. D. AND WARNER, A. M. 1995. *Natural resource abundance and economic growth.* Working paper 5398. National Bureau of Economic Research.

SACHS, J. D. AND WARNER, A. 1999. "Natural resource intensity and economic growth", *In:* Mayer, J., Chambers, B. and Farooq, A., eds *Development policies in natural resource economies.* Cheltenham: Edward Elgar, 13–38.

SACHS, J. D. AND WARNER, A. M. 2001. "The curse of natural resources", *European Economic Review*, 45 (4–6), 827–838.

SALA-I-MARTIN, X. 1997. "I just ran two million regressions (what have we learned from recent empirical growth research?)", *AEA Papers and Proceedings*, 87 (2), 178–183.

SALA-I-MARTIN, X. AND SUBRAHAMANIAN, A. 200. *"Addressing the natural resources curse: an illustration from Nigeria".* IMF working paper No. 03/139. n. Washington, DC: International Monetary Fund.

SALOMON, M. 2007. "Power and representation at the Vietnamese National Assembly: the scope and limits of political *doi moi*", *In:* Balme, S. and Sidel, M., eds *Vietnam's new order: international perspectives on the state and reform in Vietnam.* New York: Palgrave Macmillan.

SANDBU, M. E. 2006. "Natural wealth accounts: a proposal for alleviating the natural resource curse", *World Development*, 34 (7), 1153–1170.

SANTISO, C. AND BELGRANO, A. G. 2004. *Politics of budgeting in Peru: legislative budget oversight and public financial accountability in presidential systems.* SAIS working paper series. Washington, DC: Johns Hopkins University.

SARRAF, M. AND JIWANJI, M. 2003. *"Beating the resource curse: the case of Botswana".* Environment

Department Papers 1. Washington DC: World Bank.

SCHMITT, C. 2000. *Political theology.* Moscow: Canon-Press-Ts.

SHULTZ, J. 2005. *Follow the money: a guide to monitoring budgets and oil and gas.* New York: Open Society Institute.

SIMON, J. 1996. *The ultimate resource 2.* Princeton, NJ: Princeton University Press.

SINCLAIR, A. 1993. "Approaches to organisational culture and ethics", *Journal of Business Ethics*, 12 (1), 63–73.

SMIL, V. 2005. *Energy at the crossroads: global perspectives and uncertainties.* Cambridge, MA: MIT Press.

SMITH, B. 2004. "Oil wealth and regime survival in the developing world, 1960–1999", *American Journal of Political Science*, 48 (2), 232–246.

SOREMEKUN, K. 1995. *Perspectives on the Nigerian oil industry.* Lagos: Amkra Books.

SPRUDS, A. 2006. "The NEGP and Russia's gas diplomacy: Latvian perspective", *Baltic Mosaic*, 1 (5), 20.

STATE OIL FUND OF THE REPUBLIC OF AZERBIJAN (n.d.) Home page. Available online at http://www.oilfund.az/index.php?n = 164 Accessed 30 October 2008.

STIGLITZ, J. E. 2005. "Making natural resources into a blessing rather than a curse", *In:* Schutz, J., ed. *Follow the money: a guide to monitoring budgets and oil and gas revenues.* New York: Open Society Institute.

STIGLITZ, J. 2007. "What is the role of the state? The problem of diversion of resources", *In:* Humphreys, M., Sachs, J. and Stiglitz, J., eds *Escaping the resource curse.* New York: Columbia University Press and Revenue Watch Institute.

Sultanov, Ch. A. 2000. *Oil.* Vol. 1. Baku: Nafta Press.

SYRQUIN, M. AND CHENERY, H. B. 1989. "Patterns of development, 1950 to 1983", World Bank discussion paper 41,. Washington DC: World Bank.

THAYER, C. A. 2000. *"Doi moi 2?* Vietnam after the financial crisis", *Harvard Asia Quarterly*, 4(1). Available online at http://www.asiaquarterly.com/content/view/55/43/ Accessed 1 December 2007.

THE ECONOMIST 2008. *Exxon's wrathful tiger takes on Hugo Chávez.* 14 February 2008.

TIMMER, C. T. 2007. "How Indonesia connected the poor to rapid economic growth", *In:* Besley, T. and Cord, L. J., eds *Delivering on the promise of pro-poor growth.* Washington DC: World Bank, 29–57.

TIPPEE, R. 1993. *Where's the shortage?* Tulsa: PennWell.

TORVIK, R. 2002. "Natural resources, rent seeking and welfare", *Journal of Development Economics*, 67 (XX), 455–470.

TURNER, B. 1977. "The Fadama lands of central Northern Nigeria, their classification, spatial variation, present and potential use". Unpublished PhD thesis, London: University of London.

UNITED NATIONS DEVELOPMENT PROGRAMME (UNDP) (n.d.) "Vietnam human development index". Available online at http://hdr.undp.org/xmlsearch/reportSearch?y = *&c = n%3AVIET + NAM&t = *&k = &orderby = year Accessed 1 November 2008.

UNITED NATIONS DEVELOPMENT PROGRAMME (UNDP) n.d. "Human development index". Home page. Available online at http://hdr.undp.org/en/statistics/Accessed 1 November 2008.

UNITED NATIONS DEVELOPMENT PROGRAMME (UNDP) 2005. *Energizing the millennium development goals: a guide to energy's role in reducing poverty.* New York: UNDP.

UNITED NATIONS DEVELOPMENT
PROGRAMME (UNDP) 2006. *Human
development report 2006: beyond
scarcity: power, poverty, and the
global water crisis*. New York:
UNDP.

UNITED NATIONS DEVELOPMENT
PROGRAMME (UNDP) 2007. *Human
development report 2007*. New York:
UNDP.

UNITED NATIONS GLOBAL COMPACT
n.d. "Human rights". Available
online at http://www.unglobal
compact.org/Issues/human_rights/
index.html Accessed 3 November
2008.

UNITED NATIONS HIGH
COMMISSIONER ON HUMAN RIGHTS
2005. "Report of the United
Nations High Commissioner
on Human Rights on the
responsibilities of transnational
corporations and related business
enterprises with regard to human
rights". E/CN.4/2005/91, 15
February 2005.

UNITED NATIONS SECURITY COUNCIL
2002. *Final report of the panel of
experts on the illegal exploitation of
natural resources and other forms of
wealth of the Democratic Republic of
the Congo*. New York: UN.

VAN DER VEER, J. 2008. "Two energy
futures". Speech. 25 January. Shell.

VERGILYAR (2007) Newsletter.
Ministry of Taxation of the
Azerbaijan Republic, 15 August.

Voluntary Principles on Security
and Human Rights n.d. Home Page.
Available online at http://www.
voluntaryprinciples.org Accessed 3
November 2008.

WALKER, S. AND POE, S. C. 2002.
"Does cultural diversity affect
countries' respect for human
rights?", *Human Rights Quarterly*,
24 (2), 237–263.

WANTCHEKON, L. 1999. *Why do
resource dependent countries have
authoritarian governments?* New
Haven, CT: Yale University.
Available online at http://www.yale.
edu/leitner/pdf/1999–11.pdf,
accessed 1 December 2007.

WATTS, M. J. 1983. "The poverty of
theory", *In:* Hewitt, K., ed.
*Interpretations of calamity: from the
viewpoint of human ecology*. Boston,
MA: Allen & Unwin, 231–262.

WEINTHAL, E. AND JONES LUONG, P.
2006. "Combating the resource
curse: an alternative solution to
managing mineral wealth",
Perspectives on Politics, 4 (1), 35–53.

WIGGINS, V. 1999. *Comparing
XTGLS with regress cluster*. College
Station, TX: Stata Corporation.

WISE, C. 1994. "The politics of
Peruvian economic reform:
overcoming the legacies of state-led
development", *Journal of Inter-
American Studies and World Affairs*,
36 (1), 75–125.

WOOLCOCK, M., PRITCHETT, L. AND
ISHAM, J. 2001. "The social
foundations of poor economic
growth in resource-rich countries",
In: Auty, R. M., ed. *Natural
resources and economic growth*. New
York: Oxford University Press.

WORLD BANK 1989. *World tables
1988–89*. Washington DC: World
Bank.

WORLD BANK 2004. *Regulation of
associated gas flaring and venting:*

*a global overview and lessons from
international experience. Global gas
flaring reduction – a public–private
partnership. Report* No. 3.
Washington, DC: World Bank.

WORLD BANK 2006. *World
development indicators: CD-ROM*.
Washington, DC: World Bank.

WORLD BANK 2006a. *World
development indicators 2006*.
Washington DC: World Bank.

WORLD BANK 2006b. *Governance
indices 2006*. Washington DC:
World Bank.

WORLD BANK 2007a. *Vietnam public
expenditure review and integrated
fiduciary assessment*. Washington,
DC: World Bank.

WORLD BANK 2007b. *Angola: oil,
broad-based growth, and equity*.
Washington, DC: World Bank.

WORLD COMMISSION ON
ENVIRONMENT AND DEVELOPMENT
1987. *Our common future*. Oxford:
Oxford University Press.

WORLD ECONOMIC FORUM AND
CAMBRIDGE ENERGY RESEARCH
ASSOCIATES 2006. "The new energy
security paradigm", World
Economic Forum and Cambridge
Energy Research Associates.
Spring, 8. Available online at http://
www.weforum.org/pdf/Energy.pdf
Accessed 4 November 2008.

YERGIN, D. 2006. "Ensuring energy
security", *Foreign Affairs*, March–
April.

ŽIŽEK, S 2006. *The universal
exception: selected writings*. Vol 2.
Butler, R. and Stephens, S., eds.
London and New York:
Continuum.

INDEX

accountability, 49, 51, 55, 58, 59, 96, 99, 100, 109
  and domestic conditions, 58
advertising, 112
Africa, 76, 78
AGA *see* AngloGold Ashanti
aid conditionalities, 3
Alberta, 16
alternative energy systems, 79
AngloGold Ashanti, 119, 121, 122, 125, 126,
  127, 128, 129
  and business principles, 123, 124
  operations in the DCR, 4
Angola, 2, 9, 59, 60, 61, 65, 66, 76, 77
Annan, Kofi, 140
autocracies, 1, 2, 8, 45, 46, 47, 50, 52, 55, 57,
  96, 105 *see also* reforms
  and stability, 23, 24
Azerbaijan, 3, 10, 93, 95, 96, 97, 100, 104, 105, 106
Azerbaijani oil production, 93, 94
Azerbaijani policies for resource use, 94
Azerbaijani socio-economic relations, 93, 94
Baltic states, 112
Belarus, 107, 116
Botswana, 1, 2, 7, 31, 33, 35, 36, 37, 38, 39,
  40, 42, 43, 44, 48, 58, 60
BP *see* British Petroleum
Brazil, 17, 18, 19
British Petroleum, 3, 83, 101, 102, 104, 105,
  111, 138
Brundtland Commission, 77
budget transparency, 2, 57, 59, 60, 61, 64, 65, 99
businesses, 16, 42 *see* companies; multinational
  companies;
Cameroon, 60
cereal yields, 47
Chad, 19, 60
Chile, 48
China, 73, 75
civil responsibility, 101
civil society, 3, 4, 10, 59, 62, 64, 90, 97, 99, 100,
  101, 103, 104, 105, 112, 121 *see* non-governmental organisations
civil society watchdog organisations, 51
civil war, 57, 122
Colombia, 60, 135
commercial stakeholders, 7, 10, 81, 82, 83, 91,
  130 *see also* multinational companies
Commonwealth of Independent States, 41

communication breakdowns, 107
communication systems, 109
community development projects, 127, 128
community forum, 127, 128
companies 51, 120 *see* businesses
concessions, 83
conflict, 50, 119, 120, 122, 128, 136, 141
  and fuel exports, 48
  and resource wealth, 23, 24
conflicts of interest, 12, 18 *see also* state owned
  enterprises
Congo, 4, 7, 8, 50, 76
Congolese army, 121
Congolese gold mines, 122
Copenhagen School, 115
corporate social responsibility, 88, 121, 126,
  132, 133, 134, 140
corrupt governments, 49
corruption, 3, 6, 8, 10, 35, 45, 47, 49, 50, 51
  see also wealth
  and the private sector, 53, 76, 77, 81, 96, 100
corruption and social effectiveness, 109
Côte d'Ivoire, 36
Council of Europe, 97
democracies, 35, 49, 96 *see also* accountability
democratic checks and balances, 51, 52
democratic systems and human rights, 27
democratisers, 50, 51, 52, 55
depoliticisation, 108
developed countries, 16, 75
developing countries, 16, 71, 72, 75, 76, 78, 82
  and control of revenues, 81
  and oil exploitation policies, 81, 83
development, 48, 59, 77, 88
development agencies, 80
development goals, 54
development investment, 53 *see* employment
  investment initiatives
diamond rent, 36, 37, 38, 41, 43
"do no harm" lending philosophy, 52
domestic instability, 81
DRC 119, 120, 121, 126, 129 *see* Congo
Dutch disease, 22, 31, 32, 33, 35, 37, 42, 43, 45,
  57 *see* economic distortions
East Asia, 46
economic development and the quality of
  institutions, 25
economic distortions 2, 24
  and resource curse, 6
